Reading Mastery

Storybook 1

Level II

Siegfried Engelmann
Elaine C. Bruner

www.sra4kids.com

SRA/McGraw-Hill

A Division of The McGraw·Hill Companies

Send all inquiries to:
SRA/McGraw-Hill
8787 Orion Place
Columbus, OH 43240-4027

Printed in the United States of America.

ISBN 0-07-569325-9

3 4 5 6 7 8 9 RRC 06 05 04 03

A Division of The McGraw·Hill Companies

Columbus, Ohio

Contents

the cow on the rōad

lots of men went down the rōad in a little car.

a cow was sitting on the rōad. sō the men ran to the cow. "wē will lift this cow," they said.

but the men did not lift the cow. "this cow is sō fat wē can not lift it."

the cow said, "I am not sō fat. I can lift mē." then the cow got in the car.

the men said, "now wē can not get in the car." sō the men sat on the rōad and the cow went hōme in the car.

the end

pāint that nōse

a fat dog met a little dog. the fat dog had a red nōse. the little dog had a red nōse.

the fat dog said, "I have a red nōse."

the little dog said, "I wish I did not have a red nōse."

the fat dog got a can of pāint. hē said, "pāint that nōse."

sō the little dog did pāint her nōse. shē said, "now this nōse is not red." shē kissed the fat dog on the ēar. now the fat dog has pāint on his ēar.

the end

<u>rēad the Ītems</u>

1. when the tēacher says "gō,"
   stand up.

2. when the tēacher says "gō,"
   clap.

---

whȳ	the
that	shē
them	of
therₑ	fōr
wherₑ	dōn't
when	didn't
then	hērₑ
ātₑ	her

rēₐd the Ītems

1. when the tēₐcher says "now," clap.

2. when the tēₐcher says "now," stand up.

---

did	thōsₑ	arₑ
clap	thēsₑ	farm
do	therₑ	yard
of	then	her
fōr	whȳ	hērₑ
dōn't	when	at
didn't	werₑ	ātₑ
very	wherₑ	hē
every	her	shē
ēven	hērₑ	thē

rēₐd the Ītem

when the tēₐcher says "do it,"
stand up.

the talkiñg cat

the girl was gō͞iñg fōr a
walk. shē met a fat cat. "can
cats talk?" the girl said.

the cat said, "I can talk, but
I do not talk to girls. I talk to
dogs."

the girl did not l͞Ikₑ that cat.
"I do not l͞Ikₑ cats that will not
talk to mē."

the cat said, "I will not talk
to girls."

the girl said, "I do not līke that cat. and I do not give fish cāke to cats I do not līke."

the cat said, "I līke fish cāke, sō I will talk to this girl."

sō the girl and the cat āte the fish cāke.

the end

rēₐd the Ītem

when the tēₐcher says "do it,"
clap.

digging in the yard

a littlₑ man had a big dog.
the big dog livₑd in the yard. hē
dug a hōlₑ in the yard. the littlₑ
man got mad. hē said, "dogs can
not dig in this yard. I will gō
fōr a cop."

but the dog dug and dug.

the man got a cop. the man
said, "that dog dug a big hōlₑ in
the yard."

the cop said, "dogs can not dig in this yard."

the dog said, "I will stop. can I bē a cop dog?"

the cop said, "yes. I nēēd a cop dog."

the end

rēₐd the Ītem

when the tēₐcher says "gō," clap.

will the ōld car start?

a man had an ōld car. the ōld car did not start. sō hē went down the rōₐd. soon hē cāmₑ to a big man.

hē said, "can you start an ōld car?"

the big man said, "yes, I can but I will not. I am sittiñg. and I never start cars when I am sittiñg."

the man said, "you can sit in the car if you can start it."

sō the big man got in the car and māde the car start. hē said, "I līke this ōld car. sō I will kēēp sitting in it." and hē did.

the end

rēₐd the Ītems

1. when the tēₐcher says "now,"
   hōld up your hand.
2. when the tēₐcher says "gō,"
   hōld up your hands.

---

start	hēre	them
barn	there	then
shark	of	when
can't	fōr	where
can	end	whȳ
this	live	how
that	līked	didn't
the	lived	dōn't
hē	shē	did
her	they	do

<u>rēad the Ītems</u>

1. when the tēacher says "do it," hōld up your hands.
2. when the tēacher stands up, clap.

---

hard	wherₑ	fōr
farm	when	of
arₑ	then	hē
do	they	the
did	shē	that
dōn't	livₑd	this
didn't	lĪkₑd	therₑ
how	livₑ	hērₑ
whȳ	end	her

the dog and the bath

wē had a big dog. her nāme
was sal. this dog lĪked to run
and plāy. this dog did not lĪke to
take a bath.

wē said, "come in, sal. it is
tĪme to tāke a bath." wē ran
after her.

wē said, "sal, if you come
back and tāke a bath, you can
have some cōrn." but shē did not
lĪke cōrn.

wē said, "if you come back
and tāke a bath, you can have
some mēat." but shē did not lĪke
mēat.

wē said, "if you come back

and tāke a bath, you can rēad a book."

the big dog cāme back and took a bath. whȳ did sal tāke a bath? shē līked to rēad books.

this is the end.

arf the shark

arf was a barking shark. arf was a little shark, but shē had a big bark that māde the other fish swim awāy.

a shark swam up to arf and said, "you are a shark. let's plāy."

arf was happy. "arf, arf," shē said. and the other shark swam far, far awāy. arf was not happy now.

another shark swam up to arf. "you are a shark," hē said. "let's plāy."

arf was happy. "arf, arf," shē said. and the other shark

swam far, far awāy. arf was
not happy now.

then a big, big fish that līked
to ēat sharks swam up to the
other sharks.

"help, help," they yelled.

but the big fish was
swimming after them very fast.

stop

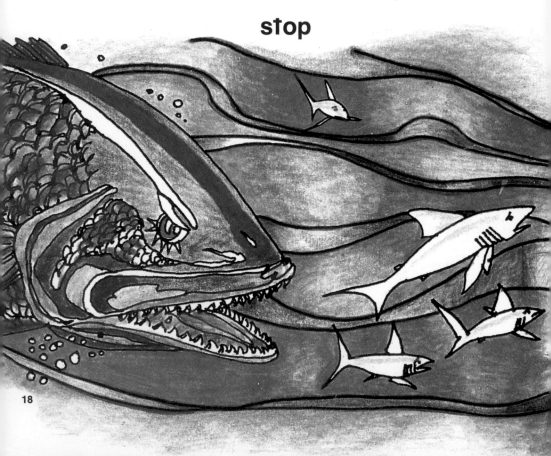

arf can help

arf was a barking shark. the other sharks did not līke her big bark. when arf went "arf, arf," the other sharks swam awāy.

but now arf had to help the other sharks. a big fish that līked to ēat sharks was gōing after the other sharks. arf swam up to the big fish and said, "arf, arf." the big fish swam far, far awāy.

the other sharks līked arf now.

"wē līke arf now," they said.

and now arf plāys with the other sharks. and if a big fish

that līkₑs to ēₐt sharks swims
up to them, arf says "arf, arf."
and the big fish swims far, far
awāy.

the end

rēₐd the Ītems

1. when the tēₐcher stands up, clap.

2. when the tēₐcher claps, hōld up your hand.

---

lĪked	barking	when
swim	that	therₑ
fōr	hērₑ	other
get	shē	funny
got	they	hōrsₑ
end	wherₑ	cāmₑ
and	how	givₑ
at	whȳ	trying
ātₑ	dōn't	rĪding
ēₐt	didn't	hard

rēₐd the Ītem

when the tēₐcher says "stand up,"
sāy "gō."

the cow boy and the cow

a cow boy was sad. hē did
not havₑ a hōrsₑ. the other cow
boys said, "hō, hō, that funny
cow boy has nō hōrsₑ."

a cow cāmₑ up to the cow
boy. the cow said, "if you arₑ a
cow boy, you nēēd a cow. I am
a cow."

the cow boy said, "do not bē
funny. cow boys do not rĪdₑ on
cows."

the cow said, "but I can run as fast as a hōrse. and I can jump better than a hōrse."

the cow boy said, "I will givₑ you a trȳ. but I will fēēl very funny rīdiñg on a cow." sō the cow boy got on the cow.

then the other cow boys cāmₑ up the rōₐd. "hō, hō," they said. "look at that funny cow boy. hē is trȳiñg to rīdₑ a cow."

stop

rēₐd the Ītem

when the tēₐcher says "now,"
pick up your book.

the cow boys havₑ
a jumpin͡g mēēt

the cow boy got on a cow.
the other cow boys said, "hō, hō.
that is funny."

the cow boy got mad. hē
said, "this cow can gō as fast as
a hōrsₑ. and shē can jump better
than a hōrsₑ."

the other cow boys said, "nō cow can jump better than mȳ hōrse." sō the cow boys rōde to a crēēk.

the cow boy on the cow said, "let's sēē if a hōrse can jump this crēēk."

"I will trȳ," a cow boy said. his hōrse went up to the crēēk. but then his hōrse stoppₑd. and the cow boy fell in the crēēk.

the cow boy on the cow said, "hō, hō. that hōrse didn't ēven trȳ to jump the crēēk."

the next cow boy said, "mȳ hōrse will trȳ. and mȳ hōrse will flȳ ōver that strēₐm.

hē will not ēven touch the strēₐm."

mōrₑ to come

rēₐd the Ītem

when the tēₐcher says "stand up," hōld up your hand.

the cow boys trȳ

some cow boys mādₑ fun of a cow boy that rōdₑ a cow. they said, "nō cow can Jump better than a hōrsₑ." sō they rōdₑ to a crēēk to sēē if a cow could Jump better than a hōrsₑ.

a cow boy fell in the crēēk. now the next cow boy was gōīng to mākₑ his hōrsₑ Jump ōver the crēēk. his hōrsₑ went very fast. the hōrsₑ cāmₑ to the bank of

the crēēk. then the hōrse jumpₑd.
did hē gō to the other sīdₑ? nō,
hē went splash in the crēēk. the
cow boy was mad.

the next cow boy said, "I
will trȳ to jump ōver that crēēk.
and I havₑ the best hōrsₑ in the
land."

but that cow boy's hōrsₑ
went splash and the cow boy fell
in the crēēk. the cow boys said,
"wē did not jump that crēēk, but
that fat cow can not jump as
far as a hōrsₑ."

"let's sēē," said the cow boy
with the cow. the cow started to
run faster and faster and

29

faster. the cow ran up to the bank of the crēēk. and then the cow jumped.

stop

rēₐd the Ītem

when the tēₐcher says "clap,"
touch your fēēt.

the happy jumpiñg cow

the cow boy on the cow was
trȳiñg to jump ōver the crēēk.
the cow ran to the bank and
jumpₑd with a big jump.

the cow jumpₑd ōver the
crēēk. the cow did not touch the
strēₐm. the other cow boys
lookₑd at the cow. they said,
"we arₑ wet and cōld." but the
cow boy on the cow was not
wet. and hē was not cōld.

hē gāve the cow a kiss. and
hē said, "now I fēēl līke a rēal
cow boy. thōse other cow boys
can have a hōrse. I will stāy with
this jumping cow." and hē did.

hē rōde the cow. hē jumped
ōver rocks with the cow. hē had
that cow fōr yēars and yēars.
and nō other cow boy ever
māde fun of his cow after the
cow jumped ōver the crēēk.

the end

rēₐd the Ītems

1. when the tēₐcher stands up, sāy "gō."

2. when the tēₐcher says "do it," hōld up your hands.

3. when the tēₐcher says "stand up," hōld up your hand.

rēₐd the Ītems

1. when the tēₐcher stands up, sāy "gō."

2. when the tēₐcher says "do it," hōld up your hands.

3. when the tēₐcher says "stand up," hōld up your hand.

of	better	circle
fōr	faster	farmer
and	you	start
how	didn't	where
other	crȳing	when
strēam	flȳing	them
this	after	then
hēre	things	what
there	gōing	that
whȳ	touch	thōse

rēₐd the Ītems

1. when the tēₐcher says "do it," touch your fēēt.
2. when the tēₐcher stands up, hōld up your hands.

jill and her sister

this is the stōry of a girl nāmₑd jill and her sister. jill trĪₑd to do thiñgs, but her sister did not trȳ.

jill said, "I can not rĪdₑ a bĪkₑ, but I will trȳ."

what did jill sāy?

her sister said, "I can not rĪdₑ, but I do not lĪkₑ to trȳ."

soon jill rōde a bīke, but her sister did not. her sister started to crȳ. jill said, "if you trȳ, you will not have to crȳ."

then jill said, "I can not jump rōpe, but I will trȳ."

what did jill sāy?

her sister said, "I can not jump rōpe, but I do not līke to trȳ."

soon jill jumped rōpe, but her sister did not. her sister said, "I can not jump rōpe, sō I will crȳ."

jill said, "if you trȳ, you will not have to crȳ."

mōre to come

rēₐd the Ītems

1. when the tēₐcher claps, touch your heₐd.
2. when the tēₐcher says "clap," touch your fēēt.

jill trĪₑd and trĪₑd

did jill trȳ to do thiñgs?

did her sister trȳ to do thiñgs?

what did jill do when shē trĪₑd?

jill said, "I can not rēₐd a book, but I will trȳ."

what did jill sāy?

her sister said, "I can not rēad a book, but I will not trȳ."

what did her sister sāy?

sō jill trīed to rēad and her sister did not trȳ.

now jill is good at rēadinͤg. but her sister can not rēad books. her sister can not rīde a bīke. her sister can not jump rōpe. and her sister can not rēad books. but her sister can do some thinͤg better than jill. her sister can rēally crȳ.

this is the end.

rēad the Ītems

1. when the tēₐcher stands up,
   pick up your book.
2. when the tēₐcher stands up,
   touch your heₐd.

Jon bākₑs a fish cākₑ

a boy nāmₑd Jon was gōiñg
to bākₑ the best cākₑ hē ever
mādₑ. hē said, "I will trȳ to
bākₑ a fish cākₑ."

hē askₑd his brother, "will
you help mē bākₑ a fish cākₑ?"

what did hē ask?

his brother said, "ick. a fish
cākₑ? I hātₑ fish cākₑ." hē ran

into the yard to plāy.

Jon askeḏ his sister, "will you help mē bāke a fish cāke?"

what did Jon ask?

his sister said, "ick. a fish cāke? I rēally do not līke fish cāke." then his sister ran into the yard to plāy.

Jon ēven askeḏ his mother, "will you help mē bāke a fish cāke?"

what did Jon ask?

but his mother said, "ick. fish cāke? ick."

sō Jon māde the fish cāke him self.

mōre to come

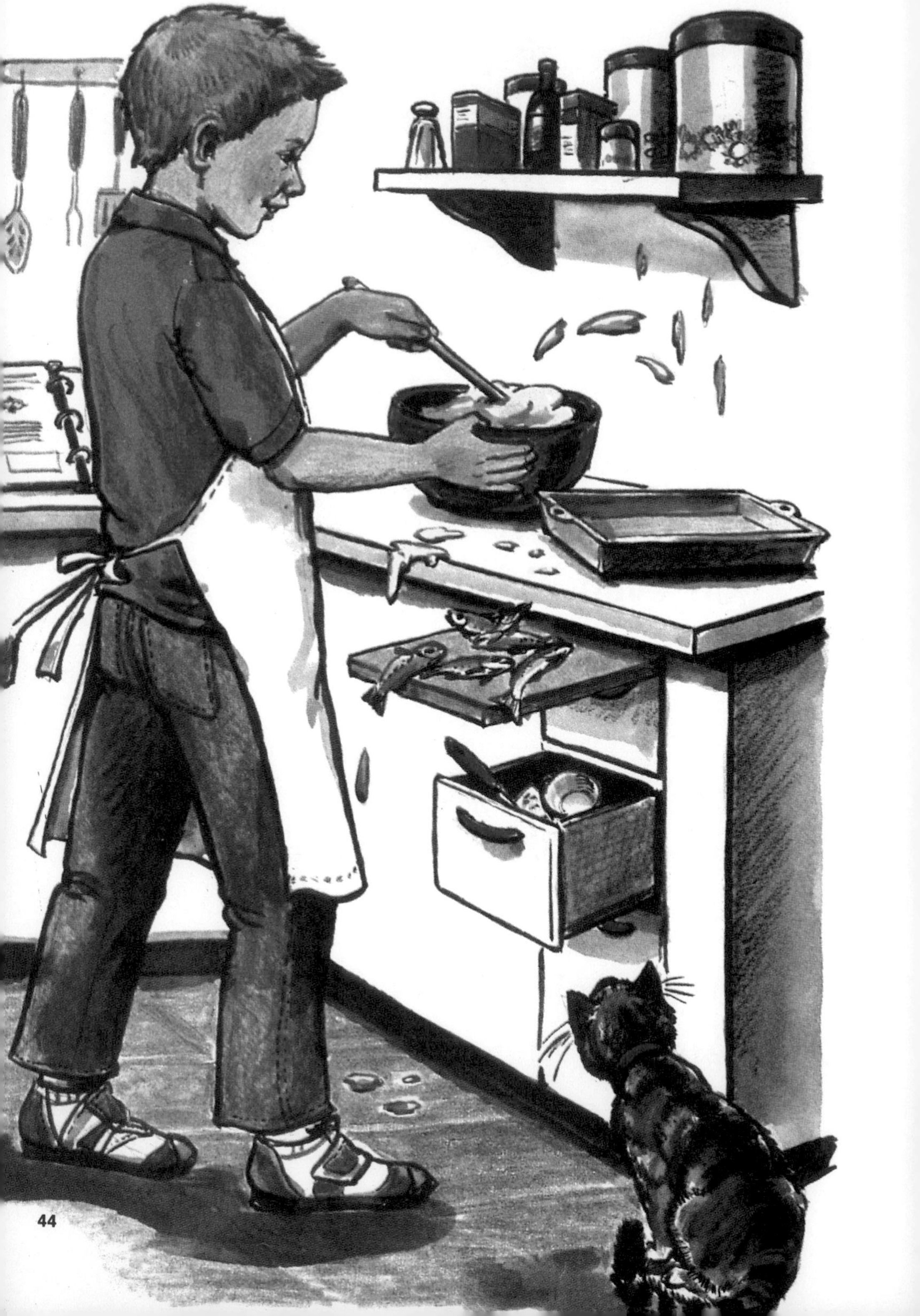

rēₐd the Ītems

1. when the tēₐcher says "clap,"
touch your nōsₑ.
2. when the tēₐcher says "gō,"
sāy "fĪvₑ."

jon hātₑs fish cākₑ

what kĪnd of cākₑ did jon
bākₑ?

did his sister help him?

did his mother help him?

jon mādₑ the fish cākₑ bȳ
him self.

when hē sat down to ēₐt the
cākₑ, his brother cāmₑ in. his

brother ask_ed, "can I trȳ some of that fish cāk_e?"

what did hē ask?

Jon said, "you didn't help mē bāk_e the cāk_e, sō you dōn't hav_e to help mē ē_at it."

Jon's mother and Jon's sister cām_e in. they ask_ed, "can wē trȳ some of that fish cāk_e?"

what did they ask?

Jon said, "you did not help mē bāk_e the cāk_e. sō you dōn't hav_e to help mē ē_at the cāk_e."

sō Jon āt_e the fish cāk_e bȳ him self. then hē got very sick. now hē hāt_es fish cāk_e. if you ask him to help you bāk_e fish

cāk_e, hē will sāy, "ick. I hāt_e
fish cāk_e."

what will hē sāy?

the end

rēad the Ītems

1. when the tēₐcher stands up, sāy "you arₑ standiñg up."
2. when the tēₐcher claps, pick up your book.

spot

this is a stōry of a dog nāmₑd spot. spot did not hēₐr well. the other dāy shē went to a stōrₑ to get some bōnₑs. the man in the stōrₑ said, "it is a fīnₑ dāy."

"what did you sāy?" spot askₑd.

tell spot what the man said.

the man got some bōnes fōr spot. hē said, "pāy mē a dīme fōr thēse bōnes."

spot askₑd, "what did you sāy?"

tell spot what the man said.

spot did not hēₐr the man and the man was getting mad at spot. the man said, "givₑ mē a dīmₑ fōr thēse bōnes."

spot askₑd, "what did you sāy?"

tell spot what the man said.

spot said, "it is tīmₑ fōr mē to lēₐvₑ. sō I will pāy you a dīmₑ fōr the bōnes and I will gō hōmₑ."

sō spot gāve the man a dīme.
then shē took the bōnes hōme
and had a fīne mēal of bōnes.

the end

rēₐd the Ītem

wһen the tēₐcher hōlds up a
hand, touch the flōōr.

spot and the cop

this is another stōry of spot
the dog.

did spot hēₐr well?

one dāy spot went fōr a
walk to the other sĪdₑ of town.
wһen shē got therₑ, shē said, "I
can not fĪnd mȳ wāy back
hōmₑ."

wһat did shē sāy?

shē walkₑd and walkₑd. but
shē did not fĪnd the strēēt

that led to her hōme. shē
started to crȳ.

then a big cop cāme up to
her. spot said, "I trīed and
trīed, but I can not fīnd mȳ
wāy back hōme."

the cop said, "wherₑ do you
livₑ?"

spot said, "what did you
sāy?" tell spot what the cop said.

spot still did not hēar what
the cop said. sō the cop got a
pad and māde a nōtₑ fōr spot.
the nōtₑ said, "wherₑ do you
livₑ?"

spot reₐd the nōtₑ and said,
"I livₑ on broom strēēt."

the cop said, "I will tāke you to broom strēēt." and hē did. spot kissed the cop and said, "some dāy I will pāy you back. you are a good cop."

the end

rēₐd the Ītems

1. when the tēₐcher stands up, pick up your book.
2. when the tēₐcher says "touch your fēēt," touch your fēēt.

the boy askₑd whȳ

a boy nāmₑd don līkₑd to ask whȳ. his mother tōld him to stāy in the yard. hē askₑd, "whȳ?" sō shē tōld him whȳ. shē said, "wē will ēₐt soon." what did shē sāy?

don dug a big hōle in the yard. his brother said, "you must not dig hōlₑs in the yard."

don asked, "whȳ?" sō his brother tōld him. his brother said, "hōles māke the yard look bad." what did his brother sāy?

don got a can of whīte pāint. "I will pāint mȳ bīke whīte," hē said. sō hē got the pāint brush and started to pāint his bīke.

his sister asked, "what are you doing?"

don answered, "pāinting mȳ bīke whīte."

what did the boy sāy?

mōre to come

rēₐd the ītem

when the tēₐcher stands up, sāy
"stand up."

don pāinted and pāinted

what did don līke to ask?

what did hē do in the yard?

what did hē start to pāint?

who askₑd him what hē was
doing with his bīke?

his sister said, "that looks
līke fun." sō shē got a pāint
brush and started to pāint don's
bīke.

don and his sister pāinted
the bīke. then don said, "whȳ

dōn't wē pāint the sīde walk?"
what did hē sāy?

so they pāinted the sīde walk.
what did they do?

then they pāinted the steps
to don's hōme.

then they pāinted a rock.

and then they pāinted ēach
other.

then don's mom went into the
yard. shē was mad. shē said, "you
pāinted the bīke, the steps, the
rock, and ēach other."

what did shē sāy?

what do you think shē did to
don and his sister?

the end

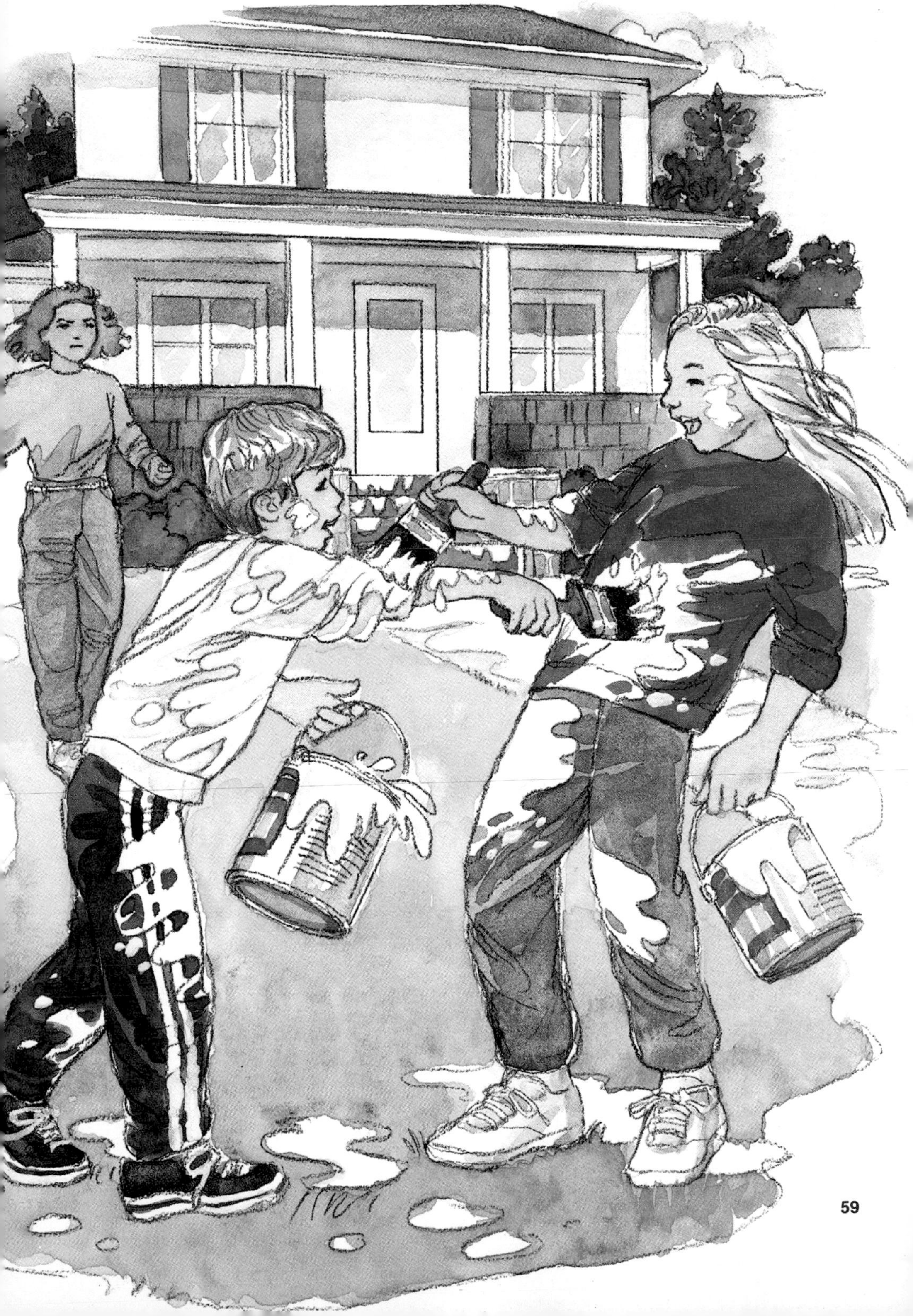

rēₐd the Ītems

1. when the tēₐcher says "fēēt," touch your fēēt.

2. when the tēₐcher says "stand up," hōld up your hands.

spot helps the cop

spot was walking nēₐr a stōrₑ. robbers cāmₑ from the stōrₑ with bags of monēy. a big cop ran to stop the robbers. hē yellₑd, "drop that monēy." but the robbers did not drop the monēy. the robbers had a big hōrn and they started to blōw it. "toot, toot," the hōrn went.

"I can not stand the 'toot, toot' of the hōrn," the cop said. "it māke͏s mȳ ēars sōre͏."

the cop held his hands ōver his ēars. then the robbers ran bȳ him. the hōrn was still gōing "toot, toot."

the hōrn did not māke͏ spot's ēars sōre͏. spot did not ēven hēar the hōrn. sō spot ran up to the robbers. spot bit them on the legs. they dropp͏ed the big hōrn. they dropp͏ed the monēy. then the cop stopp͏ed them.

hē said to spot, "you help͏ed stop the robbers." what did hē sāy?

the big cop was very happy.
the end

rēad the Item

when the tēₐcher picks up a book, sāy "hands."

flȳing is fun

a littlₑ bird had six sisters. his sisters said, "come and flȳ with us." but the littlₑ bird did not flȳ. sō hē started to crȳ.

his sisters said, "wē did not sāy to crȳ with us. wē said to flȳ with us. stop crȳing and start flȳing."

but the littlₑ bird did not stop crȳing.

his sisters said, "whȳ arₑ

you crȳiñg?" what did they sāy?

the little bird said, "I am crȳiñg bēcause I cannot flȳ."

whȳ was hē crȳiñg?

his sisters said, "wē will tēach you to flȳ if you stop crȳiñg."

sō the little bird stoppₑd crȳiñg. then his sisters grabbₑd him and took him up, up, up into the skȳ.

then they said, "you arₑ a bird, sō you can flȳ."

they let gō of him. hē yellₑd, "I can flȳ."

now when the sisters sāy "let's flȳ," the little bird jumps

up and down. hē says, "yes, flȳin͡g
is mōre fun than crȳin͡g."

then the littlе bird and his
sisters flȳ and flȳ.

what do they do?

the end

rēₐd the Ītems

1. when the tēₐcher says "go," sāy "fīvₑ."
2. when the tēₐcher stands up, sāy "now."

the farmer and his buttons

a farmer līkₑd buttons. he had red buttons and gōld buttons. he had lots of big buttons and lots of littlₑ buttons. he had buttons on his hat and buttons on his socks. he ēven had buttons on some of his buttons. but he had his best buttons on his pants. he had ten big buttons on his pants.

one dāy a man cāme to the farm. the man said, "I hаvе come to buȳ buttons." he lookеd at the buttons on the farmer's pants. "I will buȳ that big red button," he said.

so the farmer took off the big red button and sōld it. now he had nīnе big buttons on his pants.

then the man said, "now I will buȳ that big gōld button."

so the farmer took off the gōld button and sōld it. now the farmer did not hаvе nīnе buttons on his pants. do you think the

man will buȳ mōr_e buttons from
the farmer?

mōr_e to come

rēₐd the Ītem

when the tēₐcher says "go,"
touch your heₐd.

the farmer sōld his buttons

what did the farmer līkₑ?

wherₑ did he havₑ his best
buttons?

what did the man want to buȳ
from the farmer?

the man kept buȳiñg buttons
and the farmer kept selliñg them.
the man said, "now you havₑ fīvₑ
buttons. I want to buȳ that pink
button." so the farmer took off
his pink button and sōld it to
the man.

then the man wanted to buȳ the farmer's yellōw button. so the farmer sōld the yellōw button to the man.

the man said, "you still haᵥe thrēē buttons. I will buȳ them."

so the farmer took off the thrēē buttons. but when his pants had no mōrₑ buttons, his pants fell down. what did they do?

the farmer said, "mȳ pants fell down bēcause I sōld the buttons that held up mȳ pants." what did he sāy?

so now the farmer has monēy, but he has no buttons to

kēēp his pants up. how will he
kēēp his pants up?

this is the end.

r͞ead the Ītem

when the t͞eacher says "clap," touch your f͞eet.

spot t͞akes a trip

one d͞ay spot said, "I want to go on a trip in m͞y car." so she did.

she got in her car and went down the r͞oad. soon she stopped. she asked a man, "where can I get gas?"

the man said, "on best str͞eet."

spot said, "where did you s͞ay?"

tell spot what the man said.

so spot went to best str$\overline{ee}$t and got gas. then she went down the r$\overline{o}$ad some m$\overline{o}$re. soon she stopped. she asked a l$\overline{a}$dy, "where is the town of dim?"

the l$\overline{a}$dy said, "dim is f$\overline{I}$ve m$\overline{I}$les down the r$\overline{o}$ad."

spot asked, "where did you s$\overline{a}$y?"

tell spot what the l$\overline{a}$dy said.

and spot went to the town of dim. then spot stopped and asked a man, "where is a st$\overline{o}$re that sells b$\overline{o}$nes?"

the man said, "go down to m$\overline{a}$in str$\overline{ee}$t."

"where did you sāy?" spot
asked.

tell spot what the man said.

so spot went to the stōre
and got a bag of bōnes. she
had a good trip.

the end

rēₐd the Ītems

1. when the tēₐcher says "what,"
touch your nōsₑ.

2. when the tēₐcher stands up,
sāy "sit down."

3. when the tēₐcher says "do it,"
hōld up your hands.

park	hēr_e	callinͤg
ar_e	whȳ	hall
shark	līk_es	of
barn	wanted	for
farm	stopp_ed	thōs_e
what	very	thēs_e
want	ēven	that
wer_e	all	them
wher_e	fall	they
ther_e	call	when

rēₐd the Ītem

when the tēₐcher says "now,"
clap.

the dog lĪkes to talk, talk, talk

a tall man had a dog that
lĪked to talk and lĪked to rēₐd.

one dāy the dog was rēₐding
a book. the tall man was in the
hall. he callₑd the dog. he yellₑd,
"dog, come hēre and plāy ball
with me."

the dog yellₑd back at the
man, "I hēₐr you call, call, call,
but I dōn't lĪke to plāy ball,
ball, ball."

the man was getting mad. he
yelled, "dog, stop rēading that
book and start plāying ball."

she yelled, "I will not go
into the hall, hall, hall, and I will
not plāy ball, ball, ball."

the man was very mad now.
he cāme into the room and got
his cōat. he said, "well, I am
gōing for a walk. do you want to
come with me?"

the dog said, "I will not do
that, that, that, when I can sit
hēre and get fat, fat, fat."

so the tall man left and the
dog went back to her book.
she said, "I hāte to walk, walk,

walk, but I lī̄ke to talk, talk, talk."

the end

rēₐd the Ītem

when the tēₐcher says "do it,"
hōld up your hand.

the small bug went to
livₑ in a ball

therₑ was a small bug that
did not havₑ a hōmₑ. he went to
livₑ in a tall trēē. but a big
ēaglₑ said, "this is mȳ tall trēē.
go look for another hōmₑ."

then the bug livₑd in a hōlₑ.
but a mōlₑ said, "that's mȳ
hōlₑ. go look for another hōmₑ."

then the small bug livₑd on a
farm in a box of salt. but a cow

said, "that's mȳ salt. go awāy or I'll ēat you up when I lick mȳ salt."

then the small bug livₑd in a stall on the farm. but a hōrsₑ said, "whạt arₑ you doīng in mȳ stall? go fīnd another hōmₑ."

at last the bug went to a hōmₑ nēₐr the farm. he spotteₔ a ball on the flōōr. the ball had a small hōlₑ in it. the bug said, "at last I sēē a hōmₑ for me." he went into the ball and sat down. he said, "I hōpₑ that I can stāy in this ball. I līkₑ it hērₑ."

mōrₑ to come

rēad the Ītem

when the tēacher says "go," sāy
"stand up."

the bug in the ball mēēts a girl

a small bug had a hōme in a
ball. he said, "I hōpe I can stāy
in this ball. I lĪke it hēre."

he went to slēēp in the ball.
he was having a good drēam. he
was drēaming of a fĪne party.
then he sat up. the ball was
rōlling. "what is gōing on?" he
called.

he looked from the little
hōle in the ball and saw a tall

girl. she was rōllin͡g the ball on the flōōr.

"what arₑ you doin͡g?" he askₑd. "this is mȳ hōmₑ. stop rōllin͡g it on the flōōr."

the girl pickₑd up the ball and lookₑd at the small bug. then she droppₑd the ball. "ōh," she crīₑd, "therₑ is a bug in mȳ ball. I hātₑ bugs."

the ball hit the flōōr. it went up. then it went down. then it went up. the bug was gettin͡g sick.

"stop that," he callₑd. "I dōn't līkₑ a hōmₑ that gōₑs up and down."

the tall girl bent down and
looked at the bug. she said,
"this is mȳ ball. so go awāy."

the small bug looked up at
the girl and started to crȳ.

mōre to come

rēₐd the Ītem

whₑn the tēₐcher stands up, sāy
"you arₑ standiṉg up."

the bug wants to stāy
in the ball

a small buℊ wanted to livₑ
insĪdₑ a ball. but a tall ℊirl tōld
him that he must lēₐvₑ the ball
and fĪnd another hōmₑ. the small
buℊ started to crȳ. he said,
"wherₑ will I ℊo? I cannot livₑ in
a tall trēē. I cannot livₑ in a box
of salt. I cannot livₑ in a hōrsₑ
stall. and now I cannot stāy in
this ball."

"stop crȳin͡g," the girl said. "I can't stand to sēē small bugs crȳ."

the bug said, "if you let me stāy in this ball, I will plāy with you."

"no," the girl said. "I dōn't plāy with bugs. I hāte bugs."

the bug said, "I can sin͡g for you. I will ēven let you come to the party that I am gōin͡g to have in mȳ ball."

she said, "dōn't be silly. I can't fit in that ball. look at how tall I am."

the bug called, "let me stāy."

the girl sat down on the

flo͞or and looked at the small
bug. "I must think," she said.
what was she go͝ing to think
o͞ver?

mo͞re to come

rēₐd the Ītem

when the tēₐcher says "go,"
touch your arm.

the tall girl bets her brother

a tall girl wanted the bug to
lēₐve the ball and fĪnd another
hōmₑ. the bug crĪₑd and tōld
her all the thiñgs he would do if
she let him stāy in the ball. he
said that he would siñg for her.
he said that he would let her
come to his party in the ball.

the girl was sittiñg on the
flōōr thinkiñg of the bug.

then her brother cāme into
the room. he said, "what are you
doing?"

she said, "go awāy. I am
thinking."

he said, "do you think that
the ball will start rōlling if you
look at it very hard?" her
brother did not sēē the bug
insīde the ball.

the girl said, "if I want this
ball to start rōlling, it will
start rōlling. and I dōn't ēven
have to touch it."

her brother said, "I'll bet
you can't māke that ball rōll
if you dōn't touch it."

"how much will you bet?" the
girl asked. she looked at the
bug and smīled.

her brother said, "I will bet
you one football and ten toy
cars."

the girl said, "I will tāke
that bet."

mōre to come

rēₐd the Ītem

when the tēₐcher says "stop,"
touch the flōōr.

the tall girl wins the bet

the tall girl mādₑ a bet with
her brother. she bet him that she
could mākₑ the ball start rōllิng.
she said, "I dōn't ēven havₑ to
touch it."

her brother did not sēē the
bug in the ball. so he bet one
football and ten toy cars.

the girl lookₑd at the ball and
said, "start rōllิng, ball." the

bug started running insīde the ball. he ran and ran. he ran so fast that the ball started to rōll.

the girl's brother looked at the ball. he said, "wow. that ball is rōlliñg and you are not ēven touchiñg it."

the girl said, "I tōld you I could māke the ball rōll."

so the girl got one football and ten toy cars.

then she said to the small bug, "you helped me win the bet, so I will let you stāy in mȳ ball. this ball is your hōme now."

the bug was so happy that he ran from the ball and kissed

the girl on her hand. "thank you, thank you," he said.

and nēar the end of the wēēk, he had a fīne party insīde his ball. every bug on the strēēt cāme to the party, and they all said that it was the very best party they ever had.

the end

rēad the Ītem

wнen the tēacher says "go," hōld
up your hands.

the elephant gets glasses

a small elephant was not
happy bēcause he alwāys fell
down.

one dāy he went for a walk.
he could not sēē the tall trēē. so
he hit his head on the tall trēē
and fell down.

he said, "whȳ do I alwāys
fall down? I wish I would not
fall. I hāte to fall."

he walkₑd some mōrₑ. he
could not sēē a big red ball. so
he fell ōver the big red ball.

the small elephant said, "whȳ
do I alwāys fall down? I hātₑ to
fall."

he walkₑd some mōrₑ. but he
could not sēē all the boys and
girls ēatiñg hot dogs. he could
not sēē the pīlₑ of hot dogs. so
he fell into the hot dogs.

the boys and girls got mad.
"how could you fall into thōsₑ
hot dogs?" they said. "do you
nēēd glasses?"

the elephant said, "I havₑ
never sēēn glasses."

so a tall girl took her glasses
and gāve them to the elephant.
the elephant trīed on the glasses.

"mȳ, mȳ," the elephant said.
"now I can seē all kīnds of
things. I can seē tall treēs, balls,
and hot dogs."

now the small elephant is
happy bēcause he has glasses.
and he never falls down.

this is the end.

the dog loves to rēₐd,

rēₐd, rēₐd

a dog that could talk livₑd
with a tall man. the dog took a
book from the tāblₑ. the dog
said, "this book is what I nēēd,
nēēd, nēēd. I love to rēₐd, rēₐd,
rēₐd."

the tall man cāmₑ in and said,
"I look, look, look, but I cannot
sēē mȳ book, book, book."

then the man said, "mȳ book
was on the tāblₑ."

the dog said, "the book was
on the tāblₑ, but I took it from
the tāblₑ."

the tall man yellₑd at the dog.

he said, "you must not tāke mȳ book from the tāb1e."

she said, "do you want to plāy ball, ball, ball in the hall, hall, hall?"

"yes, yes," the man said.

the dog kicked the ball far, far, far down the hall. when the man ran after the ball, the dog took the book and hid it.

then she said, "let the man look, look, look. he will never fīnd his book, book, book."

the end

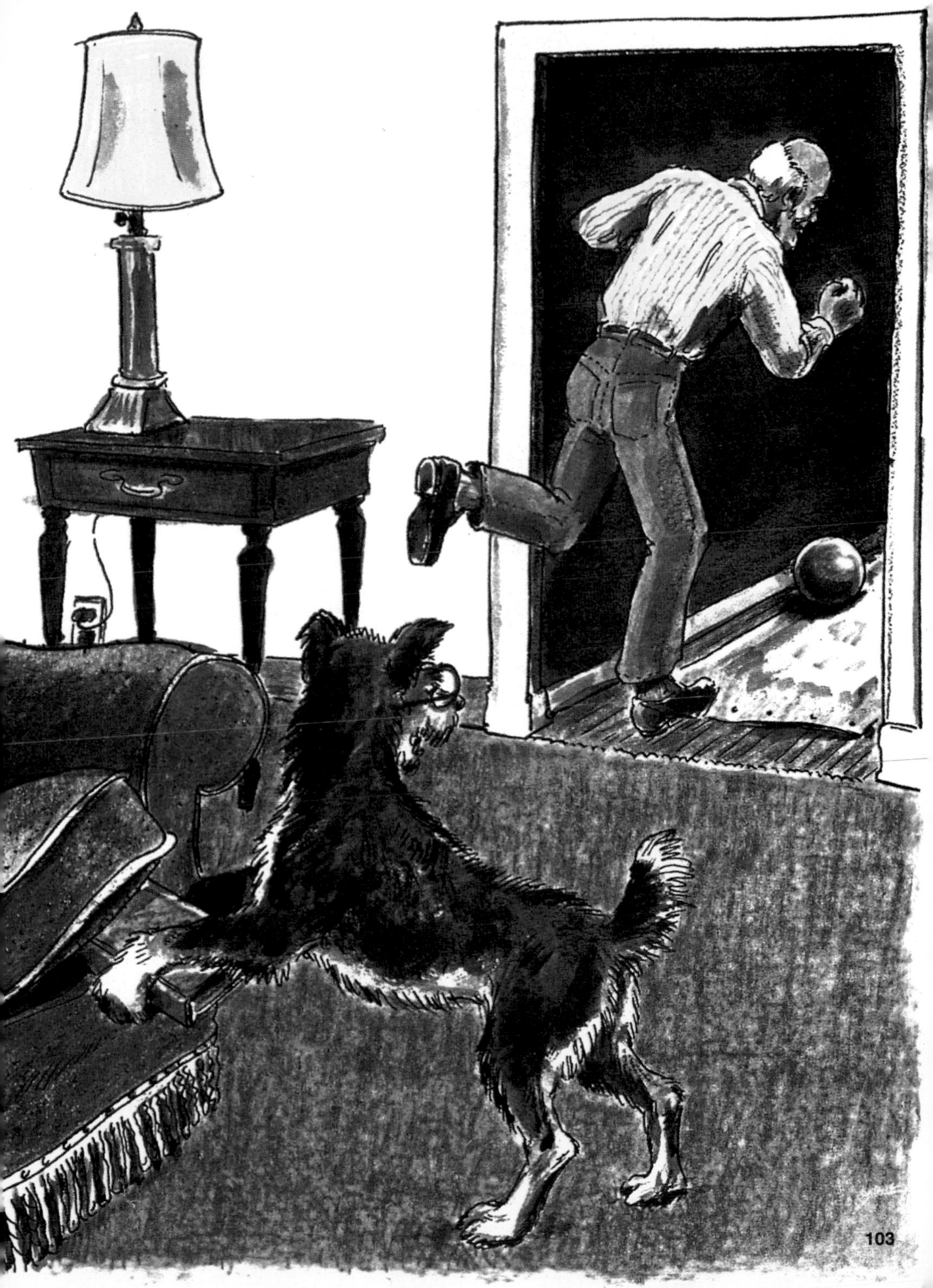

walter wanted to plāy football

walter loved to plāy football. but walter could not plāy well. he was small. and he did not run well. when he trīed to run with the ball, he fell down. "dōn't fall down," the other boys yelled. but walter kept falling and falling.

when walter ran to get a pass, he dropped the football. "dōn't drop the ball," the other boys yelled. but walter kept dropping balls.

dāy after dāy walter trīed to plāy football, but dāy after dāy he fell down and dropped the ball.

then one dāy, the other boys said, "walter, you can't plāy ball with us any mōre. you are too small.

you alwāys fall. and you alwāys
drop the football."

    walter went hōme and sat in his
yard. he was mad. he said to himself,
"I am small and I cannot run well."
walter wanted to crȳ, but he
didn't crȳ. he sat in his yard
and felt very sad. when his mom
called him for dinner, he said, "I
dōn't want to ēat. I must sit hēre
and think."

      mōre to come

walter gōes to the big gāme

walter was sad bēcause the other boys would not let him plāy football with them. walter was still sad on the dāy of the big football gāme. the boys that lived nēar walter werе plāyiñg boys from the other sĪde of town.

walter went down to the lot where the boys plāy football. he said, "I can't plāy in the gāme bēcause I alwāys fall. but I will look at the big gāme."

therе werе lots of boys and girls at the football lot. some of them werе chēēriñg for the boys that lived nēar walter. other boys and girls werе chēēriñg for the tēam that cāme from the other sĪde of town.

the gāme started. there was a tall
boy on the other tēam. that tall boy
got the football and ran all the wāy
down the lot. he scōred. the boys
and girls from the other sīde of
town chēēred.

walter's tēam got the ball. but
they could not go far. they went
fīve yards.

when the other tēam got the ball,
the tall boy kicked the ball. it went
to the end of the lot for another
scōre. walter said to himself, "that
other tēam is gōing to win. I wish
I could help mȳ tēam."

mōre to come

walter gōes in the gāme

walter was lookiñg at the big football gāme. walter's tēam was not doiñg well. the other tēam had 2 scōres. but walter's tēam did not have any scōres. as the gāme went on, walter's tēam started to plāy well. walter's tēam stopped the tall boy when he got the ball. then walter's tēam scōred. walter chēēred. he yelled, "get that ball and scōre some mōre."

but then the best plāyer on walter's tēam cut his arm. he left the gāme. walter said to himself, "now we cannot win the gāme. the best plāyer is not plāyiñg."

how could walter's tēam win if the best plāyer was not plāyiñg?

then all the boys on walter's tēam started to call. "walter, walter," they called. "come hēre."

walter ran to his tēam. one of the boys said, "walter, we nēēd one mōre plāyer. so we called you. trȳ to plāy well. we nēēd 2 scōres to win this gāme."

mōre to come

<u>walter's tēam must kick</u>

walter's tēam called him to plāy in the big gāme.

one of the boys on walter's tēam said, "we cannot run with the ball, bēcause the best runner is not in the gāme. so let's trȳ to scōre bȳ kicking the ball."

"yes, yes," the other boys said.

then the boys looked at ēach other. "one of us must kick the ball."

all the other boys said, "not me. I can't kick the ball that far."

but walter didn't sāy "no." he said, "I will trȳ. I think I could kick the ball that far."

one of the boys said, "I will hōld the ball for him."

so walter got ready to kick the
ball. some boys and girls called
from the sĪde of the lot, "dōn't let
walter do that. he can't plāy football.
he will fall down."

but walter said to himself, "I will
not fall. I will kick that ball." and
walter felt that he would kick the
ball.

mōre to come

walter kicks the ball

walter was ready to kick the ball. the boys and girls on the sīde of the lot werе sāyiñg, "dōn't let walter kick."

but walter did kick. another boy held the ball. a tall boy from the other tēam almōst got to the ball, but walter kicked the ball just in tīme. the ball went līke a shot. it went past the end of the lot. it went ōver a tall wall that was next to the lot. it almōst hit a car that was on the strēēt.

the boys on walter's tēam looked at walter. the boys on the other tēam looked at walter. one boy from the other tēam said, "that ball went all the wāy ōver the wall. I did not think that a small boy could kick a ball so far."

the boys and girls on the sīde of the lot chēēred. "that's the wāy to kick, walter," they called.

now walter's tēam nēēded one mōre scōre to win the gāme.

mōre to come

walter's tēam wins

the other tēam did not scōre. so walter's tēam got the ball.

one boy on walter's tēam said, "we must go all the wāy down the lot to scōre. but we dōn't have tīme and we can't kick the ball that far."

walter said, "I think I can kick the ball all the wāy." so the boys on walter's tēam got ready.

the ball went into plāy. a boy from walter's tēam held the ball, and walter kicked it. it went all the wāy to the end of the lot. it almōst hit the wall that was next to the lot.

the boys on walter's tēam picked him up and yelled, "walter kicked for a scōre." the boys from the other tēam said, "you are some football plāyer."

and the boys and girls on the sīde of the lot called, "walter is the star of the gāme." walter was very happy.

and now walter can plāy football with the other boys any tīme he wants.

the end

<u>rēad the Ītems</u>

1. when the tēacher says "one," hōld up one hand.

2. when the tēacher says "go," stand up.

---

mad	walter	other
māde	wall	another
hōpe	plāyer	there
hop	picked	what
fin	dropped	that
fīne	cannot	want
all	can't	went
almōst	do	were
also	dōn't	where
alwāys	didn't	whȳ

carmen the cow

this is a stōry about a cow
nāmed carmen.

when the other cows said "moo,"
the children alwāys cāme to pet
them. but when carmen said "moo,"
all the children alwāys ran awāy.
the children ran awāy bēcause
carmen had a loud moo. she trĪed to
sāy a little moo, but her moo was
alwāys a big, loud moo.

the other cows made fun of her.
they said, "we do not lĪke you
bēcause your moo is so loud."

carmen trĪed and trĪed, but her
moo was too loud.

one dāy some children cāme to
the farm with a tēacher. they cāme
to pet the cows. they petted all the

other cows, but they did not pet
carmen bēcause they did not līke
her loud moo.

one of the children started to
run up a hill, but she fell in a
dēēp, dēēp hōle. she shouted for
help. but the tēacher did not hēar
her calls. the other cows trīed to
help her. they called "moo, moo,"
but the moos were not very loud, and
the tēacher did not hēar them.

mōre to come

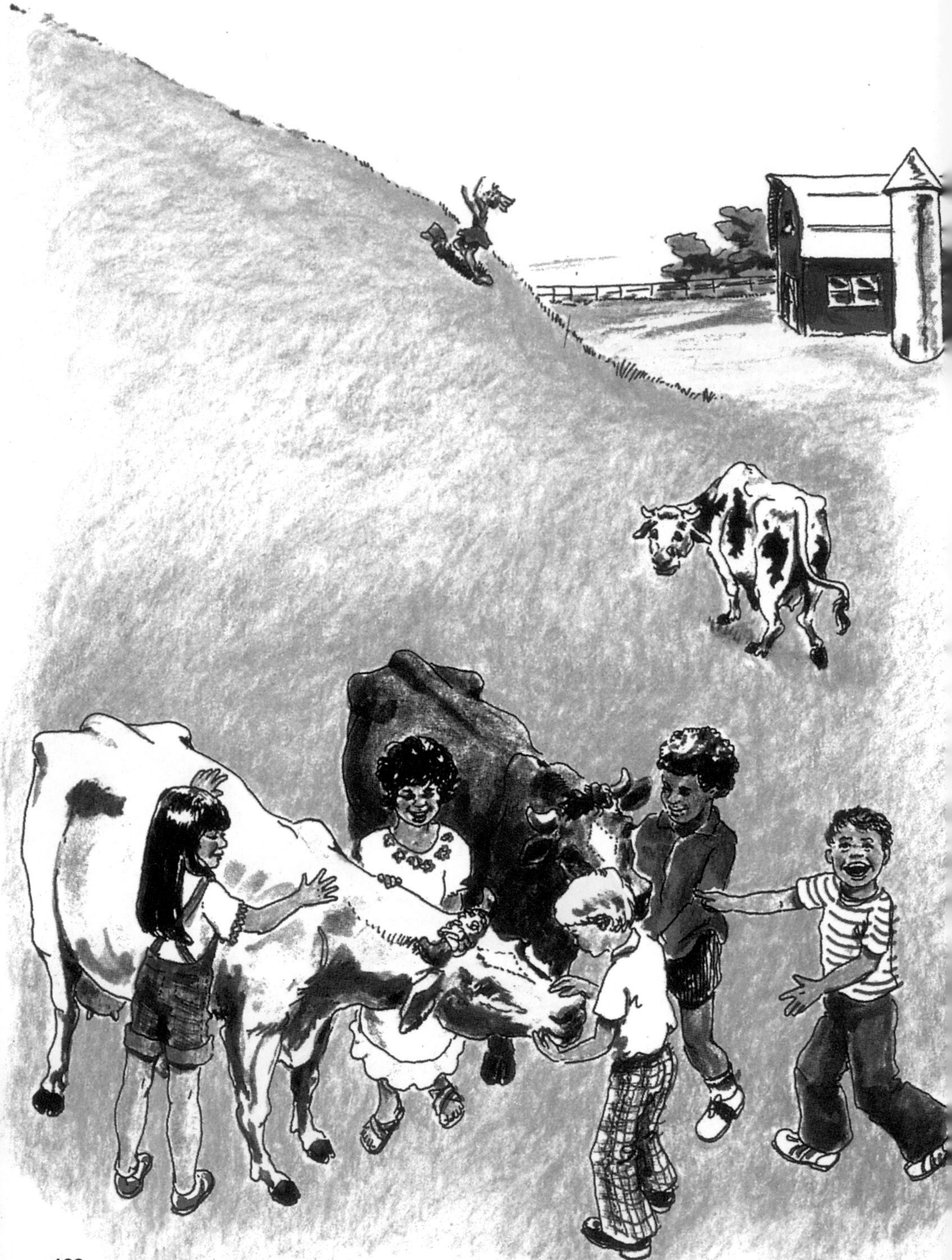

carmen calls for help

who cāme to the farm to pet
cows?

whȳ didn't the children pet
carmen?

who fell into a dēēp, dēēp hōle?

how did the other cows trȳ to
help the girl?

whȳ didn't the tēacher hēar the
cows mooīng?

then carmen saw the girl. carmen
called "moo" very loud. she called
"moo" so loud that the tēacher could
hēar her. the tēacher said, "that
sounds līke a call for help." the
tēacher ran to the little girl.

the tēacher helped the little girl
get out of the hōle. the tēacher went
ōver to carmen and said, "we are so

glad that you have a loud moo. you said 'moo' so loud that you sāved the little girl."

and what do you think the little girl did? the little girl kissed carmen and said, "thank you for mooing so loud."

now carmen has lots of children pet her. carmen is happy that she has a big, loud moo.

this is the end.

jill's mouse

jill had a pet mouse. her mouse
was little and pink. jill got a
little box for her little mouse. then
she went to her mother and said,
"look what I have. I have a pet
mouse in this box."

her mother jumped up. her
mother said, "get that mouse out of
this house."

jill said, "but I want to kēēp
this mouse."

her mother said, "you can't kēēp
that mouse in this house. I dōn't
līke that mouse."

jill asked, "would you let me
kēēp this mouse in the yard? then
the mouse would not be around you."

"yes," her mother said, "but keep that mouse out of this house."

so jill took the box and went to the yard. she said, "I will make a house for this mouse." so she piled some grass around the box.

now jill is happy and her mother is happy. and the mouse is happy.

why was jill happy?

why was her mother happy?

why was the mouse happy?

the end

1

the magic pouch

there was a little girl who lived
nēar a tall mountain. the mountain
was so tall that the top was alwāys
in the clouds. the girl wanted to
go to the top of the mountain, but
her mother tōld her, "no." she said,
"that mountain is stēep. you would
fīnd it very hard to get to the top."

but one dāy the little girl was
sittīng and lookīng at the mountain.
she said to herself, "I would līke to
see what is in thōse clouds at the
top of the mountain. I think I
will go up and see."

so the girl took her pet hound
and started up the tall mountain.
they went up and up. the sīde of

the mountain was very stēēp. up
they went. the girl said to her
hound, "do not fall. it is very far
down to the ground."

soon the little girl and her
hound cāme to the clouds nēar the
top of the mountain. she said to her
hound, "now we will see what is on
the other sīde of thōse clouds."

what do you think they will see
on the other sīde of the clouds?

mōre to come

2

the magic pouch

where did the little girl live?

what did the girl want to do?

who tōld her not to go up the mountain?

who did she tāke with her?

where did the girl go with her hound?

the little girl and her hound went into the clouds. she said, "I cannot see too well. thēse clouds māke a fog." but the girl and her hound kept gōing up and up.

all at once they cāme out of the clouds. they could not see the ground any mōre. they could ōnly see clouds under them. they were in the sun. the sun was in the girl's eyes, so she could not see well. she sat down and said to her hound, "we must sit and rest."

all at once the little girl looked up and saw a funny little house. she said, "I didn't see that house before. let's go see who lives there."

so the girl and her hound walked over to the funny little house.

all at once a loud sound came from the house.

more to come

3

the magic pouch

where did the little girl and her hound go?

what did they see when they cāme out of the clouds?

what did they hēar comiñg from the house?

when the loud sound cāme from the house, the little girl stopped. she looked all around, but she did not see anyone. the sound cāme from the house once mōre. the girl and her hound walked up to the house. she called, "is anyone insIde that house?"

all at once the dōōr of the house ōpened. the girl looked insIde the house, but she did not see anyone. slōwly she walked insĪde. slōwly her hound walked insĪde. then the dōōr slammed bēhĪnd them. the hound Jumped. the girl Jumped. she said, "let's get out of hēre." she grabbed the dōōr, but it would not ōpen. the girl said, "Ī dōn't lĪke this."

all at once the girl looked at a funny pouch hanging on the wall. and a loud sound cāme out of the pouch. it said, "ōpen this pouch and let me out."

more to come

4

the magic pouch

what did the little girl and her hound see on top of the mountain?

why didn't they leave the funny house?

what was hanging on the wall?

the girl walked over to the pouch. she said, "is there some thing in that pouch?"

"yes. I am a magic elf. I have lived in this pouch for a thousand years. please, would you open the pouch and let me out?"

the little girl asked, "how many years have you lived in that pouch?"

the elf said, "a thousand years."

the girl started to open the pouch. then she stopped. she said, "elf, I dōn't think I should let you out. this is not mȳ house. I should not be hēre."

the elf said, "this is mȳ house. so plēase ōpen the pouch and let me out. if you let me out, I will give you the pouch. it is magic."

the girl touched the pouch. she asked herself, "should I ōpen this pouch and let him out?"

mōre to come

5

the magic pouch

what was insIde the pouch?

how many yēars had the elf lived
in the pouch?

the little girl said to herself,
"should I ōpen this pouch?" she
looked at the pouch. then slōwly she
ōpened it. out jumped a little elf,
no bigger than your foot. the girl's
hound went, "owwwww." then the elf
jumped all around the room. he
jumped on the tāble and on the
flōōr. then he ran up one wall and
down the other wall. he ēven ran
around the hound. "owwwww," the
hound yelled.

"I'm out. I'm out," the elf
shouted. "I lived in that pouch a

thousand yēars and now I'm out."

at last the girl's hound stopped gōing "owwwww." the elf sat on the tāble and said, "I thank you very much. plēase tāke the magic pouch. but be cāreful. when you are good, the pouch will be good to you. but when you are bad, the pouch will be bad to you.

mōre to come

6

the magic pouch

the elf tōld the little girl, "when you are bad, the pouch will be bad to you."

the girl picked up the pouch. she said to the elf, "I have been good to you. let's see if this magic pouch will be good to me."

she rēached insīde the pouch and found ten round rocks that shīne. "thēse round rocks are gōld," she shouted. "I'm rich."

so the girl thanked the elf for the pouch.

then the girl and her hound started down the tall mountain. they went down and down. they went into the clouds. when they left the clouds, the girl could see the ground. down and down they went.

when they rēached the bottom of the mountain, the sun was settĩng. it was gettĩng lāte. the girl was tīred. but she ran to her house.

her mother met her at the dōōr. she said, "where were you? your father and I have looked all around for you."

the little girl did not tell her mother where she went. she said, "I went to slēēp in the grass. I just wōke up." she tōld a līe, and that was bad.

more to come

7

the magic pouch

did the little girl tell her mother where she was?

what did she tell her mother?

what does the pouch do when you are bad?

the girl's mother looked at the pouch. she said, "where did you get that pouch?"

"I found it on the ground," the little girl said. she tōld another līe. "but mother, there are ten rocks of gōld in this pouch. we are rich."

she rēached in the pouch and took something out. but when she looked, she saw that she was not hōlding gōld rocks. she was hōlding yellōw mud. her mother said, "you are not

funny. we are not rich. but you are
dirty. go clean your hands."

the little girl got a rag and tried
to rub the yellow mud from her
hands. but it would not come from
her hands. she rubbed and rubbed,
but the yellow mud stayed on her
hands. her mother tried to get the
mud from her hands, but she could
not do it.

then the girl started to cry.

more to come

8

the magic pouch

what did the little girl take from the pouch?

could she get the yellōw mud from her hands?

could her mother get the yellōw mud from her hands?

the girl crĪed and crĪed. then she said, "mother, I tōld you some lĪes. I did not slēēp in the grass. I went to the top of the tall mountain. and I did not fĪnd the pouch on the ground. a funny elf gave it to me." the girl tōld her mother all about the funny house and the elf.

and when she looked at her hands, she saw that they were clēan.

her mother said, "where did the mud go?"

"I dōn't see it any where," the girl said. she looked to see if there was more mud inside the pouch. and what do you think was inside the pouch? there were a thousand rocks of gōld. her mother said, "we are rich. we are very rich."

and the little girl said to herself, "that pouch is good to me because I was good. I will kēēp on doiñg good thiñgs." and she did. and every time she was good, she rēached in the pouch and found something good.

no more to come

the bugs and the elephant

five elephants went for a walk.
one elephant was very tall. that
elephant said, "I must sit and rest.
I will look for a spot of ground
where I can sit."

so she looked for a good site to
sit on the ground. at last she came to
a fine site that was in the sun. she
said, "this spot is fine." but a flȳ
was sitting in that spot. the flȳ said,
"go awāy, elephant. this is mȳ spot."

the elephant said, "hō, hō. you
cannot stop me if I want to sit in
the sun."

so the elephant sat down. that
flȳ got out of her wāy. then the
elephant said, "this is a fine site.
it is fun here."

the fl̄y said, "you took m̄y spot.
so I will fix you."

the fl̄y went awāy and the
elephant went to slēēp.

when the elephant woke up, she
saw that there were many bugs on
the ground. those bugs were all
around her.

the elephant said, "how did these
bugs get here?"

the little fl̄y said, "these bugs are
with me. they are here to take you
awāy."

and they did. they picked up the
elephant and took her to the lake.
then they dropped her in the lake.

now the fl̄y is sitting in the sun
and the elephant is sitting in the lake.
the fl̄y thinks it is fun to sit in the

sun. and the elephant thinks it is
more fun to sit in the lake.

this is the end.

the pet gōat

a girl got a pet gōat. she liked to go running with her pet gōat. she plāyed with her gōat in her house. she plāyed with the gōat in her yard.

but the gōat did some things that made the girl's dad mad. the gōat ate things. he ate cans and he ate canes. he ate pans and he ate panes. he ēven ate capes and caps.

one dāy her dad said, "that gōat must go. he ēats too many things."

the girl said, "dad, if you let the gōat stāy with us, I will see that he stops ēating all those things."

her dad said, "we will trȳ it."

so the gōat stāyed and the girl made him stop ēating cans and canes and caps and capes.

but one dāy a car robber came to the girl's house. he saw a big red car nēar the house and said, "I will stēal that car."

he ran to the car and started to ōpen the dōōr.

the girl and the gōat werе plāyiñg in the back yard. they did not see the car robber.

more to come

the gōat stops the robber

a girl had a pet gōat. her dad had a red car.

a car robber was gōing to stēal her dad's car. the girl and her gōat werₑ plāying in the back yard.

just then the gōat stoppₑd plāying. he saw the robber. he bent his heₐd down and startₑd to run for the robber. the robber was bendiñg ōver the sēat of the car. the gōat hit him with his sharp hōrns. the car robber went flȳiñg.

the girl's dad ran out of the houseₑ. he grabbₑd the robber. "you werₑ trȳiñg to stēal mȳ car," he yellₑd.

the girl said, "but mȳ gōat stoppₑd him."

"yes," her dad said. "that gōat saved mȳ car."

the car robber said, "something hit me when I was trȳing to stēal that car."

the girl said, "mȳ gōat hit you."

the girl hugged the gōat. her dad said, "that gōat can stāy with us. and he can ēat all the cans and canes and caps and capes he wants."

the girl smiled. her gōat smiled. her dad smiled. but the car robber did not smile. he said, "I am sore."

the end

jane wanted to flȳ, flȳ, flȳ

a girl named jane said, "I want to flȳ, flȳ, flȳ in the skȳ, skȳ, skȳ." her father said, "but if you fall on your head, head, head, you'll end up in bed, bed, bed."

but the girl did not stop talkiñg about flȳiñg. one dāy she went to her dad and said, "if you help me make a big kite, I can flȳ in the skȳ like the birds."

her dad said, "I will help you make a kite, but I dōn't think you should trȳ to flȳ."

jane said, "that is good, good, good. let's make a kite of wood, wood, wood."

her dad said, "we'll nēēd pāper and striñg to make this thiñg."

Jane and her dad got pāper and string and wood. they made a kite that was very, very big.

Jane said, "when the wind starts to blōw, blōw, blōw, just see me go, go, go."

her father said, "no, no, no."

more to come

jane goes up, up, up

a girl named jane wanted to flȳ, but her dad didn't want her to flȳ. he helped her make a big kite. but he tōld her that she could not flȳ with that kite.

then one dāy, the wind started to blōw. jane got her big kite. she said, "I dōn't knōw whȳ, whȳ, whȳ dad wōn't let me flȳ, flȳ, flȳ."

as she was hōlding the kite, a big wind started to blōw the kite awāy. jane said, "I must hōld on to that kite or it will go far awāy."

so she held on to the kite. but when the wind started to blōw very hard, it lifted the kite into the skȳ. she looked down and yelled, "I want mȳ dad, dad, dad, bēcause this is bad, bad, bad."

the kite went up and up. soon it was nēar the clouds. jane yelled, "now I'm ōver the town, town, town, but I want to go down, down, down."

at last the kite came down. it landed in a farm five miles from town. jane left the kite there and walked back to her home. then she tōld her dad, "now I knōw whȳ, whȳ, whȳ I should not flȳ, flȳ, flȳ."

jane never trĪed flȳing again.

the end

the little cloud

there was a little cloud. the little cloud lived in the sky with a mother cloud and a father cloud.

the father cloud was very big and very dark. every now and then the father cloud would say, "it is time to make some rain." the father cloud would shake and make loud thunder sounds—"boom, boom." then the rain would fall from the cloud. the father cloud was very proud. he was the best rain maker in the sky.

but the mother cloud was pretty good at making rain too. every now and then she would say, "I think I'll make some rain." she would make some loud thunder sounds, and out would come the rain.

but the little cloud could not
make rāin. he would sāy, "I think
I'll make some rāin." he would shake
and shake. he would trȳ as hard as
he could, but no rāin came from
that small cloud.

the mother cloud said, "dōn't
fēel bad. when you are bigger, you
will make rāin. you are too small now,
but you will grōw."

and that small cloud did grōw.
every dāy he got a little bigger and
a little darker. and every dāy he
trIed to make rāin. but he couldn't
ēven make loud sounds. and not one
drop of rāin came from that cloud.
he felt very sad.

then one dāy something happened.
the wind was blōwing very hard.

that wind bēgan to blōw the little cloud far awāy from his mother and father. he callₑd to them. but they werₑ māking loud sounds, so they couldn't hēar him.

more next time

the small cloud must help

the wind was blōwiñg the small cloud awāy from his father and mother. the small cloud couldn't ēven see them any more. "I am so sad that I will crȳ," the cloud said. but what do you think happened? when the cloud trīed to crȳ, no tēars came out. that made the cloud ēven sadder.

he said, "I am so small that I can't ēven make tēars."

just then someone called, "help, help."

the little cloud looked down. there was a small dēēr and a mother dēēr. and nēar them was a big forest fire. that small dēēr and the mother dēēr were trapped. "help, help," they called.

the little cloud said to himself,
"I must get help." then he called,
"mom and dad, come ōver here and
make some rāin on the forest." but
the mother cloud and the father
cloud were too far awāy. they
couldn't hēar the little cloud.

"what will I do?" the little cloud
asked himself. "if I could make rāin,
I could help those dēēr. but I am
too small."

the fire was getting bigger all
the time. now it was all around the
two dēēr. the small cloud said, "I
must get mȳ mother and father."

but every time the small cloud
started to flōat one wāy, the wind
took him back. the small cloud looked
down at the two dēēr. then the cloud

said, "I am the ōnly one who can help those dēēr. so I will do what I can."

more to come

the small cloud is happy

the little cloud was the ōnly one who could help the two dēēr. the small cloud said, "I will trȳ to rāin. I will trȳ as hard as I can."

the cloud bēgan to shake. he shook and shook and shook. and ēach time he shook, he became a little bigger and a little darker. he shook some more. and he became ēven bigger and darker.

then he bēgan to make loud sounds. "boom, boom," he said. the sounds he made werₑ almōst as loud as his father's sounds. "boom, boom."

and all at once rāin started to fall from the little cloud. two or

thrēē drops fell. then more drops
bēgan to fall. again the cloud made a
loud sound. "boom." the rāin was
falliñg faster and faster. it started
to fall so fast that it sōaked the
forest. it sōaked the trēēs that were
on fire. and it sōaked the two dēēr.
"thank you, thank you," they called to
the cloud. the cloud kept mākiñg rāin.
when that cloud stopped, the forest
looked like a lake. all of the fires
were out, and the dēēr were standiñg
in the water.

all at once the mother cloud and
the father cloud flōated up to
the little cloud. the father cloud said,
"we see what you did. you are a
good cloud."

the mother cloud said, "I am so
proud. todāy mȳ little cloud became
a rēal rāin cloud."

this is the end.

the tall man gets a scare

one dāy the tall man and his dog
went for a walk to the lake. the dog
said, "I hate to walk, walk, walk,
but I love to talk, talk, talk."

the tall man said, "go jump in
the lake."

the dog sat down. then she said,
"you can swim around, around,
around. I'll stāy on the ground,
ground, ground."

the tall man became very mad. he
said, "dogs love to swim. so let's go
for a swim."

the dog said, "you can swim if
you wish, wish, wish. but I dōn't
like to be with fish, fish, fish."

so the tall man went swimming
and the dog stāyed on the ground.

soon the tall man came out of the lake. he said, "now let's have something to ēat. look around for some fire wood."

the dog said, "I love to ēat things that are good, good, good. but I hate to go hunting for wood, wood, wood."

the tall man said, "if you dōn't get wood, you can't have anything to ēat."

so the dog looked for wood. when she found a big pile of wood, she called the tall man. the tall man took the wood and made a big fire. then the tall man bēgan to cook bēans and mēat. the dog sat and looked at the food.

then all at once, the dog yelled,

"ōver ther‌e, ther‌e, ther‌e. I see a
bear, bear, bear."

the tall man ‌jump‌ed into the lake.
the dog ate all of the bēans and
mēat.

the dog said, "I gave the tall
man a scare, scare, scare. ther‌e
was no bear ōver ther‌e, ther‌e, ther‌e.
hō, hō."

the end

sandy counted everything

sandy was a girl who liked to count. she counted things all the time. on her wāy to school, she would count trēēs and dogs and cats. she would count boys and girls. she ēven counted the steps she took.

sandy liked school. the part she liked best was when the tēacher said, "now we will work on counting." sandy was the best counter in the school.

one dāy sandy was walking to school and she was counting things. she was walking nēar the rāil rōad tracks. and a trāin went bȳ. so sandy counted the trāin cars. there were one hundred cars in that trāin.

there were fifty red cars and fifty yellōw cars.

after school was ōver, sandy began to walk home. she walked nēar the rāil rōad tracks. and there was the same trāin she had sēēn before. the trāin was standing on the track. there were two men and one woman in front of the trāin.

one of the men was sāying, "where are the tv sets? they should be on this trāin. but they are missing."

the woman said, "how could they be missing? this trāin has been standing here all dāy. the tv sets were on this trāin before, so they must be on this trāin now."

more to come

a trāin car was missiñg

what did sandy like to do?

how many cars were in the trāin?

how many red cars were in the trāin?

sandy was standiñg nēar the woman and the men. they were talkiñg about the trāin and the missiñg tv sets.

one man said, "how many cars are in this trāin?"

the other man said, "there are ninety-nine cars in this trāin."

sandy said, "no, there are one hundred cars in this trāin."

the woman said, "get out of here, little girl. can't you see that we are talkiñg?"

sandy said, "but I counted the cars in this trāin when I went to school. there are one hundred cars in this trāin."

"go home, little girl," the woman said. "there are ninety-nine cars in this trāin."

so sandy left. she began to count the cars in the trāin. she found out that there were not one hundred cars. there were ōnly ninety-nine cars.

sandy said to herself, "I am the best counter there is. and I counted one hundred cars. so now I must fīnd out where one of the cars went."

more to come

sandy fīnds the trāin car

when sandy counted the cars on her wāy to school, there were one hundred cars in the trāin. when she counted the cars after school, there were ninety-nine cars. one car was missing.

sandy said, "I must think about this. there were fifty red cars and fifty yellōw cars. but now there are not fifty red cars. one red car is missing."

sandy walked next to the rāil rōad track.

soon she came to a shed. there were rāil rōad tracks that led to the shed. sandy said to herself, "I will fīnd out what is in that shed."

so sandy follōwed the tracks to the shed.

she looked inside the shed and saw a red trāin car standiñg on the tracks. the car dōōr was ōpen. sandy looked around. no one was around. so sandy ran ōver to the dōōr of the red car and looked inside. the car was filled with tv sets.

she said to herself, "I found the car with the tv sets."

sandy was all set to run back to tell someone that she had found the missiñg car. but just then there was a sound nēar her. it was the sound of foot steps.

more to come

a crook stops sandy

sandy had found the missing
trāin car. but now there was a sound
behind her. it was the sound of
foot steps.

"I must hide," sandy said.

then she jumped into the red
trāin car and hid behind a big tv
set. then she looked out. a big man
came into the shed. then another
man came in.

one man said, "back your truck
up to the end of the shed. we will
lōad the tv sets into the truck. but
we must lōad them fast."

the other man said, "yes." then
the men left the shed. sandy said to
herself, "these men are crooks. they
are stēaling the tv sets."

sandy wāited. she could hēar the men talkiñg outside. then she could hēar the sound of the truck.

she said to herself, "I must get out of here." she jumped from the trāin car and began to run as fast as she could go. she ran out of the shed. and then she stopped. the big man was standiñg in front of her.

he said, "what are you doiñg here?"

sandy looked at the man. she wanted to run, but she didn't think that she could run faster than the man. she had to think of somethiñg to sāy. but she couldn't sēēm to talk. she looked at the big man and the big man looked at her.

more to come

sandy tells what she found

sandy trīed to run from the shed but the big man stopped her. he asked her, "what are you doiṇg here?"

sandy wanted to sāy somethiṇg. but she couldn't think of a thiṇg to sāy.

the big man said, "can't you hēar me? I asked you what you are doiṇg here?"

sandy said, "mȳ hound dog."

"what about your hound dog?" the man asked.

sandy said, "I can't fīnd him. he ran awāy and I was lookiṇg for him."

sandy had tōld a big līe. but she

didn't want to tell the big man whȳ she had come to the shed.

the man said, "well, get out of here, and dōn't come back. if I fīnd you plāyiñg around this shed any more, you'll be sorry."

sandy said, "ōkāy. I wōn't come back." she ran awāy from the big man as fast as she could go. she said, "I must tell someone what I found out."

sandy ran back to the trāin that had a car missiñg. the men and the woman were still standiñg nēar the trāin. a cop was with them now. sandy ran up to the cop. she yelled, "I found the car with the tv sets."

more to come

sandy and big bill

sandy ran up to the cop. she told him that she had found the missing train car.

one man said, "will you get out of here, little girl? can't you see that we are talking?"

sandy said, "but I found the train car that is missing."

the woman said, "there is no missing train car."

sandy said, "but there is a car missing and I found it." then sandy told them all about the missing car.

after she told what had happened, the cop said, "I think there were one hundred cars in that train. how can we check it?"

one man said, "that's ēasy. I'll get big bill. he counts the cars on every trāin that comes in here."

that man left. soon he came back with another man. as he walked back with the other man he shouted, "big bill counted the cars. he says that there are ninety-nine cars."

sandy looked at big bill, and big bill looked at sandy. big bill was the man who had stopped her outside the shed.

more to come

back to the shed

sandy saw that big bill was the big man who had stopped her outside the shed. she shouted, "that's one of the men who was stealing the tv sets. that's him." she told the cop that big bill had stopped her outside the shed.

big bill looked very mean. he said, "what's that girl talking about? I think she's nuts."

sandy said, "no, I'm not nuts. that is one of the men."

big bill said, "I don't know what she is talking about. I never saw her before. and I don't know anything about a shed with a red train car in it."

"yes, you do," sandy said.

the cop said, "well, whȳ dōn't we all take a walk down the tracks and fīnd out who is lȳin͡g?"

so they all walkₑd down the tracks to the shed. when they came nēₐr the shed, sandy could see a big whīte truck at one end of the shed. she said, "that must be their truck. the crooks must be inside the shed, lōₐdin͡g the truck."

big bill gave sandy a mēₐn look.

more to come

thank you, sandy

sandy and the others wer~e~ nēar
the shed. the cop said, "the rest of
you wāit here. I'll go inside that
shed and see what's gōiñg on."

so they wāited as the cop went
into the shed. as soon as the cop
was in the shed, big bill said, "I've
got work to do. I'm lēaviñg."

"you better stāy here," one of
the men said. big bill didn't answer.
bill just gave sandy a mēan look.

sandy looked at the shed and
wāited. then she saw some men start
to come from the shed. they all
had their hands up. the cop was
walkiñg behind them.

the cop shouted, "that girl found the tv sets. I think big bill is one of the crooks."

one of the men said to sandy, "thank you for fīndiñg the missiñg car." the woman also thankₑd sandy. so did the cop.

then one of the men said, "this rāil rōad would like to givₑ you a gift for fīndiñg the crooks." so the man gave her a very fine gift. what do you think that gift was?

it was a tv set.

this is the end.

sam gets a kite kit

sam liked to make things. he liked to make toy cars. so he went to the store and got a toy car kit. his mom said, "that kit has the parts of a car. you have to rēad and fīnd out how to fit the parts so that they make a car."

sam said, "I will do that."

so sam began to rēad the pāper that came with the car kit. then he began to fit the parts to make a car. soon he had a toy car.

his mom said, "that is a fine car. you are good at rēading and at making things."

sam did not like to make the same thing again. he said, "I will not make other cars. I will make something else."

so he went to the store and got a kite kit. when he got home, he showed his mom the kite kit. his mom said, "that kit has a lot of parts in it. you will have to read the paper that comes with the kit to find out how to make the kite."

sam looked inside the kit. then he said, "what paper? there is no paper in this kit."

sam's mom said, "that is too bad. how will you make the kite if there is no paper in the kit?"

sam said, "I will go back to the store and get a paper that tells how to make a kite from these parts."

when sam got to the store, the man in the store said, "I dōn't have other pāpers that tell how to make kites."

sam asked, "how can I make a kite if I dōn't have the pāper?"

the man said, "you will have to do the best you can."

sam was not happy. he went home and looked at all the parts in the kite kit.

more to come

sam makes a funny kite

sam liked to make things. he had made a toy car from a kit. he did a good job. now sam had a kite kit. but there was no p̄aper in the kit to tell how to make a kite from the parts.

sam was not very happy. he looked at ēach of the parts. then he began to trȳ to make a kite from the parts in the kit. he worked and worked.

when his mom saw the kite, she said, "hō, hō. that is a funny-looking kite."

it was funny-looking. it looked like a small tent made out of p̄aper and wood. the top of the kite was very sharp.

sam's mom said, "I'm sorry for making fun of your kite, but it looks very funny."

sam said, "I dōn't care how funny it looks. I think it will flȳ."

his mom said, "no, I dōn't think it will. it does not look like a kite that will flȳ."

"we will see," sam said.

so sam and his mom went to the park. there werₑ lots of boys and girls in the park. some of them werₑ flȳing kites. and some of the kites werₑ wāy up in the skȳ.

sam said, "I think mȳ kite will pass up all those kites."

sam's mom said, "I dōn't think your kite will go thrēē fēēt from the ground."

do you think sam's kite will flȳ?
more next time

can sam's kite rēally flȳ?

when sam made his kite, his mom said that it looked funny. so did the boys and girls in the park. they looked at the kite and said, "hō, hō, that thing looks like a tent. it wōn't flȳ."

sam said, "we will see."

sam's kite began to go up. up, up it went. it was going up very fast. sam's mom said, "well, would you look at that kite go up."

the boys and girls said, "wow, that kite can rēally flȳ."

soon sam's kite passed up all the other kites. it went up so far it looked like a little spot.

some of the boys and girls asked sam, "where did you get that kite?"

sam said, "you can get a kit for

this kite at the toy store. but I will have to tell you how to fit the parts so that they make a tent kite."

more and more boys and girls asked sam about his kite. at last sam said, "I will make a pāper that tells how to make a tent kite from the kit."

and he did. when he got home, he sat down with his mom. his mom helped him with the pāper. when they were done, his mom said, "this pāper rēads very well. you did a good job."

sam said, "that's good. now let's make a lot of these pāpers so we can give one to everybody who wants one."

the next dāy sam gave ēach boy and girl a pāper. he tōld them to rēad the pāper and do what it said.

now there are many tent kites

flÿing ōver the park. and no one
says, "hō, hō." the tent kites flÿ
better than any other kite.

the end

tim and his hat

tim had a hat. it was red and white. tim said, "I hate this hat." but his mother said, "it is cōld outside. so you must have a hat."

when tim was outside, he said, "I will take this hat and hide it." so he did. he found an ōld trēē with a hole in it. he stuck the hat in the hole. then he said, "when I come back from school, I will get mȳ hat from the trēē."

tim got to school on time. he began rēading his book. then he looked out the windōw. what do you think was falling from the skȳ? snōw was falling. when tim saw the snōw, he said, "wow, it is getting cōld out there." and it was. it was getting cōlder and cōlder.

when school was ōver, the snōw
was very dēēp. tim walked outside.
then he said, "mȳ ēars are getting
cōld. I had better run home." so
tim began to run. he ran as fast as
he could go, but the snōw was very
dēēp and it was hard to run in that
snōw. the other boys and girls were
plāying in the snōw, but tim did not
have time to plāy. he said, "I must
get home before mȳ ēars get too
cōld."

at last, tim came to the ōld trēē.
he grabbed his red and white hat.
he slipped the hat ōver his ēars.
then he said, "I dōn't hate this hat.
I like this hat now."

tim did not hate his hat after

that dāy. and he did not hide his hat
in trēēs. now tim has time to plāy
with the other boys and girls when
the snōw gets dēep.

this stōry is ōver.

212

the fox wants a cone

a little girl was sitting in the woods. she had an ice crēam cone. she was sitting on a log, ēating her ice crēam cone.

a slȳ fox was looking at her. that fox was thinking. "I will con that girl. I will con her into giving me her cone."

so the slȳ fox ran up to the girl. then he fell ōver and began to shout, "help me, help me. mȳ mouth is on fire. givе me something cool for mȳ mouth."

"close your eyes and ōpen your mouth," the girl said.

the slȳ fox was thinking, "hō, hō, I connеd that girl out of her cone."

when the fox closed his eyes, he

did not get a cone in his mouth. he
got a drink of cōld water.

"there," the girl said. "that
should make your mouth cool."

"no, no," the fox shouted. "mȳ
mouth nēēds something cōlder than
that water."

the girl said, "close your eyes
and ōpen your mouth."

the fox said to himself, "this
time I will con her out of her
cone."

but he did not con her out of a
cone. he conned her out of a bit of
ice. she dropped the ice into his
mouth. then she said, "now your
mouth must fēēl cool."

"no, no," the fox yelled. "I nēēd
a cone."

the girl said, "you can have the
cone, but I ate all the ice crēam."

but the fox did not take the
cone. she had made him so mad that
he ran back into the woods. he
never trīed to con her again.

more to come

rēad the Ītem

say "what" when the tēacher says "that."

the con fox

the slȳ fox wanted an ice crēam cone.
he couldn't con the girl out of her cone,
but he had a plan. he said, "I will go to
the ice crēam stand. when I get there, I
will con somebody out of a cone."

so that fox went to town. when he
came to the ice crēam stand, he said,
"hand me a cone."

the man at the stand made up a big
cone. then the man said, "that will be one
dime."

the fox said, "but I gave you a dime."

the man said, "no, you did not give me
a dime. I think you are trȳing to con me."

"I dōn't con men," the fox said. "I

came here for a cone. and I gave you a
dime for that cone."

the man looked at that slȳ fox. then
the man said, "if this is not a trick, I will
give you the cone."

the fox said, "I am not lȳing. I am
not trȳing to con you."

just then a little girl came up to the
ice crēam stand. it was the girl that the
fox had met in the woods. the girl said to
the fox, "you are the fox that trĪed to
con me out of mȳ cone. I am glad to
see that you are buȳing a cone."

the man at the stand said, "so you
are a con fox."

the fox was so mad that he ran back
to the woods. he never trĪed to con the
man at the cone stand again.

this is the end.

r̄ead the Ītem

s̄ay "spot" if the t̄eacher says "stop."

don was sad

   don had a job that he did not like. he worked in a hat store. he mopped up in that store at the end of ēach d̄ay. every d̄ay he mopped and mopped. when he mopped, he talked to himself. he would s̄ay, "I hate to work in this hat store. I hate to mop."

   then he would think of things that he would like to do. he said, "I wish I was big. I wish I could flȳ. I would like to be a super man. but I am just a mopper. I am not big. I cannot flȳ."

   when the store was mopped, don would sit and mope. he would think of the things he would do if he was a super man.

"I would fīnd crooks," he said. "they would shoot at me, but I would not fēēl a thing."

every dāy was the same. don would mop and mop. then he would mope and mope. when he mopped, he would think about being a super man. when he would mope, he would think about that too.

then one dāy something happened. don was mopping in the back of the store. all at once, he stopped mopping. "I think I hēar something," he said.

the sound came from the dōōr that led down the stāirs. somebody was sāying, "come down the stāirs." don ōpened the dōōr and went down the stāirs.

to be continued

rēad the Ītem

when the tēacher says "what," sāy "that."

don mēēts a woman

wherₑ did don work?

whȳ did don mope?

somebody tōld don to come down the
stāirs. so don droppₑd his mop and went
down the stāirs. it was very dim down
therₑ. but don could see a woman in the
dark. the woman had a cap and a cape.
she said, "don, do you want to be a
super man?"

"yes, Ī do," don said.

the woman said, "Ī will help you be a
super man if you tell me that you will do
good."

"Ī will do good," don said.

then the woman handed don a dime.
that dime lookₑd dim in the dark.

the woman said, "keep that dime. when you want to be a super man, tap the dime three times."

don looked at the dime, but when he looked up, he did not see the woman. "where are you?" don asked.

there was no answer. don called again, but there was no answer. then don took the dime and went up the dim stairs. he said to himself, "I must be having a dream." but then he looked at the dime and said, "if I am dreaming, how did I get this dime?"

don picked up his mop and began to mop again. then he said, "I think I will tap that dime three times and see what happens. I hope it works."

so don dropped his mop and tapped his dime one time, two times, three times.

to be continued

The Family Handyman Magazine's

HOME EMERGENCIES AND REPAIRS

The
Family
Handyman
Magazine's

HOME
EMERGENCIES
AND REPAIRS

by the Staff of

The Family Handyman Magazine

Harper & Row, Publishers

1817   NEW YORK, EVANSTON, SAN FRANCISCO, LONDON

FIRST EDITION

STANDARD BOOK NUMBER: 06-011211-5

LIBRARY OF CONGRESS CATALOG CARD NUMBER: 77-138760

Designed by Lydia Link

Contents

Tables

Acknowledgments

The compilation of this work required the help of many people. Members of the staff of *The Family Handyman* magazine who were exceedingly co-operative were Morton Waters, Franc L. Roggeri, L. LaBarge, Arnold B. Romney, Harry McClelland, and Sam Scheuer. Writers and contributing editors of this publication who were also helpful include Robert B. Berger, Robert Hemberger, J. Edward Latham, John L. Elliott, Burt Murphy, Lee Oertle, Bernard Gladstone, Mort Schultz, Stanley Schuler, Leon Theil, Raymond Schuessler, and Ralph Treves.

ARNOLD E. ABRAMSON, Publisher
The Family Handyman

The Family Handyman Magazine's

HOME EMERGENCIES AND REPAIRS

Tools and Materials for Emergency Repairs

Storms . . . rain, wind, snow, ice . . . can cause considerable damage to any home. When they strike, there is little time to gather the necessary materials to repair the damage. And it is generally essential to make those patch repairs immediately to prevent further ill effects. Later, in calmer weather, the proper repairs can be made.

There are also many home emergencies that occur at times other than during a storm. But when an emergency situation strikes, you should know how to cope with it. This, of course, is the purpose of the present book. But, before getting into the various problems that can cause discomfort and hardship in a home, let's say a word about prevention, an important phase of combating any home emergency. There are many things you can do now to prevent future trouble. And one of these is to acquire the necessary equipment and tools so that you will be ready when an emergency strikes.

EMERGENCY TOOLS AND MATERIALS

Preparation is the key to handling the home emergency. It's the unexpected things that come up, such as roof leaks, broken windows, or power failures, that can bring danger or discomfort to you and your family. We cannot predict exactly when an emergency will occur, but we can tell you how to handle any situation that may arise, so that even the worst eventuality presents no serious problem to you.

The most important part of being prepared is having a stock of emergency supplies. Knowing what to do is also important, but if you do not have the materials needed for emergency action, you may as well be totally unprepared. That is why we have assembled a list of all the things that

1

should be kept on hand. Most of the tools and materials needed for the usual types of emergencies are likely to be found in the home. But often something is lacking, making it impossible to do the job when it must be done. It's a good idea to store this equipment in one area of the basement or workshop. While you have many hand tools for everyday repairs, here is the basic equipment you need to meet unwelcome emergencies.

Table 1

BASIC TOOLS AND MATERIALS

Caulking gun	Staple gun
Claw and ball-peen hammers	Steel square
Two screwdrivers (one large one small)	Nail set ($\frac{1}{16}$-inch)
Wire-cutting pliers	Mason's trowel
Slip-joint pliers	Force cup (plumber's friend)
Handsaw (crosscut)	Three-cornered file
Two wood chisels (¼- and ⅞-inch)	Stillson wrench
Small flat paintbrush	Carpenter's pencil or crayon
Snow shovel and ice chopper	Metal shears
Jackknife	Brace and bits
Hacksaw	Soldering iron or gun
Cold chisel	Glass cutter
Folding rule	Spade
Hatchet or hand ax	Galvanized water bucket
Gimlet	Small washtub
Smoothing plane	Funnel
6-foot stepladder	Center punch
Oilcan	Wrecking bar (16- or 18-inch)
Putty knife	Adjustable wrench
Tree-pruning saw	Pipe wrench
Cleanout auger (snake)	Propane torch
Mallet	Drill and bits
Test light	Level

Materials You Need

Here are several items that are a *must* to meet some emergencies.

1. An extra length of gutter (try to get a section to match the type you now have on your home).

2. Strap hangers to hold gutters.

3. A section of downspout.

4. Downspout straps.

5. Plastic sheeting: buy either heavy vinyl plastic sheeting, the acetate sheets (often sold for tack-on storm windows), or the reinforced sheeting which uses cord or wire.

6. Strips of towel for freeing frozen pipes.

7. Pipe clamps to fit the pipes so you are ready if a pipe springs a leak. Or you can get the metal patching kits, in which

impregnated plastic sheeting can be used to make small patches.

8. Several short and medium lengths of pipe with unions, couplings, and nipples, just in case you have to replace part of a pipe line.

9. Extra lights: have some candles, kerosene lamps, or flashlights on hand in case your electricity fails.

10. Turnbuckles and wire.

11. Electric resistance cable (the heating cable used to melt ice).

12. Rock salt or ice-melting chemicals.

13. Caulking compound.

14. Soft metal alloy sheet to make patch repairs. There is one type that is rustproof, easily soldered, and easy to cut and bend.

15. About 50 to 100 feet of heavy rope; reinforced clothesline can do the job.

16. Bailing wire for tying down wind-loosened objects.

17. Fiberglass repair kit.

18. Stakes to secure bailing wire.

19. Heavy cardboard (white) for making signs to warn unwary pedestrians of hazards that could cause injury, such as downed electric wires.

20. Flares to supplement warning signs, particularly at night.

21. Tube or can of waterproof sealer.

22. Epoxy steel-dust putty to repair cracks in waste pipes.

23. Aluminum or galvanized shingle and roofing nails.

24. Sink-drain chemicals.

25. Strands of wire.

26. Faucet washers and packing.

Materials You Need for Coping with Power Failures

In addition to the materials already mentioned, here is equipment for lighting, heating, and—if you have an electric range—for cooking, when the power fails.

1. Gasoline lantern: this provides ample, safe lighting for the home.

2. Candles, however, can be used instead for room lighting.

3. Electric lantern provides needed illumination if you must work outdoors at night.

4. Electric flashlight will do as a substitute, but make certain it's the waterproof type.

5. Space heater can be a kerosene or gasoline model.

6. Matches should be kept in a tightly sealed waterproof container. Coat a few with wax or paraffin so they can be used outdoors in rain.

7. Camp stove uses gasoline or alcohol for fuel.

GLUES AND ADHESIVES

The homeowner who expects to be able to cope with various emergencies should become acquainted with such items as adhesives, glues, and patching compounds. Let's look at glues and adhesives first. Actually, in recent years, the terms "glue" and "adhesive" are used almost interchangeably. While there are still some made entirely of organic products, most glues have a synthetic plastic or resin base and can be used on a great many materials. With this new family of adhesives you can b,nd almost anything to almost anything else.

Some of these new products are designed for one specific job; others are multipurpose adhesives that solve a wide variety of bonding and sealing problems around the home and in the workshop. Some require that workpieces be clamped; some do not. Some can be used at almost any temperature; others have fairly rigid temperature limitations. Some come ready for use; others must first be mixed or blended. Some can be used over any surface; others require special surface preparation or cleaning. If you want to be sure of long-lasting, permanent results with any of them, there are two rules that must be observed: (1) be sure that you are using the right kind of glue or adhesive for the job at hand; and (2) make certain that you follow the manufacturer's recommendations exactly.

The following table lists some of the most common bonding and repair jobs homeowners are likely to encounter and recommends the adhesives that will work best on each. In many cases, several adhesives will do the job, but the table lists those that will perform well at the least possible cost.

Table 2

SELECTING THE RIGHT ADHESIVE

Typical Home Repair Problems	Polyvinyl white glue	Liquid animal glue	Casein glue	Plastic resin glue	Resorcinol glue	Contact cement	Epoxy resins	Clear household cement	Plastic-mending adhesives	Fabric-mending adhesives	Plastic rubber	Rubber silicone
General woodworking, light duty, interior	X	X										
Heavy-duty woodworking			X	X	X		X					

Table 2 (Continued)

Typical Home Repair Problems	Polyvinyl white glue	Liquid animal glue	Casein glue	Plastic resin glue	Resorcinol glue	Contact cement	Epoxy resins	Clear household cement	Plastic-mending adhesives	Fabric-mending adhesives	Plastic rubber	Rubber silicone
Waterproof wood joints					X		X					
Laminating plastics to wood or metal		X				X						
Gluing metal to wood						X	X	X			X	X
Repairing and bonding metals							X					
Ceramic and masonry repair							X					
Bonding glass to glass or metal							X					X
Bonding plastic to metal, wood, or plastic						X	X	X				X
Repairing flexible plastic								X	X			
Mending rubber											X	X
Mending leather, cloth, canvas								X		X	X	
Leather to wood or metal						X			X		X	
Rubber to metal, wood, glass						X					X	X
Cloth to wood, plaster, or cardboard	X	X				X		X				
Cardboard, paper, to itself or to wood	X							X				

Table 2 (Continued)

Typical Home Repair Problems	Polyvinyl white glue	Liquid animal glue	Casein glue	Plastic resin glue	Resorcinol glue	Contact cement	Epoxy resins	Clear household cement	Plastic-mending adhesives	Fabric-mending adhesives	Plastic rubber	Rubber silicone
Porcelain and china, light duty						X		X				
Porcelain and china, heavy duty							X					
Cork and felt to wood	X	X				X					X	
Cork and felt to metal						X					X	
Sealing joints in metal, glass											X	X

Regardless of which glue or adhesive you select, remember that there are certain rules to observe if you want to be sure of long-lasting, permanent results. Surfaces to be bonded should be clean; remove all dust, moisture, wax, and grease beforehand. Some adhesives also require the removal of all old paint or varnish as well. If the joint was previously glued and came unstuck, scrape off the old adhesive first if you want to ensure a good bond this time.

When clamping pressure is recommended, be sure that clamps are over the entire joint. Do not tighten clamps any more than necessary for firm contact. Excessive pressure may bend or warp the workpieces out of alignment and may also squeeze out so much glue as to seriously weaken the joint. If no pressure is required (as when working with epoxy adhesives), use rope, tape, or some other temporary brace to hold the pieces together while the adhesive sets.

When working with a glue that has to be mixed before use, make certain to measure the ingredients carefully; then take the time to mix them thoroughly. This is particularly true with the two-part epoxies and other synthetic resins. Thorough blending is required to start the chemical reaction that makes them harden. With some, temperature limitations must also be carefully adhered to. Using these at temperatures well below recommended limits may not necessarily interfere with their hardening, but it will greatly weaken the resulting bond.

SEALERS AND PATCHERS

A multitude of new sealers and patchers have been introduced in recent years, most of them guaranteed to do a more effective repair job and last much longer than their predecessors. For example, take that bugaboo to all homeowners—the ever-present gap around a bathtub or bathroom sink. As you know, grout is usually used for sealing this area, but it has one big disadvantage: it dries out with age, losing needed flexibility, so it crumbles and you are left with a crack.

The caulk or seal around a bathtub or sink requires this flexibility, because a bathtub or sink shifts as settling occurs. A number of companies are now marketing a bathtub caulk that is elastic and retains flexibility. The basis for it is the use of silicone or vinyl plastic as a main ingredient. These products come ready-mixed in tubes, which means that you do not have to mix them. Simply lay the tube's nozzle along the crack and fill it.

Modern bathtub silicone or vinyl plastic sealants begin curing in a few minutes and are hardened sufficiently in about one hour. In its tube form, the caulk is soluble, some brands with water, others with turpentine ("turps"). So, if you do happen to get some on the tile or on a fixture, you can wipe it away with a damp cloth or sponge. But this must be done immediately, or it becomes a matter of chipping away the excess. Most of these sealers can be used for other jobs as well, such as repairing ceramic tile that has come loose and fastening fixtures (towel rack and soap dish, for example) to ceramic tile.

In other words, if you were to buy a bathtub sealer containing silicone

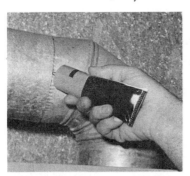 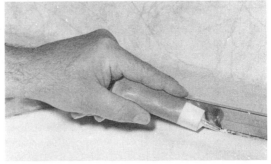

(Left) Often overlooked by the homeowner are natural cracks in heating ducts. A good deal of heat can be lost through these. A liquefied metal caulk is excellent to use for these areas. (Right) This type of bathtub/sink caulk contains a silicone rubber or vinyl plastic and will remain flexible for many years to come. It is the best way to stop water leaks around plumbing fixtures.

or vinyl plastic base, you could use it for a variety of jobs other than sealing the gap between tub and tile, in spite of the fact that the manufacturer may make products called silicone seal, clear seal, metal seal, or auto sealer for other specific jobs. The only basic difference in the sealers that contain silicone or plastic vinyl base is their color. Many manufacturers, in fact, sell their modern caulking products under one name only and in one package only. However, there are times when selecting a sealer on the basis of color could be an advantage, although you might already have a compatible sealer on hand. Suppose, for example, you wish to seal a crack in an aluminum gutter or downspout. A white or black smear on that metal would mar its appearance. Thus, you might be inclined to use so-called metal seal. This is basically the same silicone-base product as the others, but its outward appearance is designed to give an aluminum color.

Take another example. Assume you have a crack in a clapboard panel that you wish to seal, but the siding is brightly painted. You can see what black-, white-, or aluminum-colored sealant would do to clapboard siding that is brown, yellow, or some other color. But, of course, a translucent sealant would not harm the appearance at all.

Finally, the relatively new types of caulking compounds in butyl rubber or vinyl plastic are also used to seal a home's natural cracks, such as between siding and window sash and around doors. These are available in tubes or cylinders, as is regular caulk, to fit standard caulking guns.

Another product area that you should know about is the liquid (or plastic) metal products—specifically, liquid (plastic) aluminum and liquid (plastic) steel. These are actually atomized aluminum or steel, combined with epoxy resins in putty form.

Once they dry, you can drill, tap, file, or grind them. In addition, they are not affected by water, steam, oil, or gasoline and will not crumble, crack, check, peel, or shrink. Temperatures up to 400° F. will not affect them, either.

To give you some idea of what liquid aluminum or steel can be used for around the house, the following is a list of repairs that can be made with either type:

1. Leaks in sink-trap seals, pipes, tanks, and washtubs.
2. Holes and leaks in garbage cans, pans, and pails.
3. Holes in gutters, downspouts, and sheet-metal roofs, as well as cracked seals in metal gutter joints.
4. As an anchor for loose screws, nuts, and bolts.
5. As caulking around aluminum storm doors and windows.
6. To reset handles on tools and utensils.

7. To fill cracks and seals in heating ducts and furnace jackets.

Fiberglass Patches

The number one emergency patching material is fiberglass. Boatowners have long known the advantages of using it for patching their craft. Now this versatile material has been adapted for home and shop use. You can buy it in kit form in hardware and department stores. The kit consists of an epoxy resin, a hardening agent, and fiberglass cloth to cover the area being patched. These materials can also be purchased separately in any quantity from most marine supply stores and boat dealers. It's ideal for making repairs over metal or wood rain gutters. The fiberglass cloth follows the contour of the gutter willingly. You will certainly lessen a lot of your plumbing repair headaches with these patches. Frozen, split, or leaking pipes are easy to repair. One or two layers of the cloth and resin will withstand a great deal of pressure and make a permanent patch. Cracks in basement walls can also be handled easily. The fiberglass cloth should be put on so that it overlaps the crack at least 3 inches on each side.

Fiberglass eliminates the use of solder and soldering iron on all metal repairs. Pails, garbage cans, and car mufflers and radiators are only a few of the things that can be patched. Since no heat is required (as in welding or soldering), you can patch a leaky fuel oil tank without danger of explosion. One of the biggest advantages is the fact that the fiberglass and epoxy resin will adhere to and reinforce wood, glass, metal, concrete, plaster, hardboard, plastic, and most composite materials.

Regardless of the surface over which the patch is applied, the procedure is basically the same. The surface to be repaired must be clean and dry. Use steel wool to remove flaking paint or rust. The resin and its hardener should be mixed according to directions on the can and spread over the surface with a small brush or spatula. A piece of fiberglass cloth is cut to size and pressed into position over the area, and additional resin is spread to saturate it. The wrinkles and bubbles in the cloth should be smoothed out with a small squeegee or piece of cardboard. A second layer of cloth and resin can be put over the first to make the patch stronger. Allow the resin to cure before painting.

LUBRICANTS

Lubricants can forestall problems in equipment around your home and thus prevent emergencies. The following guide lists common items around the house that require regular lubrication.

Table 3

SELECTING THE RIGHT LUBRICANT

Item	Lubricant	Where to Lubricate	Frequency and Amount
Light appliances (blender, toaster, etc.)	Light household oil	Where manufacturer says	Twice a year; follow manufacturer's instructions for amount
Heavy appliances (washing machine, dryer, etc.)	Heavy oil (SAE 20 or equivalent)	Where manufacturer says	Twice a year; follow manufacturer's instructions for amount
Rusted or "frozen" equipment	Penetrating oil	As close to meeting surfaces as possible	Liberally
Locks	Powdered graphite, liquid lock, or liquid deicer	Place the latch in open position. Puff lubrication there, then puff some into the keyhole	Twice a year; as much as needed
Hand tools	Light household oil	Where manufacturer says	A thin film after each use
Power tools	Light household oil	Where manufacturer says	Twice a year; follow manufacturer's instructions for amount
Drawers	Silicone formula white grease stick or spray	On tracks and drawer rails	Twice a year; as much as needed
Windows	Silicone formula white grease stick or spray	Along guides on both sides	Twice a year; as much as needed
Small motors	Light household oil	Where manufacturer says	Twice a year; follow manufacturer's instructions for amount
Hinges	Light household oil	Remove the hinge pin, clean, apply lubricant to pin and hinge	A thin film twice a year
Wheel lugs	Combination liquid graphite/oil lubricant	Remove the lugs, clean, apply lubricant to bolt and lugs	A thin film four times a year
Outdoor tools	Combination liquid graphite/oil lubricant or light household oil	On all exposed metal	A thin film after use or twice a year
Sliding and overhead doors	Light household oil or combination liquid graphite/oil lubricant	Along tracks	Three times a year; as much as needed
Sliding screens and storm windows	Silicone formula white grease stick or spray	On sides of metal windows and screens, also in tracks	Four times a year or as needed

Lubricating properly is not simply a matter of a few squirts of oil. As part of your new attitude toward it, you should keep these three things in mind.

Do Not Use Too Much. Where manufacturers supply specific instructions as to the amount and frequency of lubricating their products, follow them to the letter. They know their products best. It's a grave mistake to think that if a little lubricant is good, a lot will be wonderful; that can be a wonderful way to botch up the equipment. If instructions are not provided, follow the chart guide.

Use the Correct Lubricant. Manufacturers have taken great pains to create lubricants ideally suited to specific jobs. Use the right one for maximum benefits.

Clean What You Are Lubricating. This is not always possible, but it is always desirable.

SAFETY WHEN MAKING EMERGENCY REPAIRS

Home emergencies cause sufficient damage without your hurting yourself while meeting the problem. Here are a few safety tips to follow.

1. Leave blown-down electrical lines alone! Even if you are *positive* that the lines are dead, do not touch them with bare hands. Use a board to move the lines *only* if they are a real hazard! Call the power company.

2. If you use power tools outdoors—an electric drill or portable handsaw —make certain they are grounded. Do not stand on damp ground or in water when using electrical tools!

3. For electrical repairs inside the house, use insulated-handle tools. Coat the handle and most of the tool with liquid rubber, or buy shockproof guards at your local hardware store. In the basement, stand on a dry piece of plywood or a few boards—not on the concrete.

4. Avoid exposed flames in the house. Keep lighted candles in deep glass bowls or jars away from curtains or other inflammable objects.

5. Keep inflammable liquids—gasoline or kerosene—in tightly sealed cans and clearly marked. Do not store them in the house! Better keep them on a high, safe shelf in the garage or, best of all, in a special storage bin in the ground.

6. Do not try to climb a ladder during a raging storm. Even after the storm, follow these ten rules for ladder safety:

- If your ladder is wood, lay it flat and walk along the rungs. You will find the weak ones—safely—this way.
- Do not use a wood ladder that has been painted. You cannot see weak spots through a coat of paint.
- Do not try to put up a ladder where there are power-line wires overhead.
- Select a level, solid resting place for the feet of the ladder.
- Place the feet of the ladder one-fourth its length away from the wall. At this angle you cannot overbalance and fall backward.

- Before you start carrying materials up the ladder, be sure you have a place to put them when you get to the top.
- Cans of liquid materials should be fitted with hooks on handles so they can be hung from the ladder.
- If there is a strong wind blowing, stay on the ground.
- Do not carry tools loosely in your pocket. They may fall on someone below.
- Do not try to reach from the ladder. Take the time to move it over.

Now, let us see how you can handle home emergencies or how they can be prevented. Of course, many of the items covered in the following chapters could not be classified as *real* emergencies, but rather as problems or sources of discomfort for your family.

CHAPTER 2

Emergency Plumbing Procedures

Perhaps the peak of frustration in any homeowner's life occurs with his valiant but futile efforts to stem the rising tide of some emergency plumbing failure. Scurrying here and there in helpless disorder, he will eventually wait, purple with rage, for the arrival of a plumber who is out on another job, meanwhile striving to convince an alarmed wife that everything will be all right. This incident may draw chuckles at the next barbecue, but the telling of the tale will nevertheless reveal bitter undertones. Much better to tell a success story—and here's how.

Not all plumbing failures are actual emergencies, of course, and not all breakdowns require a highly paid plumber. There are those you can fix yourself, and there are those you can temporarily control while awaiting the man in the panel truck. To equip yourself with this know-how saves on the pocketbook and minimizes water damage with its untold inconveniences.

Actually, your plumbing system is divided into three simple parts: the supply system, which conveys hot and cold water to the various fixtures; the drainage system, which carries away all waste and used water; and the vent system, which ensures a constant flow of fresh air through the drainage system.

Do not worry about the vent system; you will never see it. It seldom needs attention (see page 34 for exception) and has the primary function, as just stated, of allowing a circulation of fresh, clean air throughout the drainage system, tending to stop the growth of fungi which produce sewer slime. Admission of air also is used to prevent trap siphonage.

While the vent will not cause you any trouble, the supply system is subject to deterioration, leaks, faulty washers, and other annoyances in proportion to the quality of the pipe used when your plumbing was installed. The drainage system, on the other hand, is sometimes subject to stoppage and occasionally leaks at the valves.

Shutting Off Water. In an emergency, you may need to shut off the main water supply. In most cases the flow of water in a house is controlled by means of stopcocks or shutoff valves in the pipes. To shut off the main supply of water, as it enters the house, it's necessary to close the wall cock or valve which is usually in the main pipe in the basement. This cock may have a handle, or a wrench may be needed to turn it. It may be of the ground-key type with a small plugged hole bored in its side for draining the pipes after the water is shut off, or it may be a compression-stop type with a cap nut covering the drain opening. In either case, this opening should be closed when the water is turned off, for, if not closed, a stream of water will shoot from the hole with considerable force. Where means have not been provided for shutting off a drain opening, a small wooden peg driven into it will temporarily stop the flow of water until the pressure is relieved by draining the pipes through the faucets.

Additional shutoff cocks are sometimes provided below the sink, lavatory water closet, or other fixtures for convenience when repairs are to be made, so that the flow of water may be cut off from any one fixture without disturbing the flow to other parts of the system. It is important that all members of the family know where these various shutoffs are located. To help speed up this identification, mark all pipes in the basement with identifying dabs of colored paint. Use one color for all hot water lines, another color for cold water pipes, and additional colors for gas lines, waste pipes, and the like. You can also color-code them in the same way to tell which room each pipe supplies.

PLUMBING LEAKS

Wherever you have a container that holds or carries water, there is always the possibility of a leak. Often the leak is not a serious matter, but it is a nuisance and, if allowed to continue, could add considerably to your water bill. In extreme cases, the leak may lead to flooding and water damage.

Leaky Faucets

Compression water faucets are most often found in the home. Actually, water faucets and globe valves, which are also usually found on the water lines, serve the same purpose, in that they control the flow of water. The essential difference is that faucets are used at discharge points over fixtures such as sinks, lavatories, and tubs, while valves are used to close off portions of the plumbing system. In fact, faucets and globe valves are very similar in construction, and repair instructions given below apply to both. Your

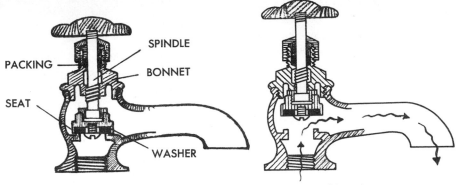

PACKING

SPINDLE

BONNET

SEAT

WASHER

Sketches show the working parts of a typical compression faucet and how they operate.

faucets or valves may differ somewhat in general design from the one shown here, because both faucets and valves come in a wide variety of styles. For instance, mixing faucets, which are found on sinks, laundry trays, and bathtubs, are actually two separate units with a common spout. Each unit is independently repaired.

If a faucet drips when closed or vibrates ("sings" or "flutters") when opened, the trouble is usually a worn washer at the lower end of the spindle. If it leaks around the spindle when opened, new packing is needed.

To replace the washer:
(See illustration on page 16.)
1. Shut off the water at the shutoff valve nearest the particular faucet.
2. Disassemble the faucet: the handle, packing nut, packing, and spindle, in that order. You may have to set the handle back on the spindle and use it to unscrew and remove the spindle.
3. Remove the screw and worn washer from the spindle. Scrape all the worn washer parts from the cup and install a new washer. If you do not have the proper size of washer, file down a larger one; do not use one that is too small.
4. Examine the seat on the faucet body. If it is nicked or rough, reface it. Hardware and plumbing supply stores carry the necessary seat-dressing tool. Hold the tool vertically when refacing the seat.
5. Reassemble the faucet. Handles of mixing faucets should be in matched positions.

To replace the packing:
Simply remove the handle, packing nut, and old packing, and install a new packing washer. If a packing washer is not available, you can wrap stranded graphite-asbestos wicking around the spindle. Turn the packing nut down tight against the wicking.

Other faucet parts may be replaced as necessary. For example:

Bonnet Washer and Packing. If there is a leak around the bonnet or stem, the washer in the bonnet may be worn, but more than likely the packing around the stem may have to be replaced. Bonnet washers are called "friction washers" and, being metal, seldom wear out. So, your first test is to tighten the bonnet *firmly* in place and check again for leaks. If

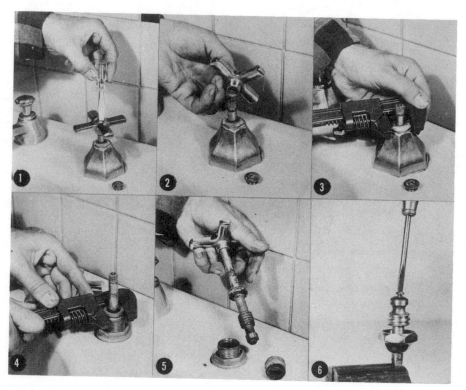

Steps in replacing a washer:

1. To open a faucet for washer replacement, unscrew the cap cover handle screw; then remove the screw.

2. The handle is then lifted off. If stuck tightly, tap the underside all round with a block of wood.

3. Use a smooth-jawed wrench to remove the large nut holding down the spindle housing. Do not scar chrome.

4. The spindle housing lifts off, exposing a nut which holds the spindle in position. Remove it with a wrench.

5. With the bearing nut gone, the spindle can be twisted out. Use the handle to turn the spindle if it sticks.

6. Holding the spindle in a vise makes removal of the brass washer screw easier. Replace washer and screw.

the leak continues, remove the bonnet, pry out the friction washer, and remove the packing beneath it. Either the packing will be preformed to fit the bonnet snugly or it will be standard cord packing. Replace with either type, but preferably the preformed.

If you use cord, first put the friction washer on the stem and wrap the packing around in a clockwise direction; do not use too much, because it could prevent the stem from moving upward, resulting in a decreased water flow.

Now, put the bonnet back on the stem, firmly squeezing the two together, compressing the package. Next, separate the bonnet and stem, and you will find the washer and packing in place in the bonnet. Reinsert the stem in the faucet, replace the bonnet and handle, and the unit is repaired.

Swing-Spout. When water seeps between the retaining nut and swing spout of a kitchen faucet, the cause may be a simple, loose fitting. If tightening does not cure it, remove the nut (some models have a knurled retaining ring), which enables you to separate the spout from the faucet unit.

Within the nut will be packing or what is called an O-ring. Remove and discard it. If you use an O-ring replacement, it fits effortlessly into place. If you use packing, wrap a new length around the spout shank, place it back in position over the faucet unit, and tighten the retaining nut, compressing the new packing.

Sink Spray. Three conditions can cause a sink spray to malfunction—a cracked hose line, a clogged spray head, or a faulty washer. The washer is the least likely cause and needs only a simple replacement. Likewise, a clogged head need only be removed and cleaned of accumulated foreign matter.

A break in the hose, which usually occurs near the head, cannot be snipped off and reinserted. Unfortunately, you will have to replace the entire length, which has factory fittings at both ends. It is impossible to transfer the old fitting.

Fuller-Type Faucet. To repair a leak in this old-fashioned type of faucet, unscrew the entire faucet from the supply pipe. In the end of the faucet you will see a cone-shaped washer. The nut or screw holding this in place is easily removed and a new Fuller ball (as the washer is called) substituted. Most plumbing supply houses still stock Fuller balls.

One-Handle Faucet. This relatively new type of faucet, because of its complex gears and pins, should be serviced only by a competent plumber.

Pipe Leaks

Generally, there are three types of plumbing pipes in the home. One carries water; a second is the drainpipe that leads to the third type; this is the waste pipe going to the sewer or septic system.

Leaks in water pipes usually result from corrosion or from damage to the pipe. Pipes may be damaged by freezing, by vibration caused by machinery operating nearby, by water hammer, or by animals bumping into the pipe. (Water hammer is discussed later in the chapter.)

Actually, pipe leaks are usually quite simple to repair. Your first step is to turn off the water at the nearest shutoff valve between the leak and water supply, and open the nearest outlet to drain the pipe. Then proceed in this fashion.

Leaks at Joints or Fittings. For easiest repair, use commercial iron cement and a special pipe clamp, both available at all hardware stores. Fit the clamp around the pipe and bolt it in place against the fitting. The cement, which comes in powder form, should then be mixed with water to the consistency of stiff putty and tamped into a groove in the clamp. As soon as the cement hardens, turn on the water.

A leak in a sink drainpipe usually occurs at the large nut holding the gooseneck. Either the nut has loosened or the packing is faulty. Try tightening the nut first (wrap tape around it to protect the finish). If this does not work, loosen it and slide it out of the way. Wrap packing around the threads and retighten the nut.

Holes and Cracks. Small holes in pipe, such as those made by accidental puncture, can often be sealed with fiberglass as described in Chapter 1 or by self-tapping screws. The latter require a gasket cut from an old inner tube or other piece of rubber. The gasket should be about twice the size of the screwhead. Punch a hole in the center of the rubber, insert the screw, and coat both sides of the rubber with iron cement; then drive the screw into the hole by turning its head with a monkey wrench, or screwdriver.

This method is not recommended for pipe under 1½-inch diameter, since the plug impedes the water flow, or for pipe too thin to form a thread as the screw is driven in. In 1½-inch pipe or larger you may prefer to use a utility plug which has its own neoprene gasket and requires no thread to hold it in place. Instead, it carries a metal "spider" which expands inside the pipe as the plug is tightened, clamping it firmly in place. Install by drilling or punching a ⅜-inch hole in the center of the leak. Insert the utility plug. Hold the plug cap with one wrench, and with another turn the screw head until tight.

Pipe Clamps. For holes in smaller pipes, and for corrosion or cracks in all pipe, your most practical remedy is an ordinary pipe clamp carried by hardware and chain stores. These are stocked for all sizes of pipe and in widths to cope with almost any type of crack, puncture, or weak spot caused by corrosion.

Apply by cutting a rubber, fiberglass, or leather gasket large enough to cover the leak amply. Coat both pipe and gasket with iron cement. If the pipe is cracked, force iron cement into the crack with a hammer. Then place the clamp around the pipe and gasket and tighten the bolts. If the crack is too long for the width of a single clamp, use two or more clamps spaced an inch or two apart over the gasket. These patches will stand up for a considerable time if water pressure is *not* too high.

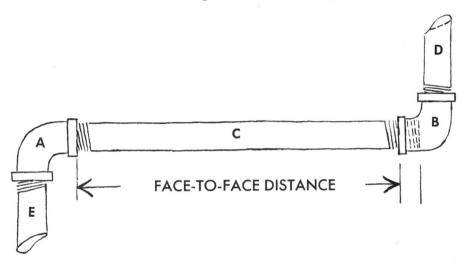

Leaking section between elbows A and B (above) is replaced by made-up union (below).

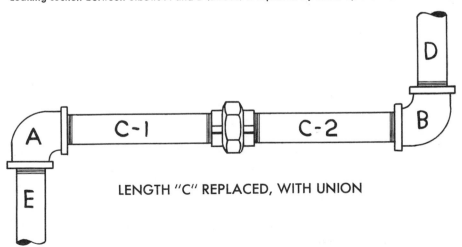

Pipe Replacement. When a pipe leaks because its wall has rusted out, the only practical repair is the replacement of the pipe, and generally all the pipe of the same length of service as well, because the occurrence of one rust leak is usually the signal for the beginning of a whole series. This should be done by a plumber, but may be temporarily repaired as described previously.

Waste-Pipe Leaks. Waste pipes, usually of cast iron, are probably the easiest to repair. Simply apply iron cement or plastic steel to the leak. Another effective repair is made with one of the plastic or fiberglass patching kits. The material is cut to size and treated with a special solvent or activating liquid from the kit. Clean the defective area with a wire brush and apply the patch.

Leaky Flush Tanks

The parts of the tank that usually require repair are the flush (outlet) valve, the intake (float) valve, and the float ball. To determine the location of a leak, remove the tank's cover. If the water level is low because water is flowing out of the tank into the toilet bowl, the flush valve is not closing properly. If the level is high, causing water to flow out of the tank through the overflow pipe, the inlet valve is not closing.

Flush Valve. A leak at the flush valve is ordinarily caused by one of three conditions: a damaged tank ball, rust or dirt on the valve seat, or damaged metal linkage. To find the trouble, shut off the water supply and flush the toilet to empty the tank. Now remove the flush ball and examine it carefully. If worn, rotted, or out of shape, it must be replaced. First, however, check the flush valve seat—the hole over which the ball fits when it is in place—for dirt or rust. If it appears rough, smooth it with a piece of emery cloth. Scrape away any scale or rust; then screw the new flush ball to the connecting rod.

Another cause of a flush valve leak could be in the linkage between the flush handle and the flush ball. Test its operation by holding the handle in the open position and releasing it to the closed position. The flush ball should drop squarely on the valve seat when the handle swings closed. If not, see if the rods are bent and replace any that are. The lower rod—the one attached to the flush ball—is held in position by a metal guide arm, one end of which is connected to the overflow pipe. This arm is adjustable and should be directly over the valve seat; otherwise the flush ball will not seat itself properly. While you are at it, replace any rods that are badly corroded or rusted, even though they appear straight.

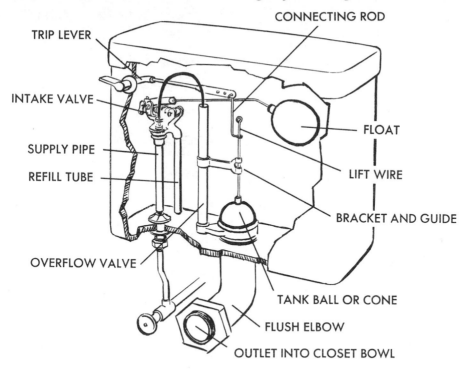

CONNECTING ROD

TRIP LEVER

INTAKE VALVE

SUPPLY PIPE

REFILL TUBE

OVERFLOW VALVE

FLOAT

LIFT WIRE

BRACKET AND GUIDE

TANK BALL OR CONE

FLUSH ELBOW

OUTLET INTO CLOSET BOWL

Typical flush tank.

When working on the flush valve, stop the flow of water by propping up the float with a piece of wood. Be careful not to bend the float rod out of its proper alignment.

Intake Valve. A leaky inlet valve—one that does not close—could be caused by a bent float rod, a hole in the float, a worn valve washer, or a rough valve seat. First inspect the rod that connects the float to the inlet valve. This controls the amount of water that will flow into the tank before the valve closes. If the rod is bent upward, the water level will be low and an insufficient supply will be delivered to the bowl. Unless the rod is badly out of shape, necessitating replacement, you can adjust it slightly in the proper direction.

Plunger Washer. To replace a worn plunger washer:

1. Shut off the water and drain the tank.

2. Unscrew the two thumbscrews that hold the levers and push out the levers.

3. Lift out the plunger, unscrew the cup on the bottom, and insert a new washer. The washer is made of material such as rubber or plastic.

4. Examine the washer seat. If nicked or rough, it may need refacing. If the float valve assembly is badly corroded, replace it.

Float Ball. The float ball may develop a leak and fail to rise to the proper position. (Correct water level is about 1 inch below the top of the overflow tube, or enough to give a good flush.) If the ball fails to rise, the intake valve will remain open and water will continue to flow. Brass float balls can sometimes be drained and the leak soldered. Other types must be replaced. When working on the float ball, be careful to keep the rod aligned so that the ball will float freely and close the valve properly.

If these measures do not stop the leak, you will have to disassemble the valve itself. Before doing this, make sure the water is shut off. The inlet valve is located near the top of most tanks, although in some older ones it may be found at the bottom. In the latter case, you must flush all the water out of the tank to get at the valve. Loosen the screw that holds the valve's plunger. On the bottom of this is a washer, which is held by a nut and, in most cases, a brass ring cap. The cap may be badly corroded; if so, replace it as well as the washer. While the valve is disassembled, check the valve seat for rough spots and smooth it with a seat-dressing tool.

Leaks in porcelain flush tanks are common enough occurrences and can be stopped easily. Having shut off the water and drained the tank, clean and dry the inside surface; follow with an application of epoxy resin to the crack. The epoxy has to be forced in with something like a kitchen knife, against both sides of the opening, to assure the best bond. After allowing the recommended drying time, refill the tank and flush several times to be sure the patch holds.

Flushometers. This is the new device for tankless toilet operation. Originally these were used exclusively in areas where high water pressures were available, but now they can be installed (where there are floor outlets) in areas where as little as a 10-pound pressure is provided. Since there is nothing visible about this type of device other than the operating handle, repairs may seem to warrant calling in professional help. However, the mechanism has been simplified and the working parts reduced in number.

Here are the major troubles that occur with a flushometer: the unit will not flush at all, or runs for too long or too short a period; the valve will not shut off at all; the mechanism is too noisy; leaks develop around the flushing handle; the toilet may flush all by itself repeatedly. The majority of these troubles stem from one or two things: the valve is not properly regulated, or the by-pass outlet is blocked, too small, or too large. Other troubles can be caused by damage or clogging of the valve seat, similar to troubles with faucet washers. Cleaning the whole mechanism and replacing washers will cure most of the troubles. Installation of special quiet valves will reduce noise.

Cement Laundry Tubs and Porcelain Enamel Fixtures

When a cement laundry tub springs a leak, it is, of course, useless until repaired. With a cold chisel, cut into the cement along the crack to make a groove about ½ inch deep. Wet down the area and fill the crack with a stiff mixture of 1 part of cement and 2 parts of sand, packing the groove liberally. Fill the tub with water and let it stand a few days to give the patch time to cure.

If the tub seems to be losing water through seepage rather than a leak, thoroughly dry it out and apply a coating of epoxy resin to the entire surface, inside and out.

Plumbing fixtures coated with porcelain enamel will chip or crack if struck a hard blow or if subjected to sudden extremes of temperature. Broken or chipped enamel can be repaired by the application of special enamel-patching compound or liquid porcelain enamel. The surface must be clean, dry, and free of grease so that the substance will bond firmly to the surface when it is applied.

Vitreous china fixtures that become cracked can sometimes be *temporarily* repaired with china cement, but the value of such repairs is questionable. Normally, the fixture will require replacement.

OPENING STOPPED DRAINS

Clogged drain lines are emergencies you can usually handle yourself, but in doing so, your approach must be methodical. That is, the first step in clearing a stoppage is to find out where the stoppage actually is. Suppose, for instance, the kitchen sink stops up; first make sure it is only the sink that is clogged. Examine other fixtures for signs of backed-up waste. Run some water into the bathroom basin and bathtub to make sure they are running off. Do not, however, flush the toilet to test for a stoppage, for if there is one you are likely to have a couple of gallons of sewage back up and overflow onto the floor. If there are any open fixtures in the basement, such as washtubs, examine them; a stoppage involving the whole house will show up here first.

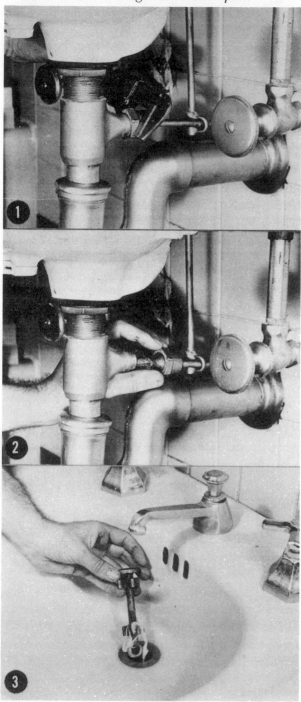

Mechanism operating the drain closure. (1) The stopper base is released by first removing the large nut. (2) The nut slides off, pulling out the interlocking device. Be sure the basin is empty before removing. (3) With the base rod freed, the closure may be withdrawn for removal of lint and other clogging debris.

When a single fixture stops up, but *all* other fixtures run off, showing that the house drain is clear, you *know* that the stoppage is in the sink drain.

Sink-Drain System. First, check the sink stopper or strainer for hair and lint. In most sink models, the stopper is removed by loosening the nut of the lift-rod coupling underneath the basin; then pull the rod back so the retainer ball is clear of the fitting. Release the catch on the stopper, and lift it out of the basin for cleaning.

If this is not the cause, the next step is to fill the basin partially with water and place the rubber cup of a plumber's plunger over the water outlet. Now work the plunger vigorously up and down for 10 to 20 strokes. Pull up the plunger and allow the waste to run off.

If the drain is still stuck, try again. You will suck waste water back into the sink: pick out any matches, paper, hair, or other solid matter that may be in it. Keep the strainer clear. Do not give up too easily; repeat the whole plunger operation 8 to 10 times before deciding it's of no use. Often, with just a plunger, you can succeed in getting the waste to run off slowly.

But if not, then—and *only* then—use a chemical solvent such as caustic potash, according to directions on the can. Chemical solvents made specially for this purpose will in most cases dissolve the grease causing the stoppage. Do *not* use solvents if the sink is completely stopped up. First, solvents take a long time to work down to the stoppage—from two hours to over-night. Second, the solvent may *not* work, and then you have an entire waste line filled with a caustic solution dangerous to your skin and eyes as the actual work of cleaning out the stoppage continues. *Do* use chemical solvents to keep clear the "sluggish" drain of any fixture which has a tendency to stop up. But play safe; make sure the drain is only "sluggish" and not completely clogged.

If the plunger will not start even a slow runoff of the waste, the next step is to check the trap underneath the sink. If it is equipped with a cleanout plug, remove the plug with a wrench. If there is no plug, you must remove the complete trap. Before doing anything, however, place a pail under the trap to catch water and dirt that will come pouring out. The chief function of a trap is to catch the debris that may flow down the drain. Also the water that remains in the trap after the sink is drained seals the pipe, locking out noxious sewer gases.

With the trap open or plug removed, run a drain-trap auger through the opening as far as it will go. The best auger to use is one 15 to 20 feet long, equipped with a crank. If you hit a tight obstacle, use short, sharp thrusts to force the flexible part of the auger through. The crank enables you to rotate the flexible line, using it to drill through obstructions when jabbing fails to free them; it is also used for guiding the line around turns or elbows in the pipe. (One purpose of the elbow trap is to prevent valuables such as rings from reaching the main drain.)

When replacing the plug, remember to replace the gasket, too. When you replace the entire trap unit, wrap packing around its threads before tightening the fittings. Use grease-impregnated fiber cord, which forms a watertight seal. You can buy packing at any hardware store.

Some bathtubs have a "drum" trap which has an access cover set even with the bathroom floor. Unscrew the cover and clean out the trap. The snake can also be worked from a drum trap. If there is no drum trap, the snake will have to be worked directly through the strainer holes, as bath traps are generally inaccessible and most of them do not have trap plugs.

Toilet Stoppage. The overflowing of a toilet is caused by a stoppage, and a clogged toilet can often be cleaned with a plumber's friend. First, however, prevent an overflow of water by removing the tank's lid and pressing the ball within downward; this ball blocks the drain, sealing off the water flow to the bowl. You may also have to use a water closet auger or snake, if the plumber's friend does not clear the trap.

Before using the auger, fill the bowl with water to just under the rim. This additional weight of water helps to flush any object which may be loosened into the drain, and it also indicates when you have cleared the stoppage. In use, the curved end of the auger is placed in the curved trap of the bowl. The auger is then forced through by pushing and turning the steel rod: it is withdrawn in the same manner, always turning in the same direction.

If the auger pulls out the stoppage, fine; if not, work it through 3 or 4 times. If the waste runs out, pour a pail of water in the bowl. If this runs off readily, flush the toilet. Now put about 5 or 6 feet of toilet paper in the bowl and let it get wet; then flush it down with a pail of water. If the toilet backs up now, you know some solid object—a toothbrush, a comb, a medicine bottle—is caught in the bowl. It allows plain water to pass, but not water and paper.

If the auger fails, it may be necessary to remove the water closet bowl and loosen the jammed object. To do this, proceed as follows:

1. Shut off the water.
2. Empty the tank and bowl by siphoning or sponging out the water.
3. Disconnect the water pipes to the tank.
4. Disconnect the tank from the bowl if the water closet is a two-piece unit. Set the tank where it cannot be damaged. Handle the tank and

bowl carefully; they are made of vitreous china or porcelain and are easily chipped or broken.

5. Remove the seat and cover from the bowl.

6. Carefully pry loose the bolt covers and remove the bolts holding the bowl to the floor flange. Jar the bowl enough to break the seal at the bottom. Set the bowl upside down on something that will not chip or break it.

7. Remove the obstruction from the discharge opening.

8. Place a new wax seal around the bowl horn and press it into place. A wax seal (or gasket) may be obtained from hardware or plumbing supply stores.

9. Set the bowl in place and press it down firmly. Install the bolts that hold it to the floor flange. Draw the bolts up snugly, but not too tight, because the bowl may break. The bowl must be level. Keep a carpenter's level on it while drawing up the bolts. If the house has settled, leaving the floor sloping, it may be necessary to use shims to make the bowl sit level. Replace the bolt covers.

10. Install the tank and connect the water pipes to it. It is advisable to replace all gaskets, after first cleaning the surfaces thoroughly.

11. Test for leaks by flushing a few times.

12. Install the seat and cover.

Incidentally, inefficient flushing can be caused by failure of the trip lever or handle to lift the ball valve to water level so it can float and settle into place as the water flows out. You can usually see what is needed by watching the flush valve and ball at work a few times. Frequently, the outlets in the upper rim of the bowl can become clogged and require brush cleaning. Also the vent may be stopped up so air does not escape freely ahead of the water flow, in which case a trip to the roof with the snake can clear the vent from the top. Less likely possibilities are a flooded municipal sewer system or an overloaded septic system, but then you would be apt to notice sluggish action in all drains.

Main House Drain. Should you find all fixtures backing up, this shows that the stoppage is in the main house drain. To correct, follow the drain to where it leaves the house. Near the wall you will find (in most cases) a U-shaped house trap. Unscrew the trap cover on the street or septic-tank side of the trap. If the drain leading outside seems clear, the stoppage may be in the bottom of the trap. You can probe this with a stick, but there is no better way of clearing a house-trap stoppage than with your hand, though you may want to wear a rubber glove. If the bottom of the trap is clear, unscrew the other trap cover, if there are two. If no stoppage is visible, screw both covers back on; when you do clear the stoppage a lot of waste will suddenly gush to the trap, and it will overflow if the covers are not on.

Now look for a cleanout plug in the house drain. This plug is usually found at the end of the pipe. You can work a snake from here, but you will need a flat steel snake for the sink drain and, preferably, a heavy one. If you cannot reach the stoppage from the cleanout, unscrew the inside trap cover and work *to* the stoppage. It may be messy, but it will do the trick.

You can also cut an access hole in the cast-iron pipe. Mark off an oval-shaped patch in the top of the pipe; then, with a sharp cold chisel, make a continuous cut along the mark. Keep going around the cut, increasing the force of the hammer blow, and the piece will pop out. Or with a hacksaw make two vertical cuts 3 or 4 inches apart. Join the cuts horizontally with a cold chisel and chip out the piece. The hole is repaired with putty in the same manner as the sink drain.

If the stoppage is between the house and the street sewer or septic tank, it is a job for the plumber. Such stoppages are almost always due to roots, and you do not have (nor would it pay you to have) the necessary tools.

Another reason for a stoppage outside the house would be a collapsed sewer line—again a job for the plumber. In either case, install a cast-iron sewer, which will neither collapse nor allow roots to enter it.

By the way, a fairly recent innovation in plumbing tools for cleaning clogged drains is the power impact gun, which allows you to clear obstructions as large as a medicine bottle without removing traps or other plumbing. One type is a jet model using compressed freon gas cartridges in a gun housing; the other is a flushing gun using air pressure from a separate compressor. Both operate on kinetic energy—that is, water impact to clear stoppages up to 250 feet—and often may be rented at plumbing supply shops.

Other Sewage Problems. As suburban areas rarely have the advantage of municipally operated sewage systems, waste disposal is generally a private matter. Nevertheless, when trouble develops, the homeowner often finds himself at sea about the steps needed to put the system back in working order again. Many homeowners are not even aware of the type of system they have, how it works, and what to do when something goes wrong.

Sewage disposal systems are generally of one of two types: septic tanks or cesspools. A septic system consists of a sealed tank into which raw sewage flows in a sealed sewer pipe from the house. Here it is acted on by bacteria or enzymes which convert it to liquid. The liquid waste, now purified partially, is led through open tile lines buried in gravel beds. About 40 percent of it seeps into the ground, and the rest evaporates or is absorbed by plants growing above the drain fields.

A cesspool, on the other hand, is open at the sides and bottom so that liquid seeps directly into the soil around and below it. There are no drain fields. There is, or can be, some bacterial action on solid waste in the cesspool.

Indications that something has gone wrong with the sewage disposal system are few but definite. Water drains slowly from household fixtures or refuses to drain at all. The soil above the system may become saturated, or sewer gases may bubble up through the ground. In extreme cases raw sewage may even be forced up through vents. Almost invariably the trouble will have been caused by one or more of these conditions:

1. The unit is too small.
2. Water consumption has been substantially increased.
3. The drain fields have been clogged by tree roots.
4. The drain fields have been smashed by heavy traffic over them.
5. The soil around the disposal points has become saturated.
6. Liquefaction in the septic tank has been slowed down or halted by excessive use of lye or strong detergents or by cold weather.

The only likely cure for point 1 is a larger tank. Where greater water consumption due to laundry installation is the cause of overloading, a dry well should be constructed for *laundry waste only* to relieve the tank of this excess.

The remaining problems can be handled, as an emergency measure at least, by the use of special-purpose chemical compounds. Root-removing chemicals are available under a number of brand names, or a solution of 2 pounds of copper sulfate in 5 gallons of water will do the job. Clogged drain fields and areas where the soil has become loaded with sediment may be cleared with drain-field cleaners. Both root- and sediment-dissolving chemicals are introduced *beyond* the tank. It's a good idea to set up a permanent pipe for this purpose. It should have a sealed lid flush with the ground. With such an arrangement, periodic treatments are easily accomplished.

Renewing bacterial activity is also a simple matter. Activators should be introduced once a month through house drains. Not only does this treatment assure clear sewer lines, but the tank that is functioning properly never needs to be cleaned.

FROZEN PIPES

If one or another of your household water or drainpipes suddenly stops working after a cold spell hits, chances are it is frozen. First thing to do? Carefully inspect as much of pipe as you can see for cracks and breaks.

Water is almost the only substance in nature that expands initially on solidifying. It is this expansion which causes the breaks often found in a frozen pipe. If thawing begins before such breaks are corrected, water spills out into your house, and water pressure may enlarge minor breaks into major ones. Should your inspection show serious bursting, call a plumber. Should you find minor cracks, repair them, even if only with temporary patching, before starting to thaw. (See *Plumbing Leaks*, earlier in this chapter.) Should you find no cracks—and just because a pipe has frozen does not necessarily mean that it has burst—you can begin thawing at once.

Supply Pipes

To thaw safely any pipe supplying hot or cold water to bathroom, kitchen, laundry, or any other faucet, first make sure that all faucets on the line are open. If in doubt, open every faucet in the house at least partially. This acts as a safety valve should your later heat application build up air and steam pressure.

Make sure all your shutoff valves are open. You may have previously closed them to prevent a flood through burst pipes while making your inspection or putting on patches. Next try to locate the frozen section. Lead or copper pipe, when frozen, gives itself away by bulging. Cast-iron pipe, however, does not bulge. But you can generally locate the frozen length because it feels colder to your hand than does the adjacent pipe.

Blowtorch or Candle. Blowtorch heat is not recommended. It is easy to build up steam pressure in the pipe, which may then burst in your face. Candle heat may be used if nothing combustible is in the pipe's vicinity. Keep the candle moving so that the pipe at no point becomes too hot for you to touch. Avoid heating the middle of a frozen section, since this may build dangerous pressure. If you are not sure where the frozen portion begins and ends, take no chances and avoid the candle.

Lamps. Do not use flame lamps of the kerosene type. Electric lamps, backed by a metal reflector, work well if positioned not more than 3 or 4 inches from the pipe. Do not permit the electric bulb to touch the pipe.

Electric Irons. An iron, if you have a sufficient extension cord, is a handy thawing tool. Lay it right on the pipe, but keep it moving.

Resistance or Heating Cable. Do not use this. There is too much danger of shock and pressure, except in expert hands.

Hot Water. This is the safest, most effective, and messiest way for the family handyman to thaw a pipe. Pour the water from a kettle—or saturate towels wrapped around the frozen section. And wear your rubbers.

Heat Lamps. For most homeowners, a heat lamp or photoflood bulb is convenient if pipe is in a wall. Its radiant heat does the trick. Be careful to avoid scorching paint or wallpaper. If you do not have a lamp, try a room heater or hair dryer. And, though it may seem ingenious, do not place a heating pad around the pipe. You may get a severe shock.

Disposal Pipes

First try running hot water into the drain. If that does not work, mix a can of lye or drainpipe cleaner with *cold water*—being extremely careful not to splash yourself. Pour the concoction slowly down the drain. By chemical action, this generates heat which may be sufficient to thaw.

If unsuccessful, apply heat as recommended above for thawing supply pipes. Work from the lower or exit end of the frozen section upward toward the input. This allows the melted ice to drain away.

Inaccessible Pipes

Underground or inaccessible pipes must be handled a little differently. With pipe wrenches, open the frozen pipe where convenient at the house end. Insert a pipe or rubber tube of a lesser diameter than the frozen section. An ordinary household medicinal water bag and tube often can serve the purpose. Push the tube in as far as it will go, preferably until the end rests against the actual ice. Pour in the hot water. The water will flush back with melted ice, which may be caught in a bucket as shown. Keep pushing the thaw tube further into the pipe as the ice melts, until the entire passage is clear. Then withdraw the thaw tube and close the shut-off valve immediately, so that the house will not be flooded; reconnect the length of thawed pipe to the water system.

Preventing Freezing

Pipes may be insulated to prevent freezing, but this is *not* a completely dependable method. Insulation does *not* stop the loss of heat from the pipe, but merely slows it down; and the water may freeze if it stands in the pipe long enough at below-freezing temperature. Also, if the insulation becomes wet, it may lose its effectiveness.

Electric heating cable can supply the continual heat needed to prevent pipes from freezing. The cable should be wrapped around the pipe as shown on page 32 and covered with insulation.

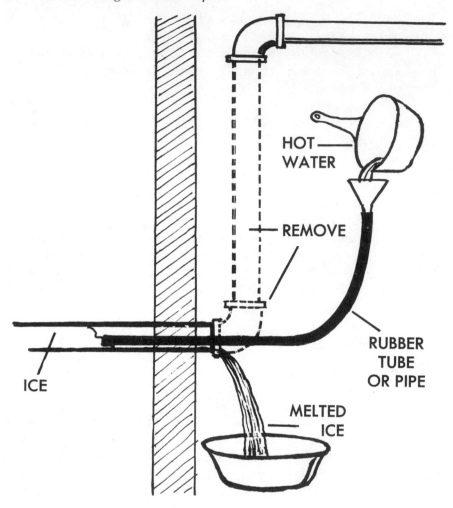

HOT WATER

REMOVE

RUBBER TUBE OR PIPE

ICE

MELTED ICE

How to thaw out an inaccessible pipe.

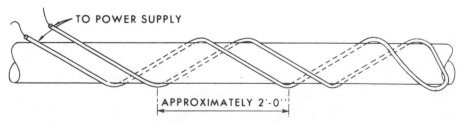

TO POWER SUPPLY

APPROXIMATELY 2'-0"

Application of heating cable to a pipe to prevent freezing.

NOISY PLUMBING

Noisy plumbing can give you a headache in more than one way. Not only is it rough on the nerves, but it also raises havoc with the home's piping system. For instance, water hammer sometimes occurs when a faucet is suddenly closed. When the flow of water is abruptly stopped, its kinetic energy is expended against the walls of the piping. This causes the piping to vibrate, and leaks or other damage may result.

Water hammer may be prevented or its severity reduced by installing an air chamber just ahead of the faucet. The air chamber may be a piece of air-filled pipe or tubing, about 2 feet long, extending vertically from the pipe. It must be airtight. Commercial devices designed to prevent water hammer are also available.

An air chamber requires occasional replenishing of the air to prevent it from becoming waterlogged—that is, full of water instead of air.

A hydropneumatic tank, such as the type used in individual water systems, serves as an air chamber, preventing or reducing water hammer.

A whistling faucet often results from excessive water pressure. It can be alleviated with a water-pressure regulating device only. Never try to reduce water pressure by partly closing the main water valve. These valves are not built to operate under these conditions and soon become damaged. A whistle in a faucet can also be caused by a poorly closed valve, which results when a washer becomes worn. Replace the washer.

Two methods of silencing pipes:
(Left) a capped pipe air chamber and (right) a coil-type air chamber.

If a faucet squeals when you turn it on, the stem should be lubricated with valve grease or Vaseline. It's very possible that noise in a faucet is also caused by poor design. A whistle, for example, usually indicates that the clearance between the valve and its seat is too small. The best and only cure for this is to replace the faucet with a make or model of better design.

The humming sound in a toilet is due to a slight but constant flow of water. Flushing the toilet or turning on water elsewhere reduces the flow to the point where the noise cannot be heard, but very likely does not halt the flow entirely. The ball valve that stops flow to the toilet bowl may be damaged, permitting a slow trickle of water to flow into the bowl, and this keeps the intake valve open just enough to replace the amount flowing out. Or the intake valve may be damaged, permitting water to flow into the tank and then out of the overflow pipe into the bowl. First check the ball valve. This is usually on a wire stem or chain and covers an opening in the center of the bottom of the tank about 2 inches in diameter. If the rim of the opening is rough or the ball surface dented or roughened, replace the ball with a new soft-rubber one. If this fails, replace the whole mechanism.

Noises in drains—gurgling sounds—are probably due to absence of a proper air vent system or one that is partially clogged. It may be that birds or wasps have built nests near the top, or a backflow of grease that has hardened may have caused partial stoppage in the vent. This job calls for cleanout operations directed from the roof through the vent. Boiling water, lye, or a stiff wire or snake directed down the vent will clear the drain easily, once the trouble is correctly diagnosed.

WATER HEATER EMERGENCIES

If you see water escaping from a water heater safety valve—or water leaking from the tank—immediately turn off the heat source, close the water supply to the heater, and drain the tank. This action prevents a flood and, if the unit is gas-fired, a possible explosion from escaping gases. Next, call a heating specialist. Do not attempt to replace the water heater unit yourself.

Water dripping from the tank usually means the tank has to be replaced. The tank, however, can be *temporarily* repaired by using a boiler repair plug. First, shut off the supply of cold water to the tank by closing the shutoff valve on the cold water supply line. Also shut off the heating unit.

To drain the tank, open the drain cock at the bottom of the tank. It's best to let the water cool a while unless the leak is bad. Be careful if you use a plastic garden hose to drain the tank by connecting to the drain cock. Hot water will weaken the plastic and may ruin the hose. If you have a rubber hose, use it instead. You can also reduce the amount of water to be taken out, if you open the hot water faucets in the house to remove the hot water in the pipes. It is best to open the hot water faucet at the lowest part of the system, possibly the one near the laundry tubs, if you have them in the basement.

There are two basic types of boiler or utility repair plugs. One has a sheet-metal screw at one end and is screwed into the opening by using an open-end wrench to turn the head. (A washer helps plug the leak.) The other type, used for bigger holes, is similar to a toggle bolt and nut; it grips the inside of the tank as the bolt is tightened with a screwdriver. (This procedure is not suitable for glass-lined tanks.) It is *not* recommended that you try repairs on cracks or corroded spots. These require reinforcing patches difficult for the amateur to install. Call in an expert. In general, corrosion repairs of any sort are, at best, only a temporary expedient.

Once the repair is completed, you can refill the system as follows.

1. Shut the drain cock.

2. Open the hot water faucet at the sink or a tub.

3. Open the cold water shutoff valve at the inlet pipe.

4. Let the cold water flow into the tank and wait until the water starts to flow out of the open faucet.

5. With the system full, you can now shut off the faucet.

6. Open the remaining hot water faucets in the house until the air is removed from the line. As soon as water starts to flow evenly, shut each faucet.

7. Turn on the heating unit. (See *When a Water Heater Fails to Operate.*)

When hot water pressure is low, the coil in your heater is usually at fault. You can probably open either end of the heating coil for examination. If clogged, your answer is right there. Generally, the coil can best be replaced by a plumber. It cannot be cleaned out either quickly, cheaply, or with any assurance that the cleaning job will not cause it to leak in a short while.

A rumbling noise in a hot water tank is likely to be a sign of overheating which could lead to the development of explosive pressure. (Another indication of overheating is hot water backing up in the cold water supply pipe.) Cut off the burner immediately. Be sure that the pressure-relief valve is operative. Then check (with a thermometer) the temperature of the water at the nearest outlet. If above that for which the gauge is set, check the thermostat that controls burner cutoff. If you cannot correct the trouble, call a plumber.

Tanks in "hard" water areas are susceptible to scaling and corrosion. If you live in such an area, you might consider the addition of a water softener to your plumbing system. This easily installed device reduces corrosion by minimizing scaling.

Water softening can be accomplished in three basic ways. The most popular type consists of a chamber or tank installed on your water intake line through which the water passes and is filtered and treated to remove the majority of unwanted chemical substances in the water. Another type of water-softening device is connected on the main water line, where all water passes through the process and comes out cleansed of chemicals and rust-creating deposits. The third consists of placing the unit only on hot water lines, preferably between the cold water intake and heating plant. This saves the boiler, storage tank, and pipe lines from clogging with chemicals and keeps the most seriously affected lines free from trouble. It has only this disadvantage: that mixing cold with hot water at the point of use will result in less completely filtered water. Soap consumption will be somewhat higher.

About the only things to go "wrong" with water-softening devices are the clogging of the filters and leaks in the tanks. The former can be replaced or periodically renewed as directed in the manufacturer's instruction booklet, while the latter can be fixed temporarily with boiler or utility repair plugs.

PUMPING SYSTEMS

In rural areas, there is normally no public utility to supply water, and the homeowner must have his own water supply system. This is generally accomplished by means of a pumping system consisting of a drilled well, a water pump, and a water storage tank. Mechanical adjustments or major repairs of such pumping systems should be left to trained servicemen. With proper lubrication and the maintenance of proper belt tension, a pump should provide years of trouble-free service. Be sure to keep the manufacturer's instruction manual handy, and follow his directions for oiling the pump and the motor. But before attempting to adjust or oil a pump, shut off the electricity. Otherwise, it may start when you least expect it, and you may be injured. Remember: never lubricate a running machine!

Major Emergencies

Problems you will face and their causes are listed here.

Pump Runs but Does Not Deliver Water. This could be due to a closed shutoff valve (between the pump and the water storage tank), low water level in the well itself, valves in the pump piston (or plunger in a deep-well pump) sticking open, loss of prime in the pump, or clogged strainer at the bottom of the well. Usually, a trained serviceman should be called in to check valves in the piston or plunger, but the pump may be primed by removing the priming plug and adding water. Follow the manufacturer's instructions for priming as the procedure differs with various types of pump.

Pump Does Not Deliver Full Capacity. This could be due to any of the causes discussed in the previous paragraph, plus a loose or worn drive belt, worn valves or plunger leathers, worn motor, or insufficient voltage at the motor. This last condition could occur as a result of excessively long wires to the motor, or of installation of other additional equipment without increasing wire size. The light company can check that for you.

Frequent Starting and Stopping of Pump. Sometimes when the tank does not have quite enough air in it, the pump will start and run a few moments even though no water is being used. This is not abnormal if it happens only occasionally. However, if it happens frequently and the pump runs for any length of time, it may be due to a leaky faucet or valve in the water closet. It could also be due to a leaky valve in the pump itself which permits water to leak back down into the well from the tank.

Air Spurts from Faucet. If air spurts from the faucet, it could be due to an excessively low water level in the well or to loose fittings or connections in the line, which permit air to enter. Also, the air-control valve may not be functioning properly so that excessive air is being allowed to enter the tank.

Noise. Noise often indicates worn parts. To be on the safe side, the pump should be checked by an experienced serviceman if the trouble is not readily located. The trouble could be due to worn bearings or gears, pump pulley too tight, loose mounting of motor or pump, pump rod whipping against the pipe in a deep-well pump, loose drive belt, sticking valves, oil level low, and so on.

CHAPTER 3

Electrical Emergencies

Electricity is an important part of today's living, and when an electrical emergency arises it can disrupt our whole way of life.

It is important to remember that electric current can be lethal. Therefore, minor repairs to the electrical system and equipment of a house are the only ones which should be undertaken by the home repairman. They may include such tasks as replacing a blown-out fuse, replacing broken or frayed appliance cords, or overhauling an electric bell system. The householder should not attempt to disturb permanent wiring or make extensions thereto, even though he may be familiar with such work. Work of this nature should be done by a licensed or experienced electrician in accordance with local regulations or the provisions of the latest edition of the National Electrical Code.

THE ELECTRICAL SYSTEM

All electric wires in the house pass through the main fuse box. The wires going to different rooms are, however, controlled by individual fuses, with several light fixtures and wall outlets to each fuse.

The fuse is an electrical safety valve; if too much current passes through it, a wire inside melts and stops the flow of current. Generally, the size of fuse is governed by the size of wire used in the house and the electrical load it can carry safely. Never replace a fuse with one larger than its amperage. That is, if the fuse is rated 15 amperes, replace it with one of the same amperage.

When a fuse blows out, it's a sign of danger. Either the line has been overloaded or there is a break in the wires somewhere along the line— in an appliance cord, a switch, or possibly the wall.

Do not try to replace a fuse in the dark. Use a flashlight. On the side of some fuse boxes is a switch handle. Pull this handle to the OFF position before you open the box or touch any fuses. If there is no handle, when you open the door you may find one or two cartridge-fuse holders at the top of the box. Pull both of them out. This turns the current off. Do not worry if there is a small spark when you do this.

It's easy to recognize a "blown" plug-type fuse. Either the window in the fuse is blackened or the wire is parted. A blown fuse should be replaced with one of the same ampere size.

If none of the plug fuses is blown and all are firmly screwed in their sockets, insert new cartridge fuses. It is usually difficult to spot a defective cartridge fuse by eye examination alone. Cartridge fuses snap into clamps.

If you find a blown plug-type fuse, remove it by turning counterclockwise. Insert a 25-watt bulb and put the current back on. If the light bulb shines dimly, there is an overload. Turn off the current, disconnect an appliance or two to eliminate the overload, and replace the fuse. But if the bulb shines brightly, there is a short circuit. One by one, disconnect appliances and lamps and switch off lights. When the test bulb goes out, you have located the troublemaker. Turn off the current and replace the fuse. If the fuse blows again, the trouble may be inside the wires; and that is a job only for an expert.

There should be a wiring diagram of the entire house pasted inside or near the fuse-box cover. This diagram is easy to prepare. To determine which outlets and switches are controlled by each plug-type fuse, remove one fuse at a time and see which lights do not go on. Use a test light to check each outlet. List next to the fuse the fixtures and outlets that fuse serves.

In some areas, circuit breakers may be used in place of fuses. They work like switches, popping off automatically when a short circuit or overload occurs. A small plug-type circuit breaker is available for use on individual branch lines as a screw-in replacement for a fuse. When a short occurs, a button in the center pops out. Remove the source of the short, push the button in, and current is restored.

Here are some other emergencies you can handle.

Defective Electric Outlet. Shut off the current at the power source. Next, remove the screws from the outlet plate, and then from the outlet box. Pull out the outlet from the box, being careful not to break the wires. After removing the wires from the outlet, install a new one. Attach the white wire to the silver screw, the black wire to the gold one. When pushing the outlet into the box, make certain that the bare wires and terminal screws do not touch the sides of the box.

Defective Electric Switch. Shut off the current at the power source. Then remove the screws and take out the switch from the box. Next, remove the

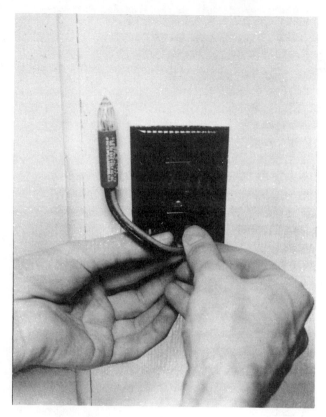

An electrical tester indicates whether current is present. Lamps that work also can be used. If no indication, check the house fuse.

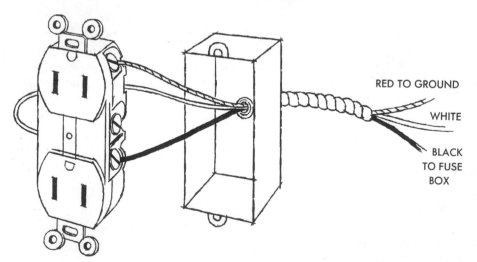

RED TO GROUND

WHITE

BLACK
TO FUSE
BOX

The wiring diagram of a convenience outlet.

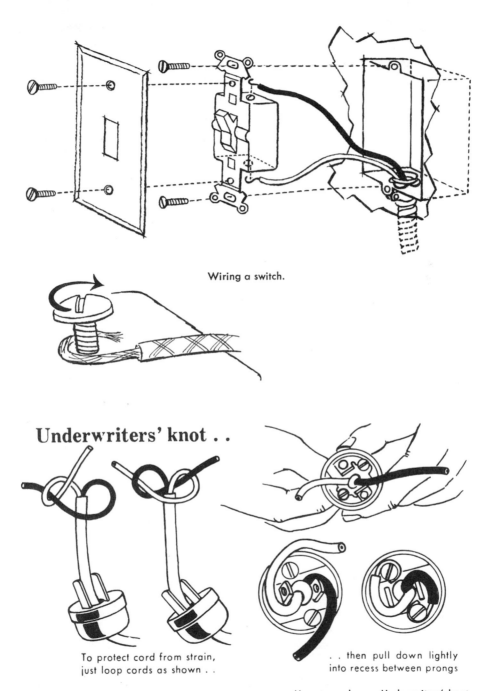

Wiring a switch.

Underwriters' knot . .

To protect cord from strain,
just loop cords as shown . .

. . then pull down lightly
into recess between prongs

How to make an Underwriters' knot.

wires from the switch. When replacing the defective switch with the new one, attach the wires in exactly the same way the old ones were. Then set the switch in place and fasten it, making sure that the screws and bare wires do not touch the sides of the box.

Defective Lamp-Fixture Socket. Shut off the current at the power source. Then use a screwdriver to pry apart the upper part of the socket; you will see where dents are made for the upper part to fit over the lower, and it is by pushing up on the dents that you can separate the two parts. Inside the socket you will find the terminal screws where the switch mechanism is connected. Loosen these screws; then remove the defective switch and re-place it with a new one by connecting it to the wires. The two wires are inserted through the socket cap. Tie the two wire ends with a double Under-writers' knot. There are two reasons for this: it relieves strain of the weight on the connection, and it enables the wire ends to fit tightly into the socket cap.

When the two wires are knotted, with a knife scrape off the outer covering on the ends of the two wires. Then attach the two wire ends to the terminal screws, winding the wire around the screws in a clockwise direction. Now tighten the screws and snip off loose wire ends. Replace the fiber insulating shell, and finally put on the outer metal shell, being sure the upper and lower parts fit very securely at the dents where they meet.

Pull-Chain Broken below Light. Turn off the current at the power source. Buy a new chain with a split clamp. Open one end of the clamp, slip the bottom bead of the old chain into it, and squeeze the clamp together.

Pull-Chain Broken within Light. Turn off the current at the power source. Pull the socket apart and note how the chain is threaded into it. Open or pry out the clamp holding the last bead of the chain, thread the new chain into the socket, and place the end bead in the clamp. Reassemble the socket.

Fluorescent Lamp

The fluorescent tube or lamp gives 2500 to 5000 hours of service. It gives warning of the approaching end of its service by flashing on and off for several hours. You can have a new lamp ready by then and make the change-over quickly.

If you turn on the switch and the fluorescent tube does not go on, you should follow this procedure:

1. Check other lights on the same circuit to see that current is flowing in the line.

2. If there is current in the line and the tube does not go on, replace the starter.

3. Should the tube still fail to go on, remove the fluorescent tube and check the contact points at the end. They may be dirty and should be sanded lightly.

4. Replace the tube and try again.

5. If the light does not go on, shut off the power to the circuit by removing the fuse.

6. Check the contact points in the fixture. They may be bent or corroded. Sand the contact points or straighten them, if bent.

7. Should the lamp not go on after it is replaced in the fixture and the current turned on, remove the fuse again.

8. With the current off, remove the fixture and check the wiring inside to make certain that all connections are properly made.

9. Test the switch by removing it and checking it with a test light in your workshop. The switch may be faulty; if it is, replace it.

10. If the switch is working, the ballast inside the fixture is probably at fault, and a new one should be substituted.

If you have checked carefully as you worked along, you should be able to replace the entire unit, set the tube in the sockets, and turn on the current.

LARGE HOME APPLIANCES

In the case of large appliances, it generally is a good idea to call an *authorized* service representative for the brand of machine you have. Generally, he has better knowledge of the appliance and can fix it more quickly and properly than a "jack-of-all-trades" serviceman. When you call, give him the model number and a description of the problem so that he can bring the proper parts and tools with him.

In addition, if you are not pleased with the service you have received from this representative—whether it was inept or slow, or he was not courteous—the manufacturer should be informed about it. A letter will usually ensure better service the next time.

With a better knowledge of your appliances, you can sometimes correct the problem without professional help or can make emergency repairs until the serviceman comes. Of course, the life of all appliances can be greatly prolonged by preventive maintenance. This consists of two parts:

1. Check the vital parts regularly and observe each unit in operation. This can be done quickly by putting the machine through each phase of its cycle period.

2. A regular schedule of lubrication should be maintained with the help of the lubrication charts in the appliance manufacturer's instruction manual

for each type of unit. In most machines, the following require lubrication with oil or grease: motor, pump, shaft bearings, transmissions (if not sealed).

With *all* major appliances, here are three checks that you should always make before calling a serviceman:

Check No. 1—*Pulled-Out Plug.* Number one cause of any inoperative electrical appliance is an electrical plug inadvertently pulled loose or out of its wall outlet. No plug in; no current out. It's embarrassing to wait out a serviceman's scheduled call and be billed a service charge for pushing a plug back where it belongs.

Check No. 2—*Normal Cutoffs.* After ascertaining that the machine is plugged in tightly, check next whether one of the built-in safety cutout switches on the machine has opened the circuit. Any such switch can stop the action to inform you of an unsafe condition. You may not be aware of these safeguards, but the instruction book or machine demonstrator usually brings them to the purchaser's attention. They may include, for example, in a washing machine:

1. A door switch, which opens the circuit if the door is opened while the machine is running (in some models only during the spin-dry cycle). Just close the door.

2. An unbalanced load switch, which opens the circuit if the clothes are lumped to one side of the cylinder during the spin cycle and is causing excessive vibration. Rearrange the clothes in balance, reset the switch, and on she goes.

3. A motor overload, thermal cutout on the circuit-breaker switch (it's all the same thing) which opens if the motor overheats due to excessive load. When the motor cools in a few minutes, the switch may be reset manually. The reset may be a button or a popout action of the cycle dial. But first remove some clothes to lighten the load. If the cutout recurs, the motor and other electrical components must be checked for overheating due to other causes. These may be a jammed pump, a worn main bearing, or low voltage trouble.

Check No. 3—*Wall Outlet.* If the switches are all right, try the next test. The lights on the same circuit with the machine outlet may have gone out at the same time that the machine did. This sign tells you that the machine is not on an individual circuit; you will have to go to the fuse box or circuit breaker, or you can check for a live circuit at the outlet first.

All you need is a test light. A home-made tester, such as a plug-in wall socket with a light bulb, desk lamp, or portable light, will do in a pinch. Put the prongs of the test light into the machine outlet, and if the light does not go on, check the fuse. Change it (or reset the circuit breaker) if blown, but do *not* plug in the machine until the short is found. If, however, the fuse has not blown, you had better test the light itself in a working outlet. Now, if it lights in that outlet but not the machine's, you will have to look for a loose connection in the outlet or a break in the house wiring that needs repair.

When all tests have turned out favorably, check the cord and plug for visible breaks or shorted wires. If none, further checks must be made, and the following is a table of symptoms and possible causes. The list is by no means complete, but it will serve as a guide to the more common failures and causes of failure in a washing machine. Also, since the check list in this chapter applies to general categories of appliances rather than to specific models or brands, not every item may apply to your particular appliance. In addition to using our lists, always refer to the owner's manual that comes with an appliance. Most manufacturers include service information that applies specifically to their brand and your model.

Table 4

WASHING MACHINE EMERGENCIES

Symptoms	Causes
Washer will not start.	1. Branch-line fuse blown or circuit breaker tripped. Replace or reset.
	2. Overload protector tripped due to a thermal overload. Wait for thermal disks to cool, and then try the motor again. If an overload trips again, search elsewhere for the overload condition.
	3. Hot and cold water faucets at the washer are not turned on. (These faucets should always be turned off when the washer is not in use to guard against potential water leakage and pressure in the hoses.)
	4. One of the controls is not properly set—a button not completely depressed or a control dial in a wrong position.
	5. Lid or door not closed. (Safety devices on some washers prevent the washer from operating while the lid or door is open.)
Water not entering machine.	1. Water faucets closed.
	2. Clogged inlet valve screen. Remove and clean the screen. Be careful not to bend or distort the screen surface when performing this operation.
	3. Miscellaneous causes, such as loose leads on electrical components, kinked hoses, trouble in the house water supply, etc. Make a visual check to spot and correct the trouble.

Table 4 (Continued)

Symptoms	Causes
Washer will not spin or stops during the spin.	1. Load unbalanced. Many washers have a protective feature to stop the washer if the load is spinning unevenly. Rearrange the load and reset the machine. 2. Lid not closed. 3. Loose or broken belt. Inspect and replace or adjust. Grease or oil on the clutch plate or on the drive belt will result in slow spin or no spin.
Washer will not drain.	Kinked drain hose, air lock, or suds lock. Air lock may be caused by a baffle missing on the tub at the drain port. Suds lock is caused by excessive suds. Add cold water to the tub and scoop out suds.
Improper water temperature.	1. One of the faucets not turned on. 2. Water hoses attached to the wrong inlet—hot to cold and cold to hot. 3. Faucets require adjusting for proper hot water temperature. If hot water is too cold, do not open the cold water faucet completely. If the hot water is too hot, do not open the hot water faucet completely. 4. Temperature controls not set properly. 5. Water heater not delivering hot water. Check by running hot water from a nearby faucet.
Excessive vibration.	Some washers have an unbalanced-load cutoff switch which will stop the washer if an excessively unbalanced load occurs. In other machines, the washer may "walk" with an unbalanced load. Correct the walking by adjusting and tightening the leveling legs. The walking condition may also be caused by sympathetic vibrations being set up in a weakened floor. Correct the floor condition.
Agitator frozen on post.	If you cannot remove the cap that holds it on, call a serviceman. Henceforth, remove the cap every two weeks, lift out the agitator, clean the post, and apply Vaseline to the screw threads under the cap.
Water leak at bottom center of outer tub.	1. Kinked drain hose. 2. Stuck pump. 3. Obstruction in the outer tub drain hose or at the outlet in the bottom of the outer tub. 4. Faulty seal in the outer tub. 5. Seal boot punctured or clamps loose. 6. Outer tub partially full of water.
Water leak at gasket on top edge of outer tub.	1. Loose washer top. 2. Hold-down clips not holding the top tight against the gasket. Re-form the clips for a positive seal. 3. Gasket may not be in position at the top of the outer tub. Tape the gasket in place, entirely around the top edge of the tub.
Water leak at lid gasket.	1. Faulty gasket. 2. Gasket not properly aligned under porcelain clamp. Loosen clamp screws and align gasket or clamp. 3. Lid not aligned in the top opening. Loosen the hinge screws and align the lid.

Table 4 (*Continued*)

Symptoms	Causes
Washer does not empty.	Check whether a garment has been thrown out of the basket. Some machines have a tendency to do this, but you can often remove the garment by disconnecting the machine, removing the entire top, and reaching down under the basket.

Table 5

DRYER EMERGENCIES—GAS OR ELECTRIC

Symptoms	Causes
Dryer will not start.	1. Power failure. Look for a blown fuse or tripped circuit breaker. 2. The motor has overheated, causing motor-overload protector to cycle. For dryers with this device, wait a few minutes for the motor to cool before starting dryer again. 3. Controls not properly set. Be sure buttons are completely depressed and dials turned to the proper settings. 4. Door not securely closed.
Clothes will not dry or take an excessive time to dry (although the dryer starts and the drum turns).	1. Lint filter requires cleaning. 2. Controls are set on a no-heat or other improper heat setting. 3. In vented dryers, ducting may need cleaning or the damper on the other end of the vent line is not opening properly. 4. Clothes were unusually wet when placed in the dryer (caused by wringing them out by hand or by an unbalanced spin in the washer). 5. Dryer overloaded. 6. A fuse is blown or circuit breaker is open. 7. Gas dryers: (a) Gas service has been interrupted—check to see whether other gas equipment is operating; (b) gas supply is not turned on at the dryer; (c) pilot light is out. (Some dryers have electric ignition.)

Table 6

DISHWASHER EMERGENCIES

Symptoms	Causes
Dishwasher will not run or water does not enter.	1. Power failure. Look for a blown fuse or tripped circuit breaker. 2. Door or lid not closed or latched securely. 3. Water not turned on at appliance (portable models). 4. Control dial not properly set, or push button not fully depressed.
Machine does not wash clean.	1. Water temperature too low (it should be at least 140° F.). 2. Dishwasher is loaded incorrectly or is overloaded. Check your dishwasher guide for loading instructions or diagrams.

Table 6 (Continued)

Symptoms	Causes
	3. Dishes not properly precleaned. 4. Too little detergent, or detergent being used is old or caked. (Old dishwasher detergent can lose its potency.) 5. Wrong detergent; use only an approved detergent. 6. Soap dispenser does not open. To correct, clean it thoroughly. Make sure that the catch which holds the dispenser closed has not been bent. 7. Spray arm not rotating freely. 8. Wrong cycle selected for the load being washed. 9. Water pressure may be low and too little water entering the dishwasher. This is usually a temporary condition, sometimes caused by running water for other purposes while the dishwasher is operating.
Machine hums but does not operate.	1. Strainer in the outlet portion clogged. 2. Something is jamming the impeller.
Dishes do not dry thoroughly.	1. Water temperature too low. 2. Wrong cycle selected. 3. Dishwasher overloaded or dishes nested together. 4. Heating element inoperative (professional service required).
Dishes and glassware have water spots or film.	1. Wrong detergent being used. 2. Wrong amount of detergent being used, either too little or too much. 3. Water temperature too low. 4. A rinse additive (wetting agent) is needed. If your dishwasher has a reservoir or dispenser for this type of product, the container may be empty. 5. Hard water can leave mineral deposits on dishes or glasses after the water has evaporated. Check your instruction manual for instructions on how to remove mineral deposits.
Insufficient water fill.	Low water pressure. If this condition does not quickly correct itself, call a serviceman. You may then have to call in a plumber.
Noisy operation.	1. Objects, not placed securely in the racks, rattle from water action. 2. Dish or utensil dislodged by water action. 3. Item moved and touches spray arm or prevents it from rotating properly. 4. Unlevel floor causes vibration (portable models).

ELECTRIC IRONERS

Except for the loss of power—a blown fuse or open circuit breaker—there is little that the average homeowner should attempt to repair on an electric ironer. Call an authorized serviceman.

RANGES—ELECTRIC

Like most major appliances, a range that does not work properly needs a serviceman. Of course, you may check out several items first. If the range does not heat and lights are off, for instance, check the fuse box or circuit breaker. Or, if a single surface unit does not heat, raise this unit, remove the reflector, and check whether the wires are connected to the terminals or whether one or more of them is broken. Reconnect the wires. If the unit still does not heat, it is probably burned out. Of course, before touching any heating element, make sure the switch is off and the element is actually cold.

Oven Repair. A cold oven will not cook the Sunday roast, nor will an oven that is not operating at peak efficiency—at least not to satisfy anyone's taste. If your electric oven is guilty of either of these, chances are that the trouble lies in a burned-out heating coil or a coil that has become so encrusted with carbon deposits (from combustion of cooking vapors) that its efficiency is seriously lowered.

The diagnosis and cure are simple: Remove the heating unit (just pull it loose from the plug-in receptacle at the rear of the oven) and inspect the coil for damage. Also check for broken insulators—the buttons through which the coil is laced. Replacements may be purchased at your hardware or appliance store. Take along a piece of the old coil and a sample insulator to make sure you get the right size.

Before removing the old coil, make a sketch of the way it is laced through the insulators; do not trust your memory. Then cut the coil loose. The new coil will need stretching to the right length. Measure with a piece of string the path the coil will take, allowing for loose turns; then stretch the coil to match the string. Lace the coil through the insulators according to your diagram, and attach the ends to the terminals. Before putting the unit back into the oven, check to make sure that the new heating coil is suspended tautly between all the insulators and that there is no contact at any point with the wire frame.

It is often possible to make an emergency repair so that you can finish, for example, a half-cooked Sunday roast. First disconnect the range or wall oven or shut off the power at the main switch panel. Remove the burned-out heating unit and examine it from one end to the other, looking for a break. A light pencil-prodding is helpful, as the broken ends often remain so perfectly aligned that they do not show.

If you find a break somewhere along the length of the resistance wire, between insulators, straighten about ½ inch of each broken section, using pliers, and clean this portion with steel wool. This removes any oxide coating and thus permits you to make a good electrical contact when reconnecting the break. When there is space, it's a good idea to join the broken ends with a small bolt and nut. Just loop the cleaned wire ends under the head of a roundheaded bolt, and tighten the nut to hold them together. Remember that the loops should be made in a clockwise direction so that tightening the nut will tighten the loops.

Should the break in the heating-unit wire occur close to one of the insulators or terminal screws, just loosen that screw and remove the broken portion of wire. Then straighten out about ½ or ¾ of an inch of the wire with your pliers, clean it with steel wool, and loop it under the screw. Tighten the screw in place. But remember that these are *emergency* repairs, and it's important to replace the damaged unit with a new one. Here are some other problems that you can handle:

Table 7

RANGE AND OVEN EMERGENCIES

Symptoms	Causes
Inaccurate results from thermostatically controlled surface unit or burner.	1. Temperature control is set incorrectly. 2. Sensing device needs cleaning. 3. Utensil being used does not have a flat bottom. 4. Utensil does not conduct heat evenly.
Uneven baking results.	1. Pan too large for the oven, preventing proper circulation of heat. 2. Pans set too close to the sides, top, or bottom of the oven, or utensil is of the wrong shape or size for the food.

Table 7 (Continued)

Symptoms	Causes
	3. Oven overcrowded.
	4. Oven not at the proper temperature.
	5. Range not level.
Appliance outlet on the range will not operate.	1. The small appliance being used could possibly be defective. Check by plugging the appliance into another outlet.
	2. Fuse has blown or a circuit breaker is open. (The appliance outlet may have its own separate fuse or circuit breaker within the range that will blow or open. Check your owner's manual for the type of device and its location.)
	3. In the case of a *timed* appliance outlet, controls not set properly.

RANGES—GAS

As was stated in Chapter 2, it's best to leave gas appliances alone; call the utility company immediately if there is trouble. If either the surface units or burner and/or oven will not heat, check the pilot light. Most gas stoves have two different types of pilot lights. On one, pressing a button shoots long streams of flame over the burners so that when the burners are turned on, they will light. This type of pilot has a small flame that burns all the time. When the button is pressed, considerable gas is admitted into the pilot-light jet and the flames shoot out. The second type of pilot light makes use of a small flame which burns all the time, but does not have a button arrangement to increase the size of the flame. Instead, tubes lead from the burners to the pilot light. When a burner is turned on, gas travels along one of the tubes to the pilot light. It ignites, and the flame travels back to the burner and lights it. In either case, from the pilot light, follow the little gas inlet tube back to the manifold, where you will find an adjusting screw. Hold a lighted match at the pilot and turn the screw on the manifold counterclockwise until the gas ignites. Then turn the screw clockwise till the flame is three-quarters of the height of the flash tube leading to the burner.

Some gas ovens have electric ignition. In such cases, if the top burners light but the oven does not, check whether the electric fuse on the house circuit into which the range is connected has blown. If it has not, call a serviceman.

It's important to remember that the operating efficiency of a gas range depends on the proper mixture of gas and air. The correct amount of gas reaching a burner is generally controlled by a six-sided nut located on the gas cock. The volume of air is controlled by the air shutter on this gas cock. Usually the shutter itself is held securely with a set screw. The burner, of course, should be lighted when adjustments are being made.

The proper flame from a standpoint of heat and gas economy is one with a green cone and darker blue edges. It should be approximately 1½ inches high. If the flame is too short, its size can be increased by turning the six-sided nut. If the flame has a yellow tip, the air shutter should be moved to allow more air to mix with the gas. A flame that sputters and jumps indicates too much air. This is corrected by closing the air shutter enough to make the flame burn steadily with proper height and color. As soon as the proper flame has been obtained, the setscrew on the air shutter should be tightened to prevent the shutter from being put out of adjustment.

REFRIGERATOR AND FREEZER

The household refrigerator and freezer, in common with any other appliance, requires a certain amount of attention for maximum operating efficiency at minimum cost. Here are four important facts to keep in mind.

1. Door openings and duration of opening should be kept to a minimum. Constant opening and closing of the door will cause the unit to operate longer and more frequently and also result in more wear on the door gasket, hinges, strike, and catch.

2. Models without automatic defrosting should be defrosted regularly—about twice as frequently in hot as in cold weather. Frost should never be permitted to build up to a thick coating on the evaporator, because this reduces heat transfer and impairs the efficiency of the unit. Frost also traps and holds food odors.

3. Clean the interior regularly; wash the cabinet inside and out; also wash shelves and containers.

4. Keep the forced-draft condenser clean. Dust and dirt accumulations on the fins result in lower operating efficiency and higher operating cost.

In spite of good care, emergencies do arise. Here is a table of the major ones and some of the things you can do.

Table 8

REFRIGERATOR AND FREEZER EMERGENCIES

Symptoms	Causes
Unit will not operate, and no interior light.	1. Power cord removed from or loose in the wall outlet. 2. Blown fuse or circuit breaker tripped. Check for an excessive number of appliances working off the same branch line. Replace the fuse or reset the circuit breaker.
Unit will not operate, but interior light on.	Temperature control in OFF position.
Unit runs too long or too frequently.	1. Extreme hot weather conditions may contribute to this. 2. Temperature control at too cold a setting. 3. Condenser or grille (or both) needs cleaning. 4. Door has been opened and shut more frequently than normal, or was left open. 5. Poor door seal at the gasket. Wash the gasket with soap and water. If this does not help, call a serviceman to check a magnetic-door gasket. In refrigerators with conventional latches, loosen the strike plate and move it into the box a fraction of an inch so that it pulls the latch and door tight shut. 6. Interior light may stay on when the door is closed. Check the door light switch.
Noisy operation.	1. Evaporator or defrost disposal pan not in proper position. 2. Unit not level. Some leveling screws can be turned by a screwdriver without lifting the unit. 3. Certain sounds are normal: an occasional gurgling from the unit or a change in sound level when the motor starts. On no-frost models, normal sounds include a slight air-flow noise and a change in the sound level when the defrosting cycle is in progress.
Interior has odor.	1. Some foods produce odor and must be kept in covered containers. 2. Food compartment needs cleaning. 3. Evaporator or defrost pan needs cleaning.

Table 8 (Continued)

Symptoms	Causes
Unit heats up.	Provide more air circulation at the sides and especially at the top if the refrigerator exhausts heat from the back. If you have a modern front-exhaust box, call a serviceman.
Moisture collects inside.	1. Weather is hot and humid. 2. Temperature control set too cold. 3. Door opened too frequently or left open too long.
Unit seems to labor.	Clean out dust and cobwebs from the operating mechanism with a vacuum cleaner hose.
Fresh-food temperature too cold.	Temperature control set too cold.
Fresh-food temperature too warm.	1. Temperature control set too warm. 2. Condenser or grille (or both) needs cleaning. 3. Door opened and shut too frequently or left open.
Frost on frozen foods.	1. Freezer needs defrosting (if not self-defrosting). 2. Hot, humid weather or high room temperature has increased the rate of frost build-up. 3. Door opened and shut too frequently or left open.
Freezer unit too warm.	1. Temperature control set too warm. 2. Condenser or grille (or both) needs cleaning. 3. Door opened and shut too frequently or left open. 4. Freezer needs defrosting (if not self-defrosting).

Most of the problems and suggested cures apply in the case of home freezer units, too.

Gas Refrigerator. Some household refrigerators are operated by gas and depend on the burning of a tiny pilot flame to produce circulation of the refrigerant. This circulation cools the interior of the refrigerator just as in the electric-pump circulated refrigerant.

As with other gas appliances, it is advisable to have these units repaired by utility company servicemen.

Table 9

GARBAGE DISPOSAL EMERGENCIES

Symptoms	Causes
Will not operate.	1. Disposer switch not turned on or lid not in proper position. 2. Control switch defective and needs replacement. 3. Flow interlock stuck or out of adjustment.
Stops during operation.	1. A heavy bone or an object that should not be put into the disposer (metal, ceramic, glass) is obstructing operation. 2. The disposer has been overloaded by forcing or packing wastes into the unit. In either 1 or 2, when the motor is stalled, turn off the unit and remove the obstructing object or part of the packed food waste. Wait several minutes for the motor to cool; then press the reset button on the disposer (some disposers reset automatically), and resume operation.

Table 9 (Continued)

Symptoms	Causes
Motor will not stop.	Defective control switch or a short around the starting switch. Disconnect the unit from the power source or turn off unit at the main power switch; then call a serviceman.
Drain stoppage.	It should be cleaned, and this can usually be done as described in Chapter 2.
Water leak.	This is generally caused by either the mounting screws loosening, or the putty seal being broken. To repair, caulk the seal and tighten the screws.
Slow grinding.	This is generally caused by a badly worn shredder or impellers and usually requires the services of a repairman.

Other large home applicances, such as air conditioners, dehumidifiers, and attic fans, are fully covered in the next chapter.

ELECTRIC MOTORS

Until an appliance or other electrical device breaks down in your home, you are not even aware of the motor—or how it operates the appliances that keep your home functioning. When an electric motor fails to work, as with all electrical appliances, check the source of electric power. If, after this, the motor still fails to operate, take it to a repair shop, unless you have the knowledge necessary to do the repair work yourself.

There are, however, a few *minor* repairs that you can do. For instance, some types of electric motor are equipped with removable brushes. These carbon brushes are under spring tension and provide current for the commutator of the motor. The spring is held in a small opening by means of a plastic cap. Sometimes these brushes wear down to such a point that the spring cannot give sufficient pressure to provide a good electrical contact between brush and commutator, and the motor will fail to operate properly. A new brush can be easily installed by removing the cap and taking out the spring and old brush. Often, it's possible to stretch the spring enough to give the proper amount of tension if there is enough of the brush left. If the contact between the brushes and the commutator is not good, there is some sparking and there is an unpleasant odor given off while the motor is running. A brush that is partially broken or worn unevenly can cause this condition. Replace the brush with a new one.

Motors that are not totally enclosed often accumulate dust inside the casing which, in time, may interfere with the operation of the starting mechanism. Sometimes they can be cleaned sufficiently by forcing a jet of air through the casing, but often the motor has to be disassembled and washed with a solvent, such as carbon tetrachloride, to remove the accumulated dust and grease on the interior.

You can use a vacuum cleaner to remove the accumulated dust around a motor. But when you do, it is best to shut off the current to the motor just to prevent a possible short circuit. A metal nozzle on the vacuum cleaner, or the cleaner touching the motor while the current is in both, may cause a short.

If you cannot clean the motor with an air stream and it has to be taken apart, it is recommended that you have a professional do the job unless you are skilled in handling motors. Electric motors are expensive and can be dangerous if not handled properly. It's difficult for the average handyman to take a motor apart and put it together again properly.

Generally, most electric motors require an occasional oiling, although some new motors are equipped with sealed bearings which do not require oiling for several years or the life of the motor. Should the motor be of the older type which has oil cups, it will require occasional oiling to prevent the bearings from burning out. Large household electric motors, such as are used for washing machines and water pumps, should be filled with automotive type SAE 20 oil. Do not use a light grade of oil on heavy-duty motors, since the oil will evaporate too quickly and leave the bearings unprotected. Fill the cup to the top and allow about five minutes for the oil to soak down into the wicking. The wicking is usually located near the bearing and absorbs the oil to release it to the bearing when needed. Refill the oil cup to the top. The oil cups are the only points on a motor that receive oil. Keep oil out of the motor and off the rubber-insulated cord. Oil will rot rubber and cause extensive damage if permitted to enter the motor. Since oiling instructions sometimes differ, be sure to follow directions in the owner's manual.

Motors that operate household appliances by means of a belt should be inspected occasionally to make certain that the belt is not slipping or broken. A loose or broken belt will not permit a motor to run properly. Most belts used on electric household motors are of the V type and can be obtained at most hardware and electrical stores and gas stations. Since these belts come in various sizes, take along the old belt to make certain that the right size is purchased. It's most important that the belt fit correctly. If it's too loose, it will slip and be of no value. If it's too tight, it could cause a burned-out bearing.

You can repair a worn belt temporarily by wrapping it with friction tape. But remember that this is only an emergency repair, and the belt should be replaced with a new one as quickly as possible.

SMALL ELECTRICAL APPLIANCES

Small electrical appliances play a most important role in today's homes. They prepare our meals, toast our bread, iron our clothes, and perform a host of other household functions. When they break down, they can cause a *slight* emergency.

Most appliance troubles are due to a defective power cord or plug, since these are exposed and receive the most wear. When either of these is the cause of the trouble, repairs are simple. The electrical tester or test light can be used to determine quickly whether or not the break is hidden in the appliance's power cord, somewhere along its length. To test the entire cord as a unit, disconnect it from the appliance, first making sure the plug is removed from the socket. Twist each bare end of the cord around one of the tester's wires, being careful to keep the exposed ends from making contact with each other. When this has been done, place a heavy book over the wire to make sure it will not fall off the worktable, possibly resulting in the two ends touching. Now you are ready to test. Plug in the cord just as if it were still connected to the appliance. If the tester glows, the cord is good. If it does not, the cord is faulty and must be replaced. As soon as the test is ended, disconnect the plug. Care must be used throughout. Do not allow the hands or any part of the body to come in contact with the exposed wire ends while the plug is connected.

When rewiring a plug, it is best to use an Underwriters' knot. Or you can use some of the newer electrical plugs which require no special knot; in fact, some require no stripping, or cleaning of the cover off the wires, and some need no tools.

To replace an electric iron or broiler-type plug is an easy repair job, if you have an extra plug in the house. But more often the wires just come loose. In such an event, use a small screwdriver to loosen the nuts and bolts holding the two sides together. But make sure the ironing cord is not connected to a wall receptacle. The plug is now open; it usually looks like the one shown on the next page. Loosen the inside screws and disconnect the wires. Cut off about 2 inches of wire; separate the two inside wires protected by the webbing. Clean off all coverings of each for about $\frac{1}{2}$ inch from the end. Twist the wires and connect them to the screws; reassemble the plug with two small nuts and bolts.

(1) If the cord is damaged near the point where it enters the appliance, cut the cord just below the damaged portion. (Unplug before cutting.) (2) Disassemble the appliance anyway and look inside for any loose or broken connections. (3) Repair with wire strands.

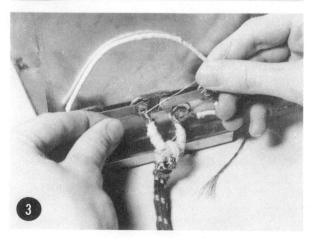

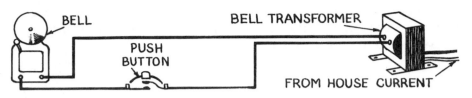

Basic doorbell circuit.

How to Repair a Silent Doorbell

While a silent doorbell *cannot* be classed as an emergency, it can cause inconvenience. Actually, your home signaling system may be equipped with doorbell, buzzer, or chimes, but the basic power circuit is the same. Other than the wiring, there are three components: the transformer, which takes ordinary house current in at one side, reduces it to the 16 volts or less required by your system, and puts the low voltage out at other side; the push button; the bell, buzzer, or chimes.

When your signaling system fails, first check the fuse on that circuit to determine if it has blown. Next, inspect all visible wiring, beginning at the transformer, over to the button, on to the bell or chimes. and back to the transformer. Look for broken or frayed insulation (repair with friction tape), wires touching each other (separate and tape apart), or obvious wire breaks (splice and tape).

If the wiring passes inspection, look at the transformer. The high-voltage input side will be wired with heavily insulated 14-gauge wire; the low-voltage output side will be wired with thinly insulated, small-size 18-gauge bell wire. Using a 110-volt tester—two wires connected to a socket and bulb, with a bit of insulation removed from the free ends of the wires— check the input side of the transformer by making contact with the two terminals. *Be careful not to touch any exposed wires, on either the tester or the transformer.* If the bulb does not light, check back on the wiring and fuse, because some irregularity is breaking the flow of current. If it does light, you know that current is being supplied that far, so use a smaller, 12-volt testing light to check the output of the transformer. If this lights, everything is good up to this point. If the smaller bulb does not light, the transformer is probably defective and current is not being passed through; it should be replaced.

There is practically no danger when handling the low-voltage side of a transformer, but shocks can easily be received from the 110-volt side. To eliminate this hazard, remove the fuse from the line supplying the transformer before attempting to replace the unit. Be sure your replacement transformer is of proper capacity. Normally, a 10-volt unit is sufficient for ordinary circuits. However, a circuit with more than one bell or chime will probably require a 16-volt transformer, capable of handling a 10-watt load. Where there is any doubt about capacity, your hardware dealer can supply the correct answer to your requirements.

If the transformer checks out, test the push button. Inspect its functional system, comprised of the button, a contact plate, and two fixed contact screw positions. Press the button, and if the contact plate is not being pushed down far enough to firmly engage the two screws, bend it until good contact is established. Make certain the two screws are firmly holding the wires and that exposed ends of the wires are not touching each other.

Place the tip of an insulated-handle screwdriver across the two screws. If the bell rings without the button being depressed, the button is faulty. Should you detect noticeable sparking when the two connectors are bridged, but the bell does not ring, there is probably a short circuit in the wiring, or the contact points in the bell are not working properly. If the button is rusted inside or found to be faulty, replace it. Buttons are inexpensive, and a new one will give your entrance a fresh look.

The next step is the bell itself. Remove the bell cover, and while someone pushes the button, closely observe the mechanism. Should the clapper strike the bell only once (or not at all), adjustment of the contact points is indicated. You will find two points, one on the clapper arm, the other on a stationary bracket next to the arm. These are adjusted either by turning a screw that is held by a locknut, or by slightly bending the stationary bracket. Check the alignment of the clapper arm; if it is out of position, the arm can be bent with gentle finger pressure. Clean the contact points with fine sandpaper, making sure to blow out the resulting dust particles. Should the bell still not function, the trouble probably lies in the small coils. In this case, it is best to replace the bell.

Depending on the make and design, chimes are actuated by a magnetically operated rod or rods which strike metal bars or tubes. For good performance they must be perfectly clean, so remove and thoroughly clean them with a rough-textured cloth and a dry-cleaning solvent, such as carbon tetrachloride. Wipe them dry with a clean, smooth cloth and return them to their positions. Oil or other lubricants should never be applied to chimes. Further inspection and trouble shooting on chimes are the same as with bells.

If your system still does not operate, the odds are that there is an undetected short circuit. To find this, disconnect one of the bell-circuit wires at the transformer and fit the low-voltage tester lamp between the transformer and the wire. If the testing bulb lights, there is definitely a short circuit. Since you have already checked visible bell wiring, the short must be hidden in the wall. This could be a fire hazard, with the hot, short-circuited wire in touch with lath, so the old wire should be disconnected as quickly as possible.

Double-strand bell wire, available at all hardware stores, costs only a few cents per foot. Use the old wire to pull the new wire through walls and partitions, being especially careful not to damage the insulation when pulling it through holes or around bends or corners.

CHAPTER 4

Heating, Ventilating, and Air Conditioning Problems

Heating, ventilating, and air conditioning all have the common purpose of treating the air in a house so that it has a comfortable temperature and humidity. But this equipment does break down and can cause an emergency in your home.

AUTOMATIC CONTROLS

Each type of heating plant requires special features in its control system. But even the simplest control system should include high-limit controls to prevent overheating. Limit controls are usually recommended by the equipment manufacturer.

The high-limit control, which is usually a furnace or boiler thermostat, shuts down the fire before the furnace or boiler becomes dangerously or wastefully hot. In steam systems, it responds to pressure; in other systems, it responds to temperature. The high-limit control is often combined with the fan or pump controls. In a forced warm air or forced hot water system, these controls are usually set to start the fan or the pump circulating when the furnace or boiler warms up and to stop it when the heating plant cools down. They are ordinarily set just high enough to ensure heating without overshooting the desired temperature, and they can be adjusted to suit weather conditions.

Other controls ensure that all operations take place in the right order. Room thermostats control the burner or stoker on most automatic systems. They are sometimes equipped with timing devices that can be set to change automatically the temperatures desired at night and in the daytime.

Oil Burner Controls. The oil burner controls allow electricity to pass through the motor and ignition transformer and shut them off in the right order. They also stop the motor if the oil does not ignite or if the flame goes out. This is done by means of a stack thermostat built into the relay. The sensing element of the stack control is inserted into the smoke pipe near the furnace or boiler. Some heating units are equipped with electric eye (cadmium sulfide) flame detectors, which are used in place of a stack control.

Without the protection of the stack thermostat or electric eye, a gun- or rotary-type burner could flood the basement with oil if it failed to ignite. With such protection, the relay allows the motor to run only a short time if the oil fails to ignite; then it opens the motor circuit and keeps it open until it is reset by hand. The illustration here shows controls for an oil burner with a forced hot water system. The boiler thermostat acts as high-limit control if the water in the boiler gets too hot.

Stoker-Fired Coal Burner Controls. The control system for a coal stoker is much like that for an oil burner. However, an automatic timer is usually included to operate the stoker for a few minutes every hour or so to keep the fire alive during cool weather when little heat is required.

A stack thermostat is not always used, but in communities where electric power failures may be long enough to let the fire go out, a stack thermostat or other control device is needed to keep the stoker from filling the cold fire pot with coal when the electricity comes on again. Sometimes a light-sensitive electronic device such as an electric eye is used. In the stoker-control setup for a forced warm air system, the furnace thermostat acts as a high-limit and fan control.

Gas Burner Controls. Gas, when used in home heating, is supplied at low pressure to a burner head, where it is mixed with the right amount of air for combustion. A room thermostat controls the gas valve. A pilot light is required. It may be lighted at the beginning of the heating season and shut off when heat is no longer required. However, if it is kept burning during nonheating seasons, condensation and rapid corrosion of the system will be prevented.

The pilot light should be equipped with a safety thermostat to keep the gas valve from opening if the pilot goes out; no gas can then escape into the room. (The pilot light of all automatic gas-burning appliances should be equipped with this safety device.)

BURNER EMERGENCIES

Automatic heating equipment sometimes needs adjustment or repair that the householder is unable to make. If trouble occurs, the adjustments and

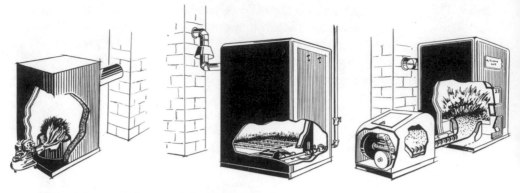

Three major types of automatic fueling equipment.

Oil-fired. (Left) The pressure-type oil burner sprays fuel in a mist, igniting by an electric spark. A thermostat starts the burner when heat is needed.

Gas-fired. (Center) The pilot light burns at all times. A thermostat turns on the main gas supply when heat is called for, and the pilot ignites the burner.

Coal-fired. (Right) A modern coal furnace is stoked automatically to keep the fire going. When the thermostat calls, the stoker builds up the fire.

repairs should preferably be made by the contractor or dealer who installed the equipment or by the utility company that services it. However, in the case of an emergency, here are steps you should take to get your automatic heating system back into operation.

When an Oil Burner Stops

The first thing the family ought to understand before you attempt any trouble-shooting is the nature of the ailing beast; fuel oil is *not* an explosive, so you will not be blowing up the burner, the house, or yourself. But it's possible for a sound like an explosion to occur. Called "puff," it is caused when the fuel-air mixture is not in proper proportion, the mix being hit by a spark from the ignition or an improperly timed spark. Although it's not dangerous it sometimes spreads soot around the furnace area.

With this thought aside, take the following steps in the order given here.

1. Call the serviceman, just in case. Chances are you will find and correct the trouble yourself, and if it's minor, you can always cancel the call. If it's something you cannot handle, no time will have been wasted by summoning help.

2. Check all the switches, most burners having two: one near the stairway leading to the cellar (or above the cellar door, outside) and one on the burner. One switch could have been accidentally flipped off, causing the shutdown.

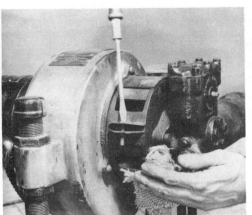 

(Left) Your furnace needs air to burn. Air is taken in through openings of this housing. A screw, loosened by vibration, may close the air intake. Adjust, while the furnace is burning, until the flame is clean, bright, and smokeless. Next time your serviceman calls he can make an accurate adjustment, but meanwhile the furnace will operate. (Right) The large nut opposite the oil intake covers the fuel-control valve. If the nut is tight, forget it. The trouble is elsewhere. If loose, remove it by hand, and adjust the setscrew this nut covers —while the furnace is operating—until you have a large, clear flame. Have this adjusted and tightened correctly on the next call of your serviceman.

3. Check the thermostat by first turning the control 5 degrees above the indicated room temperature, waiting to see what happens. If you have an automatic day-night thermostat, be sure the cycle has not been reversed accidentally. If the burner still does not go on, open the thermostat cover and check the type of control. If contact points are used, dirt could be hindering operation. Clean the points by passing a crisp, new bill or business card between them, being sure never to use an abrasive which would, of course, scratch and damage the contacts. If you have a mercury vial control, it is unlikely that anything will ever go wrong with it, as it is sealed at the time of manufacture.

4. Examine the fuse or circuit breaker which controls the burner. A fuse may loosen with vibration, or it may blow because of age and repeated surging. So keep spares handy. It's always a good idea to try a new fuse, as you may not be able to tell whether it has blown. A fuse that blows continually or a circuit breaker that repeatedly trips signifies an electrical malfunction. Have it checked as soon as possible.

5. How is the oil? Although the gauge of an inside tank may read partly full, the register needle can stick. So rap the gauge or bang on the side of the tank near its location; then check the reading again. If the cap for an

outside tank is not impossibly covered with snow, check the contents with a dip stick.

6. The oil-line valve controls the flow to the burner, and if it's closed, there will be no feed. Therefore, check the valve: for an inside tank, it is on the line connecting the tank to the burner; for an outside tank, it is usually on the wall where the line enters the house.

7. For steam systems, check the boiler. If the water level is low, the burner will have shut off automatically, so check the gauge. Allow the boiler to cool first; then refill until the gauge registers half full, and the burner should start operating.

8. For hot water systems only, check the circulator, as it often balks through lack of lubrication. So lubricate the circulator with the recommended grade of oil, and try restarting the unit; some circulators have a reset switch, so be sure to activate that. If there is no switch, give the unit a sharp rap with the flat of your hand; with luck, it will kick on.

Another cause of circulator failure could be a broken coupling. If so, the oil burner will continue to function, but there will be no hot water circulation. You can diagnose a broken coupling by listening for a loud noise in the circulator, signifying that the hookup between motor and pump has separated. Remove the cover plate and examine the coupling. You can repair it, at least temporarily, by wiring the crosspieces together.

In still another example, the oil burner continues to operate, but the circulator has definitely failed. Fear not, for you can still manage to get heat into the house, providing there is a flow valve on the water to be gravity-fed to the radiation system. Normally, the flow valve is automatically activated, opening when hit by water pumped to it by the circulator. When the circulator shuts off, no more water is being driven, and the valve closes. If you manually open the valve, as above, you override the automatic feature and maintain a continuous hot water flow.

9. Filters in forced air systems must be cleaned frequently in order to maintain efficient heating. A wholly clogged filter will not cause the burner to shut down automatically, but it can keep heat from reaching the registers. Make it a habit to remove the filter from time to time, rapping it sharply, dislodging dirt that blocks the pores. Keep a new filter in reserve at all times. All this applies to the "permanent"-type filter. If yours is the throwaway kind, replace it as often as needed. A clogged filter can reduce air flow to the point where only insignificant amounts of warmed air can pass, causing waste through neglect.

10. Check the blower of forced air systems, particularly the fan belt. It may be snapped, and a new one will have to be installed (buy the common

(Left) Check the oil flow. You may have plenty of oil, but it is not getting to the furnace. On top of the blower-unit pump there is a cap firmly held down by a series of six or eight nuts. First, shut off the burner switch; then remove these nuts and lift off the cap. There is a gasket between the cap and the pump. (Right) With the cap off, you can lift out the twin filters that screen dirt from your oil supply. There are usually grit from the oil and rust scale from the inside of the tank. You will see these coating the filter and preventing the free flow of oil. Rinse the filter in clean oil or kerosene and replace filter, gasket, and cap.

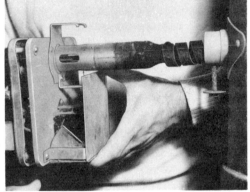

(Left) The aquastat of steam and water systems controls water temperature. You can look into this with current off by removing the cover and blowing out dust. Check the tilting lever to see that mercury switches operate freely. If set too low, the aquastat may be preventing a supply of properly heated water from being delivered, even if the furnace works well. The setting should be about 180°F. (Right) Inside view of the stack switch. This keeps the furnace shut down when the smoke pipe is too hot for safety. A coil curls and uncurls as temperatures change, thus operating the furnace. Smoky fires coat the coil with soot and prevent proper action. Clean away soot with kerosene. The switch will not turn the furnace on if the stack is too hot; you will have to wait 5 to 30 minutes for the stack to cool to see whether the switch is working correctly.

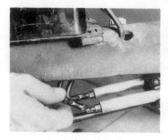  

(Left) In order to remove the nozzle assembly completely, you must disconnect the high-tension lead to the spark gap. Note the lack of insulation around the lead in the forward part of the picture. If it were to touch the metal framework, it would short out and cut down the spark, which would reduce the firing of the furnace. A new insulator is needed.
(Center) The jet, or nozzle tip, is next removed. If clogged with soot, it should be blown clear, not picked at with a pin, which would enlarge the jet opening. Spark points should be clean and placed about ¼ inch apart. If too close, a poor spark results. If too far apart or dirty, no spark may be the result. (Right) The nozzle completely disassembled to show its component parts. Burners under service contract have this replaced annually free of charge. The nozzle is cleaned of carbon by soaking in kerosene and wiping dry.

V type available at hardware and electrical stores and gas stations and keep a spare in reserve). If the blower is shorted, detected by going on and off in short cycles, or does not operate at all, you should still get some heat, for blower malfunction does not affect burner operation until the furnace heat reaches a specific minimum temperature. Remove the filter and fan belt from the blower, allowing the burner to continue operations. Partial heat will flow to registers because hot air rises. Remember, however, that oil burners automatically shut off when temperature in the furnace reaches about 200° F., resuming operation automatically when the temperature goes down about 20 or 30 degrees.

11. Most motors are equipped with an overload switch, thus preventing damage to the unit if trouble occurs in the electrical circuit. The switch control is in the electrical circuit. The switch-control button, usually painted red, is located on the motor housing. Press it. The motor should start. If not, press the stack-control relay and see what happens. If the motor starts and stops—or does not start at all—do not press the button again, because there is definitely an electrical malfunction. Wait for the serviceman.

12. The stack-control relay is a safety switch that shuts off the furnace when, for example, there is a drop in electrical line voltage to the house. Located either on the smoke pipe (that runs to the chimney) or on the furnace, it should be reset once only, by pressing the button or pushing the

tab. If the furnace starts, fine. If it starts but shuts down again, the trouble is internal, calling for a professional.

13. Examine two burner controls which could cause trouble: the nozzle and the electrodes. But, first, be absolutely sure all emergency switches are off before proceeding. Unscrew the access plate or transformer, whichever one permits you to reach inside the unit. Unscrew the oil-line connection with a wrench and disconnect the transformer-electrode wires, usually held by simple, snap-on devices. Remove the electrode-nozzle assembly, being careful not to disturb the electrode's setting. Unscrew the nozzle. On one end, you will find the filter, which must also be unscrewed and washed in warm water (it may be clogged, reducing or stopping the oil flow). Inside the nozzle is a small setscrew, which you must unscrew and wash in water, also. Blow into the nozzle. If air passes through freely, it is clean and operative. If the nozzle is clogged, you are out of luck, unless you have a spare on hand. Any attempts to probe an opening will damage it permanently.

Clean the electrodes carefully with a rag or steel wool, being sure not to change the setting accidentally. Now you can reassemble everything, turn the emergency switches on, and press the stack-control relay, starting the burner. If your model is a rotary burner, it will not have a nozzle. All you have to do with this type is reach in with a rag and wipe the electrodes clean—but be sure *all* switches are off.

When a Gas-Fired Burner Stops

Unlike oil, gas *is* explosive and must be handled with extreme care. Follow steps 1 through 4. Then check whether the pilot light is out. If it is, first shut off the A valve, which is the main gas valve to the burner, and the B pilot valve. Wait five minutes. Then turn on the B valve and ignite the pilot with a match. (In some burners there is a magnetic valve directly in front of the burner, and the B valve is attached to or built into a solenoid valve. A red button represents the B valve. Depress this and then put a match to the pilot tip. Keep the red button depressed for 1 minute to energize the magnetic valve.) Finally, turn on the A valve. In case the pilot light becomes extinguished for an unknown reason, the furnace operation should be watched carefully for a time after relighting it to determine whether further maintenance or repair may be necessary. Incidentally, if you have an electric pilot on the burner, relighting is a simple task: just follow the instructions attached to the unit.

The most frequent difficulties with gas burners are the sticking of the plunger of the main gas valve, the accumulation of gum or other foreign matter in the pressure regulator, and the extinguishing of the pilot light. Repairs to the gas valve and regulator should be made only by the utility company's representative.

Another source of trouble is improper adjustment of the primary air nozzle. If too much air is supplied, the flame will burn above the burner ports and not be in contact with the burner ports as it should be. If, on the other hand, too little air is supplied, the flame tips may become yellowish. Adjustments of the primary air shutters should be made by a representative of the utility company.

It is rare for gas leaks to develop in the gas lines; if a leak does occur, open all windows and doors, and do not under any condition have any open flames around. Turn off the main gas-control valve at the meter and call the utility company immediately. In all probability, they will have a service-man on hand in short order. Leakage of gas is exceedingly dangerous be-cause the gas is very explosive and is poisonous to breathe. Do not try to make repairs yourself except in an emergency. Never look for a leak with a lighted match; use a hand flashlight. It is even dangerous to turn a regular electric light on and off in the presence of free gas, since the tiny sparks in the light switch resulting from the action of the switch could set off an explosion.

A leak can be found by applying soapy water to the line. The gas leak will blow bubbles from the soapy water and indicate its location. For emergency repair, a small leak can be temporarily plugged with putty or soft soap worked around it and wrapped with a cloth.

When a Coal Stoker Stops

Stokers are intended to feed coal automatically into a furnace or boiler. The most common residential stoker is the underfeed type where a coal-feed screw, driven by an electric motor, supplies fresh coal from either a hopper or a storage bin into the fire pot of the furnace. Air necessary for combustion is forced by a motor-driven fan through openings in the fire pot.

If the stoker stops operation, follow the same first four steps as for the oil burner. If this fails to start the stoker, check the shear pin. This pin is usually provided in the shaft of the coal-fired screw to protect the other parts of the mechanism in case the feed screw becomes jammed with large pieces of coal or other solid material which may be in the coal. If this occurs, the obstruction should be removed and the shear pin replaced. Fol-low the manufacturer's instructions in both these matters.

Sometimes the "hold-fire" control, the purpose of which is to maintain the fire in the fire pot, whether or not heat is required, feeds too little coal, allowing the fire to go out, or feeds too much coal, causing the house to be overheated in mild weather. Adjustments to correct this condition should be made by someone experienced in such matters.

The limit control stops the stoker should the furnace or boiler temperature or boiler pressure become greater than the setting of the control. Furnace limit switches on warm air gravity installations usually require setting above 300°F. Hot water limit switches on hot water systems usually require settings above 160°F. Steam pressure controls on steam pressure installations usually require settings of 2 to 5 pounds. If the limit-control contacts open, allow the boiler to cool. Then start the fire again and see if the problem recurs. If it does, the serviceman will have to make the proper repair.

If you have a steam boiler with a low-water cutoff, the water level in the boiler may be too low. Should this happen, raise the water level to the proper height. Incidentally, if the gear case has been exposed to water in any way, do not run the stoker. Drain and flush out the gear case immediately and refill with fresh oil.

The following is a list of some of the less common troubles that could occur in a coal stoker system.

Motor Will Not Start. The most common trouble is a hard clinker over or in the retort. Another possible cause is foreign matter caught in the feed screw. If the stoker has seen long or hard usage, the end of the feed screw may be worn, causing packing of coal in the retort.

Furnace Filled with Unburned Coal. The coal feed is set too high, or an air damper is not properly set. The wind box is filled with "fines." Clinkers are over or in the retort. Digging in the retort with a bar may cause air ports to become clogged, thereby shutting air off from the fire.

Abnormal Noises. Look for loose pulleys or belt. Motor bearings are dry and need oiling. Gears may be worn or dry from lack of oil.

Smoke Backs into Hopper. The hopper is empty or very low in coal. Clinkers are over the retort. Fire is burning down in the retort, indicating too much air or too little coal feed. The smoke back connection is clogged up.

Fire Is Out. The hopper is empty. The motor has cut off automatically from overload condition. Clinkers are over the retort. The switch is off. A fuse is blown. Failure of electric controls.

To restart a fire after an emergency repair has been made, fill the hopper with coal. Let the stoker operate on maximum coal feed until the retort is filled with coal. Use paper and kindling in the same manner as you would start the fire in your hand-fired furnace. Close the air adjustment, light the paper, and throw in the line switch.

As the fuel bed builds up to the desired condition, the air adjustment should be made in the following manner: Open or close the manual air damper to give a yellow and practically smokeless flame (not white-hot) and a fire fed with no intense blasts from air ports in the burner. Sufficient air must be delivered to maintain an even-burning fuel bed with a fairly consistent depth. Once the fire is burning properly, the automatic air control will take over.

THE REST OF THE HEATING SYSTEM

Sometimes trouble may appear not in the firing apparatus, but in the part of the system which circulates the steam, water, or air. How to cure or prevent such trouble?

Steam Systems

Steam systems most frequently develop trouble in the radiator valves and radiators, or in the way of noise.

Radiators. If a steam radiator fails to heat up, make sure that the radiator is turned on, that is, that the radiator shutoff valve is open. The valve is open when the handle is turned as far to the left, or counterclockwise, as it will go. This precaution is admittedly simple. So, just in case, let's first make sure the radiator valve is turned on.

If the radiator still does not heat up, the trouble is almost sure to be in the air valve. This valve does two things: it allows the cold air in the radiator to be pushed out by the steam coming up from the boiler; and when the steam hits the valve, the rise in temperature automatically closes the valve to keep steam from escaping into the room.

By way of illustration, you know that if you take an empty water glass and place it open end down in a pan of water, the water cannot enter the glass. Exactly the same thing happens in a radiator if the air valve is stuck because of rust, grit, or corrosion. Air cannot escape, steam cannot enter, and the radiator is, as plumbers say, "airbound." To remove the grit, *first* close the radiator shutoff valve; then unscrew the air valve—this can be done by hand—by turning it counterclockwise. Shake the valve vigorously— this may loosen rust—then try to blow through it, placing the lips around the threaded end. If air passes through, reinstall the valve; if not, boil it in a strong solution of washing soda and water for about 20 minutes.

Now, you may put the valve back on the same radiator to see whether it works, but a much better test for the amateur is to put the valve on a radiator which is heating well. If this radiator continues to heat, fine; if not, obviously the valve is no good and will have to be replaced. You have, meanwhile, in the exchange, installed the good air valve in the radiator which formerly would not heat up. If this radiator still does not heat—and you *know*, now, that the air valve is all right—the radiator is water-bound. To fix this, put small blocks of wood about an inch high under the radiator legs furthest away from the shutoff valve. If you have a level, make sure the radiator is tilted slightly toward the shutoff valve. This will not only allow the radiator to heat but cure the hammering noise which it probably has been making. If the hammering continues, put blocks under all four legs, but make sure the radiator is at least level.

Sometimes an air valve will sputter steam and water. Once again, try it on another radiator. If the valve still allows water to escape, the thermostatic device inside the valve is broken, and the valve will have to be replaced.

If a radiator heats slowly, or only after all other radiators are hot, the air valve has too small an air escape opening. You can buy an air valve with an adjustable opening and set the opening wide enough so that the radiator heats along with the others. The greater the distance between radiator and boiler, the wider the opening will have to be. With several of these adjustable valves, the system can be "balanced" so that all radiators heat equally, or for that matter, some radiators can be regulated so as to heat before any others. Do not try to balance a steam system by partly closing the radiator shutoff valves, as this is likely to cause hammering. Keep steam radiator valves completely open or completely shut.

Radiator valves sometimes leak around the packing nut. Tighten the nut a couple of turns. If it still leaks, shut the valve and allow it to cool. Unscrew the packing nut and slide it up on the valve shaft. Wind some valve packing, which you can buy in any hardware store, around the shaft under the nut. Be sure you wind the packing in the same direction (clockwise) in which you are going to turn the nut. Then tighten the nut and turn on the valve.

If a radiator springs a leak, shut off the entire system. With a steam heat system the flow of water should cease shortly after heat has been turned off. But if water continues to flow, drain off the water from the boiler through the drain valve. Remember, this water is hot; do not use plastic garden hose to carry hot water; it cannot take it. You can repair a small leak in the radiator proper with iron cement. (It's obtainable in any hardware store; just follow directions on the box. In fact, this cement should be part of the basic supplies in any home.)

Noise. Hammering in steampipes is caused by water trapped in pipes no longer having enough slant back toward the boiler. This happens most often in old houses, due to settling of the floors, sagging beams, or pipe hangers and supports rotting away. The cure is to locate the low section where water can collect and then raise the pipe so as to restore proper pitch. Since only a little movement of the pipe is needed to make a water "trap," by the same token only a little movement is needed to correct it.

Noise can also result from dirty boiler water. To correct, open the drain cock at the bottom of the boiler and allow sediment and dirty water to drain out.

Refill the system with a like amount of clean water. Or you can add boiler-cleaning compounds to the water—but only if this is recommended in the manufacturer's instructions, as these compounds may damage certain boilers. Try to avoid draining boiler water, since the air has been boiled out of it and it is better for the system. If necessary to add water to the system, do so in small amounts when the fire is low, in order not to crack the boiler.

Hot Water Systems

Hot water systems have one common headache: air in the lines and radiators. Until all the air is displaced by water, the radiators will not heat evenly.

Venting. Radiators in a hot water system may also become airbound. Indeed, the regular venting of radiators is a routine job in the operation of a hot water system. Air, freed from freshly added water as it is heated for the first time, will rise and trap itself in the radiators. These air valves are hand-operated: simply open the valve with a venting key until water comes out; then close the valve. This must be done to each radiator. Recommended, therefore, is a new automatic valve, low-priced and easy to install, which does away with venting by hand.

Hot water radiator valves sometimes leak around the packing nut. The repair is the same as for a steam valve, except that the water in the hot water system must be drained out until it is below the valve you want to fix. Unlike steam valves, hot water shutoff valves may be set partly open or closed and used as throttling valves to regulate the amount of heat to each radiator. The entire system should be balanced in this manner to favor radiators which do not heat enough and cut down on those which are too hot.

If a radiator springs a leak, shut off the entire system. With hot water heat, especially with an expansion tank, it's necessary to:

1. Shut off the water feed to the boiler;
2. Let water out of the system by opening either the relief valve or clean-

out valve on the expansion tank (be careful: this water is *very* hot);

3. Then proceed to repair the radiator temporarily as described on page 71.

Water Level. If properly vented, closed-type expansion tank and forced circulation systems will maintain automatically the proper amount of water in the system. If yours is the open expansion tank type, check the water level to see whether the system is full, judging by the gauge glass on the tank at the high point of the system. If yours is a closed expansion tank system, the gauge is probably of the two-needle kind and located on the boiler. One needle indicates the temperature of water in the system. The second needle (usually black) indicates the altitude of the water (height in feet from the heating boiler to the highest point in the system).

Expansion Tank Draining. In a closed system, though not usually necessary during the winter season, if you forgot to do so before, it is best to drain the expansion tank as soon as possible. Shut off the water supply into your boiler. *Be sure the heat is off!* Drain out water and sediment. Then turn on the water supply, putting the plant into action again. If your system has a valve between the boiler and the expansion tank, *never shut it off.* Always keep it open.

Here is how to drain or lower the water level of a hot water system boiler.

1. Shut off the water supply inlet to the boiler. Attach a hose to the drain outlet at the lowest level in the system—generally at the base of the boiler. Lead the hose out to the yard or street. Open the drain outlet.

2. When water begins to flow through the hose, open the venting valves on the highest radiators.

3. When water drops to the level required, shut off the drain outlet at the base of the boiler.

4. To refill, open the water supply inlet to the boiler. Keep open the venting valves on the highest radiators until you hear water filling the pipes. Close the venting valves. Later in the day, vent all valves to release trapped air.

Warm Air Systems

Warm air systems chiefly require attention to cleanliness, since they are subject to soot circulation through the air ducts. Also, even more than other heating systems, they require thorough insulation, and close attention to possible leakage.

Soot. In parts of the system other than the furnace and adjacent areas, the cleaning usually can be done by the family handyman only through the registers. Remove the grille, insert a vacuum cleaner as far as it will go, and draw off the soot. Do this once per month.

One of the most common warm air failures is caused by neglect of filters, which gradually clog with soot and dust. The permanent-type filters should be cleaned monthly. The throwaway-type filter should be inspected monthly and replaced if necessary.

If your system contains blowers, inspect fans for excessive dirt and lint on blades. Clean regularly.

Leakage. At monthly intervals also, go over all ducts in view, inspecting for leakage: this generally occurs in duct joints. Repair by laying on commercial asbestos or furnace cement.

Insulation. To insulate the furnace or ducts, consult your serviceman.

Humidifier. Most forced hot air furnace systems are equipped with humidifiers. The purpose of these humidifiers is to moisten the normally dry, hot air forced into the house. Unless the humidifier is in working order, the hot, dry air cause you and your family to have dry throats and burning eyes.

The humidifier pan contains plates that absorb water from the pan. As the hot air passes through the ductwork, it picks up moisture from the plates and circulates it through the house. The pan must be filled with water to the prescribed level at all times. Controlling the flow of water into the pan is a valve, which is connected to the main water line by a piece of copper tubing. When the water reaches the correct level in the pan, it is shut off automatically by a float level. When the water valve becomes clogged, the humidifier cannot work efficiently. And in midwinter, the chances of this happening from all the foreign matter that collects in the humidifier pan are great.

To check, first remove all electrical plugs. Depending on model variations, it would be best to make a habit of not only removing the plug supplying the humidity controller (the unit is technically without power after this step) but also removing the plug connecting the humidifier motor to the humidistat or humidity controller. The latter step allows you to take the top half of the humidifier over to the sink for a thorough cleaning, which is the next step.

The top half or lid of the humidifier in this model contains the motor and the pump and the delicate vaporizing ring. The hole at the bottom of the pump must be cleaned with a little round brush (usually supplied by the manufacturer) and the holes at the base of the stem on the disk must be cleared and cleaned.

Rinse the entire area with warm water, dislodging gooey accumulations, chip away any mineral deposits, and be sure all the slits in the vaporizing ring are clear. Do all of this without getting any water on the topside of the lid, because this contains the motor. All you have to do here is brush or wipe away lint and dirt from the housing louvers. Now you can set the top half of the humidifier to one side.

The bottom half of the humidifier is hooked onto the ductwork, and the water supply is still connected: First, shut off the little valve at the opposite end of the brass tubing supplying the water to the unit. Then disconnect the tubing at the humidifier by simply loosening the brass nut fitting with a wrench. The bottom half of the unit can now be lifted or unhooked and carried to the sink for cleaning.

Dump the water in the bottom half of the unit and run plenty of warm water over the sides, the bottom of the basin, the float, and the little brass housing that contains the float valve. There will probably be mineral deposits on the brass housing, the wing nut (which allows adjustment of the float), and the water line of the basin. All these locations in the humidifier should be thoroughly scrubbed and cleaned.

There is probably a drain plug in the bottom of the unit, which will have scum accumulations that should be cleaned away. This plug is for draining and cleaning the humidifier while it is attached to the ductwork—a method that does not really allow a good cleaning job. So do not use it; just make sure it is well seated.

The humidity adjustment control is a simple blade which governs the distribution pattern of the water being sprayed into the ductwork by the pump. The blade is easily removed and cleaned and slips back into notches when the unit is reassembled.

With everything cleaned, simply put things back in the reverse order: put the bottom half of the humidifier back on the ductwork, reconnect the water line, and refill the basin to the water level indicated. Test the float-valve action by lifting it gently to see that it admits water. Pop in a water-conditioning tablet, and replace the top half of the unit.

One of the last steps consists of checking the "sail" in the return duct. The sail switch, linked to the humidity controller, must operate freely. Very little can happen to it beyond the disengaging of a component spring (the hooks do work loose from the constant action of the sail), so check to be sure it is secure. Also be very sure to clean the hinge action of the sail: dirt accumulations or corrosion will hamper the free movement of the sail.

In hard-water areas, make minor maintenance checks as frequently as once a month. But when visual inspections reveal a lot of mineral deposits and dirt in the basin, the time has come for a thorough cleanup. Finally, be sure to lubricate the bearings of the electric motor according to the manufacturer's instructions.

If your humidifier is different from the one described above, here are some maintenance suggestions which you will find helpful with most of the electrically operated models that are currently available to homeowners.

1. Disconnect water and electric lines that go into the humidifier. Be sure to shut off electricity at the fuse box for the circuit that supplies current to the humidifier before you disconnect any wires.

2. Empty and clean the water reservoir.

3. Check the water intake valve that supplies the reservoir. Very often this is a needle valve operated by a hollow plastic float. The hole in this valve that admits water is usually quite small and easily clogged by lime deposits. Use a thin, stiff wire to clear the hole if necessary.

4. Some humidifiers have a revolving wheel that picks up water from the reservoir. The wheel may be covered with a mesh or thin layer of plastic foam. Lime deposits on the mesh or foam prevent the humidifier from working efficiently. If you cannot remove the lime or mineral deposits, it is best to replace the mesh or plastic foam. Remove all accumulations of lime or minerals from the interior of the humidifier wherever you can.

5. The electric motor should be lubricated at least once a year. Usually two or three drops of light machine oil in each bearing are sufficient. Check the manufacturer's lubrication instructions. If these are not available, look for a small hole on each side of the motor. Frequently, the word OIL is stamped next to the hole.

When a Water Heater Fails to Operate

In Chapter 2, we discussed such hot water problems as rust in the water, sediment in the water, not delivering enough hot water, and a leak in the storage tank. If the water is too hot or too cold, the temperature setting of the thermostat(s) is usually the trouble. Should this adjustment fail to correct the situation, call a serviceman.

Remember that when you shut off the water supply for repairs, the heating equipment that fires the water heater should also be shut off. This is because most repairs require that water be at least partially drained while the repairs are being made, and since the unit is probably thermostatically controlled, the fire would continue to burn—a bad thing for an empty tank. Of course, if repairs to the water system are superficial, such as the replacement of a faucet washer, the water heater will not be drained enough to matter, and this rule can be ignored. Placement of the various fixtures involved plays a part, of course. If the water heater is on the first floor or basement, and you want to repair faucets or the like on an upper floor, the heater can remain in service, for it will not be drained at all. Some water heaters (but by no means all) have two shutoff valves, one controlling inflow and the other on the outlet side. If these two are closed, all the water will remain in the heater, allowing it to be kept in service even if all the rest of the line is drained. The proper way of refilling a hot water system is given in Chapter 2.

If a gas-fired water heater fails to operate, chances are that the pilot light is out. To relight, follow the instructions given on page 50. If heater still does not work, the utility company should be called. As with a gas-fired furnace, do not "monkey" around with a gas water heater.

Should an electric water heater not function, first check the electric circuit—fuses, circuit breaker, wiring, terminal blocks. If the heater still does not work, chances are that the heater element has burned. Some of these unscrew like a light bulb and are easily replaced. If the heater is equipped with another type, summon a serviceman.

Chimneys. If you see smoke curling out of the sides of a chimney or if a chimney feels uncomfortably hot to the touch, damp the fire and call in a masonry contractor immediately. You have a real fire hazard. If you suspect that a chimney is leaking, you can test it by building a smoky fire in the fireplace and blocking the outlet at the top of the chimney with a wet blanket. Smoke escaping through the masonry shows the location of leaks.

Should you see a leak, remember that it's a definite fire hazard. It should be patched immediately. Pick out the old, crumbling mortar with a pointing trowel, and fill in with new mortar of 1 part of Portland cement, 1 part of hydrated lime, and 6 parts of sand, thoroughly mixed with water. Keep the mixture fairly stiff—about the consistency of cake dough—and make sure to scrape off any excess.

It pays, too, to go over your entire chimney occasionally, feeling the exterior hot spots with your hand. Remember, any spot which is too hot for your hand is too hot for your house. Do not try to fix these hot spots yourself. They may indicate a broken flue, and the whole lining may need rebuilding. Call in a mason.

Furnace smoke pipes and those in use on stoves, as well as the vent pipes on various types of heaters, are subject to attack by rust outside and corroding gases inside. They develop pinhole leaks and then collapse entirely. Smoke piped through leaks is easily detected, but invisible and deadly gases generally cannot even be smelled. Close examination of pipes periodically is important. Of course, an attack of rust on the outside of the pipe can be slowed or halted entirely by a coating of rust-preventive paints. During periods when the unit is shut down, dismantle the pipe and coat the interior with oil. This burns off when the heating unit is placed back in service, but the treatment may add a year or two to the life of the pipe.

At the first sign of pinhole damage, the pipe may be restored to safe use with an application of a prepared-metal and liquid-metal compound which hardens into an actual metal capable of withstanding heat. For major damage, a sleeve of sheet metal, obtainable in any sheet-metal shop, can be wrapped around the damaged portion of the pipe. This sleeve has two flanges at the ends, at right angles to the main strip, both flanges pierced with matching holes. Thread bolts through the holes and add a nut which, when tightened, pulls the sleeve tightly around the pipe. For a sure fit, and to prevent the escape of gases, place a thin sheet of asbestos on the inner surface of the sleeve before the application.

VENTILATING SYSTEMS

The simplest method of ventilating your home is to open the windows and doors. A more positive way of replacing the house air with fresh air from the outside is to employ an attic fan. This type of fan is arranged to blow the air out so that the heated attic air is discharged from the house and is replaced by cooler air from downstairs. This air is replaced, in turn, by outside air. Thus, after a hot day, as the outside air cools, it can be drawn in by turning on the attic fan to cool the structure.

Four maintenance tasks are usually common to all attic fans to get them ready for summer use. There could be an additional one, depending on the type of fan you have.

The first thing to do on getting into the attic is to inspect the fan itself and the shutter louvers for birds' nests and nests of animals, such as squirrels.

Do *not* switch the fan on. Instead, activate the blade by hand and notice whether it spins freely and easily without any binding. If not, there is a chance that bearings are frozen. Operating it under these conditions can cause serious damage, so get the fan checked by a serviceman.

Check the fan belt for damage and proper play. Keep in mind that most attic fans do have belts. If yours does not, it is probably a large ventilating fan which you have pressed into service as an attic fan. Look for cracks, frayed areas, and glaze on the belt. If the belt shows damage, remove it and get a new one of the same size at an appliance store. If the belt is in good condition, press it in the middle. It should give from ¾ to 1 inch under relatively light pressure. If it is too loose or too tight, adjust to about 1 inch of free play. A belt that is too loose can slip, causing inadequate fan operation. One that is too tight could damage the bearings.

Turn your attention now to the shutters. Since these open and close in relation to the air produced by the fan blade, they have to be operating freely. A layoff of six months or so can cause them to rust at pivot points. So, free the louvers, activating the shutters by hand. Wriggle them open and closed a few times. Using SAE 20 motor oil, lubricate every pivot point of that shutter. Only a drop or two on each point is necessary. After oil is applied, wriggle the louvers open and closed a few times.

The way to determine whether you have a fan that needs oiling, and where and how to oil, is to check the instruction plate attached to the fan body or frame. In general, many fans have a grease cup which does *not* take grease manually. In other words, these are designed so you do not have to add grease. All you do is turn a grease plug one revolution. A grease-saturated wick inside the fan does the actual lubricating.

In spite of good care, an attic fan does break down on occasion. Here are the emergencies generally faced with this type of fan and what you should do.

1. *Does not operate.* Check to be sure the switch is on. Check whether the fuse or circuit breaker has blown. Then call a serviceman.

2. *Runs slowly.* Apply oil at oiling points to make sure the fan is properly lubricated. Check the drive belt and adjust its tension. Check the motor. Then call a serviceman if the condition continues.

3. *Vibrates noisily.* Make certain that the fan is securely mounted. Check vibration dampeners under the unit and replace them if necessary. If the noise continues, call a serviceman.

4. *Fan blades loose.* Make sure the fan blades are in proper position; then tighten the screw that holds them to the shaft. You may require an Allen wrench of the proper size to do this.

AIR CONDITIONING

Most modern air conditioning equipment needs the same maintenance to make ready for summer. The first thing you want to do is replace the filter that traps dust, dirt, and pollen from incoming air, if it was not replaced last autumn when you shut down the equipment. Keep in mind that the effectiveness of the filter and of the system is diminished when the filter in a window becomes clogged. So the filter must be changed or washed when it blocks the air movement in the system.

In central systems, the filters are located in the furnace, just above the blower or in the return duct just before the blower. Care should be taken that replacements are installed with the directional arrows (on the edge of the filter package) pointing in the direction of the air flow. Do not attempt to wash or vacuum-clean dirty furnace filters; replace them when they become clogged with excess dirt.

Filters in portable window units are located just behind the face panel, which is easily removed in a snap action or as indicated in the operating manual. Some of these models use permanent, washable filters.

Oiling of the compressor and/or blower motor is easy, but this maintenance must not be overdone. For central systems, every six months is just about right. And only a few drops at a time. Most window units are permanently lubricated at the factory and require no oiling.

Drive belts have a way of breaking. Apparently serviceable belts can snap at any time, depending on age and weathering. Inspection must be more than visual. Flex the belt with the hand. Turn it a few revolutions—with the power off—and twist the backing. This will usually show if cracking has begun. If so, buy a new one.

In central systems, the tension of the drive wheel against the belt may have to be adjusted. If so, the hooked spring (located about halfway up the drive shaft, leading to the fan) can be adjusted one hole above or one hole below its present location. Belts in window units are of a different type, but replacements can usually be had from vacuum cleaner parts dealers or by writing to the manufacturer's service agency.

And last, vents. Unless vents or passages are free of accumulated matter, the system has to work harder (as in the example of the dirty filter). As a result, there will be less than total comfort. So regularly clear all vents of dust balls and clots, removing the grilles and vacuuming deep into the opening. On window units, go outside and clear the coils of debris. Air movement designed for the system must be unhampered; otherwise the homeowner is paying more in power and deterioration.

Like many other major pieces of equipment in the house, an air conditioner is too complicated for the average person to fool with. Several things can fail during its operation. For example, the compressor and fan motor may fail to start; the fan may run, but the compressor may start but stop in a few seconds. Or you may find that everything runs well enough, but the equipment makes all sorts of weird noises. If so, shut it down immediately before serious damage results. Now is the time to call a serviceman; but before you do, try a few things. They may not work, but they are worth a try.

If you switch the unit on and nothing happens, check the fuse or circuit breaker to make sure it's operative. If it is, look at the plug on the end of the line cord. The prongs may be too close together or too far apart. If so, align them and try again.

If the fan runs, but the compressor does not start, make sure the thermostat is not set too low. If the unit still fails to operate properly, do not take a chance repairing it yourself unless you are trained in such work. Call a specialist.

If the compressor is not cycling properly, but is turning on and off at short intervals, move the thermostat up two points. If the unit tends to freeze, turn off the conditioner at once. Then restart after a few hours. If the freezing condition continues, call the serviceman. Sometimes, in a window conditioner, the cooling efficiency drops when the sun shines on it for any length of time. To correct this, hang an awning over it.

Should a window unit become noisy, check whether the grille or window is loose. Shim up the conditioner with wedges if it's not level.

CHAPTER 5

Exterior Surface Emergencies You May Face

The major emergency that a homeowner must face is when the elements—wind, rain, and snow—enter the house. They will enter if your home's exterior surfaces—roof, outer walls, and foundation—fail. Let's see what you can do if this occurs and how you can prevent it.

ROOF PROBLEMS

If during a storm you notice wet, discolored spots on walls and ceilings, the chances are that the roof is leaking. To correct, the first step, of course, is to find the spot or spots where the roof leaks. Careful examination should be made of the underside of the roof over the wet ceiling area. If the cause of the leak is found there, the handyman should consider himself lucky because he can make a simple repair and forget the source of trouble. What could be worse is that the leak is often somewhere else higher on the roof, on the opposite side of the roof, and sometimes even in a section of an outside wall above the ceiling joists. This last is the usual result of ice in gutters. Roof runoff water, unable to go further due to gutter ice, "backs up" under shingles and into the house.

If the house has an open attic with easy access to the underside of the roof, locating the leak is an easy task. Trace the marks made by trickling water to its source. It may run along a strip of roof sheathing or a rafter and then course along a joist, or the leak may originate in the flashing on a chimney, a dormer, the plumbing system's vent pipe, an adjoining wall, or a valley formed by the junction of two roof sections at an angle. Upon locating the leak from the inside, take a crayon or indelible pencil and circle the hole. This circle will tell you where the hole is located when the storm subsides, permitting you to go on the roof and reinforce the temporary repair you make from the inside.

82

The inside repair is made by applying a waterproof sealer or a thick coating of caulk to the hole, working it well into and around the area to keep water from leaking into the house until the storm stops at least.

Once the storm subsides, you must complete the temporary repair from the roof unless the roof is coated with ice and you cannot reach the damage from a ladder. If it is not too cold and you wish to take the time, you can make the permanent repair now. If, however, the permanent repair must wait, return to the attic and find the hole-locating crayon mark. Take a thin strand of wire from your first-aid kit and push it through the hole. This enables you to spot the hole when you are on the roof.

Should the space between the joists and the roof be enclosed, an examination must be made of the roof itself. Look for cracked, rotted, or missing wood shingles, cracked tile or slate, curled or torn composition shingles and roll roofing, rust and crevices in a metal roof, and openings and defects in flashing. A loose or cracked board high under a gable may be the source of trouble. And, of course, the gutters.

Take ample precaution against falling before going on any roof with a steep slope. If two ladders are available, get a hook from a hardware store and clamp it to one end of a ladder so the hook will rest against the opposite side of the roof. Too, one may construct a roof ladder by taking a board 6 inches wide or wider and as long as the roof slope and nailing cleats (¾ x 2 inches and at least 6 inches long) across the board at right angles. They should be spaced 12 inches or more apart. Here, again, a hook must be fastened to one end to support the flat, rungless ladder on the roof.

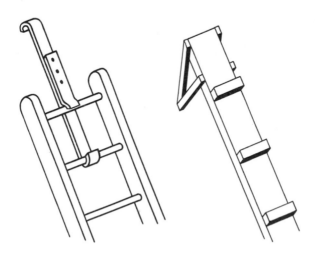

Ladder arrangements for working on a roof.

Steps in replacing a roof slate:

1. A necessary tool is a slate puller —a piece of strap iron bent and notched as shown. You may have to make one or have it made for you.

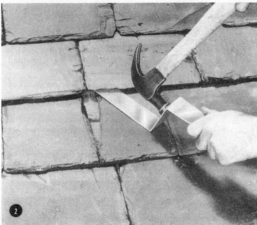

2. Insert the puller under a slate; hook the notches over nails; then drive the puller back with a hammer to draw out the nails. There are two nails per slate.

3. If a slate must be cut to fit, first score each side deeply with a screwdriver or a cold chisel. Scored lines should be matched up evenly.

4. Hold the scored slate on some solid base and tap lightly along scored lines with a hammer. This deepens the scored mark.

5. Lay the slate flat after tapping the mark. The slate will break evenly, but with a ragged edge; the raggedness is smoothed. Slip the new slate into position temporarily and mark its surface with a nail or awl where nail holes are to be drilled.

Once on the roof, a leak can often be located by pouring water on suspicious spots and having someone watch for it inside the house. If this and previous methods do not bring quick results, there is no recourse except to make an opening somewhere for more thorough examination.

As a temporary measure, climb the ladder, armed with a sheet of plastic or rubber, a stapler, and a caulking gun. Slip the plastic or rubber under the shingles that are directly above the leaking area and fasten the sheet in place with staples. To finish the temporary repair, caulk around the edges of the plastic or rubber to keep water from being blown under and down through the hole.

Permanent methods of stopping leaks and making a final repair vary with the type of materials used for roofing, but all are simple. Here is a summary of roof problems and their permanent repair.

Table 10

ROOF EMERGENCIES

Type of roof	Damage	Repair
Composition (asphalt) shingles	Small breaks in shingle	Patch the break with a thorough coating of black plastic roof cement. Remove excess cement with kerosene.
	Curled shingle	Carefully nail down the curled edge, and cover the nailhead with roof cement.
	Badly torn or missing shingle	Remove remnants of the old shingle, if any, by carefully lifting the good shingle above and drawing out nails with a pry bar. Slip a new shingle into place and nail it down with roofing nails, making sure a nail is placed at least in each corner and in the center.
	Breaks in hip and ridge shingles	Coat small breaks with black plastic roof cement. If part of a shingle is missing, cover the damaged area with plastic roof cement and lay a new shingle on top of the cement, pressing it down and lapping it over the ridge. Nail down the top corners.
Wood shingles	Loose shingle	Nail into place.
	Curled shingle	Split the shingle down the center and position a piece of tar paper beneath, overlapping the side of the split at least 1½ to 2 inches. Nail the edges of the split shingle down and cover the nailhead with roof cement.
	Badly splintered or missing shingles	Remove any of the old shingle by sawing off the nailheads with a hacksaw or by prying the nails loose with a pry bar. Install a new shingle and nail it into place.
	To prevent drying and wood rot	Now is a good time to replenish the oil in the wood. Spread linseed oil thinned with turpentine over the roof.

Table 10 (*Continued*)

Type of roof	Damage	Repair
Built-up roofs (several layers of roofing paper and tar or roof cement, generally used on flat or nearly flat surfaces)	Breaks in the layer	Cut the break back with a linoleum knife and remove all loose material. Spread black plastic cement over the bare spot, extending it about 2 inches on each side of the damage. Cut a piece of asbestos-impregnated felt to the size of the cement; spread and press it into place. Fasten with nails around the edge; then spread cement around the edges.
	Roofing curls at edges	Spread black plastic cement beneath the curled edge and press it back into place. Hammer a few nails along the edge and spread cement along the edge.
Slate and tile roofs	Slightly cracked shingles	Seal the crack with a coating of roof cement.
	Badly cracked shingles	Replacement necessary. This usually requires the services of a professional.
Flashing	Pulled loose from chimney joint	Rake out joint to a depth of ¾ inch and clean out old mortar with a wire brush. Push flashing edge all the way into the joint and fill with mortar.
	Pulled apart at chimney corner	Spread black plastic cement around, over, and under all flashing edges and corners. Wrap a piece of asbestos-saturated felt or fiberglass flashing around the area, overlapping by at least 2 inches. Lap another piece of the material around, so it overlaps the first patch. Press the material into the cement; then cover it all with a good layer of cement.
	Pulled away from vent pipe	Spread black plastic cement around the base of the pipe, extending it halfway up. Cut a patch of asbestos-saturated felt or fiberglass flashing and press it into place so it extends around the base and halfway up the pipe. Cover with cement.
	Reinforcing valleys and joints	Spread cement down the entire length of the valley or joint, overlapping at least 3 inches. Put in place asbestos-saturated felt or fiberglass along the joint to a width of 3 inches on each side. Cover with cement.

Roof Ice and Snow

On gently pitched roofs, drainage of ice or snow often gets to be overly sluggish in cold areas of the country. To be sure, there are ways to combat dangerous accumulation of ice in the gutters. (See *Gutters and Downspouts,* page 92.) But what the homeowner often experiences is a build-up of ice on the edge of the roof, blocking draining water from ever reaching the gutter. This occurs because under a blanket of snow there may be considerable melting, whereupon water trickles down toward the roof edge. Refreezing takes place as soon as it creeps out from under the snow blanket along the edge and receives the full force of wind and cold air. The result is a solid barrier of ice preventing the roof from draining at all. Water backs up under the shingles, where it may do damage. It may gradually undermine the barrier, causing the latter to let go in chunks—threatening even greater damage.

To thwart these ice dams and keep water evenly draining off the roof, the best recourse is the same electric heating cable used to protect gutters. Covering the entire roof would be prohibitively expensive—and, as it happens, wholly unnecessary. Simply plug into an electric outlet sufficient length of cable to form a zigzag line along the roof edge. This will not melt the whole wall of ice, but it will cut through it to form a sufficient number of drainage channels.

The cable, which consists of a single insulated resistance wire enclosed in a lead sheath, comes in any length at a cost of about 10 cents a foot. It is also sold in 60- and 120-foot kits, complete with plug. Thermostats can be added, but the expense is hardly justified, since the cable can be easily plugged in by hand during stormy weather.

Steep Roofs. On steeply sloping roofs—especially those made of slate, tile, asbestos cement, or metal—the homeowner runs into an entirely different situation. Here the chief danger is that of an avalanche. Snow and ice may start sliding down in big chunks which can actually rip out the roofing, tear away gutters, and wreck anything they hit on the ground below. To prevent such slides, install snow guards. These are tough little metal gadgets which stick up a couple of inches from the roof surface and stop ice or snow which otherwise would slide down. Installation is easy and depends on the type of roof. For instance, guards meant for new roofs have a sharp hook to be driven into the sheathing before the shingles are laid; those for use on old roofs have a tongue which hooks around nails under the shingles; those for metal roofs come with lugs for soldering.

For adequate protection, do not just put a line or two of snow guards

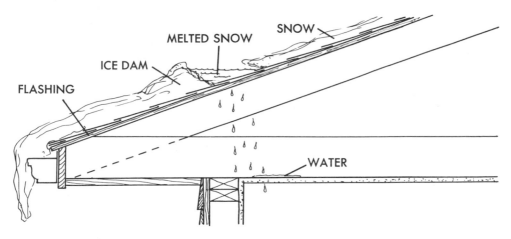

Ice dams such as shown here are a major cause of winter roof leaks.

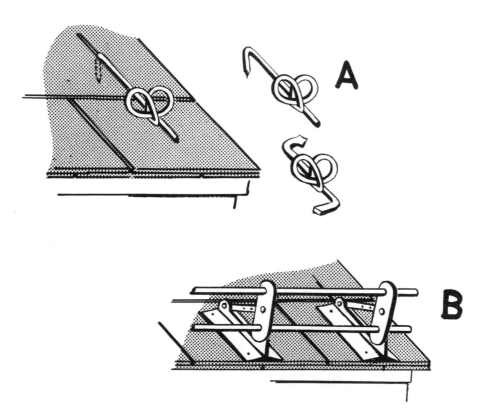

Two common types of metal snow guards.

immediately above the eaves. These are too few to be depended on to withstand the very considerable force of a snow slide starting, say, at the ridge. The rule is to space out evenly over each 100 square feet of roof surface the following number of guards: 50 on a one-quarter pitch roof; 75 on a one-third pitch roof; 125 on a one-half pitch roof. Thus distributed, these will do about as good a job, at less expense, than the more elaborate —and more conspicuous—pipe guards seen on some homes. These consist of two brackets, holding a pair of brass or iron pipe lengths so as to form a short double rail. However, if you prefer this type of guard, it is easily installed merely by slipping the brackets under the shingles and nailing in place.

GUTTERS AND DOWNSPOUTS

The gutters and downspouts each year carry off thousands of gallons of rain and perhaps melted snow from a roof. Without such drainage, tons of water would run down exterior walls, resulting in stain and rot and ultimately working inside the walls to cause even more serious damage. Moisture would appear in interiors, dampness in the cellar. In time, the foundation could be permanently marred. Yet gutters and downspouts are commonly neglected in the routine of home upkeep and repair, simply because householders forget their importance. Actually, they are easy to keep in top shape, provided you follow this seven-point check-and-repair program:

1. Clean out all loose foreign matter, such as leaves. These tend to clog the gutter and absorb water from spring rains, making the weight in the trough so heavy that the gutter could be ripped from its hangers.

2. Inspect the gutters carefully. Galvanized gutters may rust, and wood gutters may show rotted areas. A damaged area can be repaired by first scraping away any rust or rotted wood with a wire brush. Remove the fine particles and other small foreign matter with a tank-type vacuum cleaner. Spread a liberal coating of roof cement over the damaged area. Cover this with a patch of heavy-weight aluminum sheeting or tar paper. A second layer of roof cement is then spread over the top of the patch and carried past the edges to create a waterproof seal. Leaking joints can also be repaired in this manner.

Other patching materials specifically designed for repairing leaky areas on wood and metal gutters can also be used. These consist of fiberglass or plastic-impregnated fabric that is saturated with a special resin solvent. As stated in Chapter 1, ready-to-use repair kits, containing all the necessary materials, are available at your local home supply or hardware store.

3. A gutter that permits water to stand in a certain spot is not doing its job. If water tends to stand, the gutter is probably not pitched properly, or there is a low spot. To determine whether a gutter is draining correctly, pour several bucketfuls of water into the trough or run water from a hose through it. If the water does not drain off promptly, adjustments should be made.

Metal gutters are supported either by hanger straps or by spikes driven through ferrules in the gutter into the house. To correct improper drainage, loosen or tighten the straps, as required, or remove and renail the gutter spikes to give the gutter a greater pitch. As a general rule, a gutter should pitch toward the downspout about 1/16-inch for every foot of length. With a level, you can determine the pitch of a given section of the gutter. Then sight along the gutter to see that it maintains this pitch for its entire length.

Wooden gutters are nailed to wooden spacers right to the house. It's unusual for these to change pitch, but they may warp, preventing water from flowing properly. If the condition becomes too bad, replace the troublesome section of gutter.

4. After all repairs have been made to wooden gutters, preventive maintenance in the form of a preservative should be applied. Special protective coatings help to preserve and lengthen the life of the gutter and to stop warping. These preservatives are applied to the inside of the gutter with an ordinary paintbrush. One type of preservative has a rubber base and forms a resilient coating that resists cracking and checking. Another type consists of a combination of wood preservatives and asphalt. Ordinary exterior house paint can also be used effectively. Never use a primer here, however, as primer seals the pores of wood and will not let that wood "breathe."

Galvanized metal gutters should be wire-brushed and given a coat of good metal paint. Aluminum, copper, and plastic gutters, because of their high resistance to damage caused by the elements, do not have to be coated with any type of preservative.

5. If you live in an area where there are many trees, you can keep gutters free of leaves by covering them with wire-mesh guards that are available at hardware and home supply stores. The mesh is tucked under the roof shingles and rests on the gutter lip, or it is snapped or clamped in place, depending on the shape of your gutters and the type of guard you purchase.

6. To determine whether a downspout is clogged, pour water down it. If the water does not drain properly and quickly, it indicates that leaves or trash have accumulated at some point. Obstructions of this kind can often be freed by tapping the sides of the downspout along its entire length,

An easy way to remove snow from gutters.

using a wood block or hammer handle. If this does not work, flush the downspout with a strong stream from a hose. Direct the stream up from the bottom.

7. Downspout openings can be protected from clogging leaves or other matter by installing a simple strainer or caplike device that fits into the opening on the inside of the gutter. This strainer must be periodically inspected and cleaned of the trash that it collects.

Gutter and downspout real emergencies usually occur during the winter, when water from thawing snow on the roof cannot run off because the gutters are frozen. Next, the water backs up and, seeking an outlet, often finds its way under the shingles into the house and down an interior wall, ruining paint or wallpaper and nearby furnishings. The best way to avoid damage of this type is to prevent it from occurring. First, be sure that gutters and downspouts are clear; water held back by an obstruction will quickly freeze. There is less likelihood of ice when water is kept moving.

Clean drainage systems alone are not sufficient to protect against freeze-ups or blockages. As previously stated, an electric heating cable, designed for this specific purpose, may be strung along the lower edge of the roof, right above the gutters. The heater should be turned on as soon as an accu-

mulation of snow begins during a storm. It will keep at least the edges of
the roof clear, preventing backups that clog gutters.

But let's suppose you have not had the foresight to install such a heating
system, and trouble develops. You need not sit there wringing your hands;
make an attempt to clear them out. There is one elementary, but effective,
method: hot water will flush out the ice and halt the flood temporarily, at
least. Just one or two buckets probably will not be enough. Improvise a
coupling of sorts so that you can connect a rubber hose to a hot water
faucet. Its continuous stream should do the job in short order. Be sure,
though, to thaw the downspout first. Ice melted in the gutter will aggravate
the damage if the runoff has nowhere to go.

Instead of this method, there are also ice-melting chemicals, such as those
used on cement walks, which will help, but may corrode metal gutters. If
used, the drainage system should be well flushed out with clear water at the
very first opportunity when the storm ends. In the worst cases, even if the
gutters become so corroded that they must be replaced, it will probably cost
less than to repair the interior damage that may have otherwise occurred.

Sometimes you can clear a downspout of ice by poking through the drain
with a pole. If this does not clear the passage (and the ice in the drain is
in chunk form only), you can try probing with a pipe auger from below. It
just may clear the downspouts and permit drainage.

If a downspout goes into a dry well and no water is cominng through, it
may be essential to saw the pipe through near bottom to prevent excessive
water from overflowing the gutter. Slip a tar paper shoe over the end to
direct the flow of water away from the house.

Should the downspout's seam split or joint break when it is clogged with
ice—or even leaves and twigs—the metal can be bent back in shape and
the seam or joint resoldered. To do this, clean the metal with steel wool.
Then heat with a blowtorch and apply sufficient solder to seal the split or
joint. Use aluminum solder if downspout is made of aluminum.

If a gutter splits or gives way under the weight of ice, there is little that
can be done to correct this damage during a storm. But as soon as the
storm lets up, get an assistant to hold a ladder. With a hacksaw, cut out the
damaged section and insert a new piece, using slip connectors at each end.
Add a few strap hangers to hold new pieces and to give old sections additional strength. Caulk around nail holes where hangers were set into the
roof. Small damaged sections can be put into shape until full repairs are
possible by lining inside with glass membrane and coating with asphalt. Do
not forget to add strap hangers for support.

PREVENTION OF SIDING EMERGENCIES

Wood, metal, masonry—these three terms sum up the types of siding used in most homes today. Of the three, wood is by far the most common. Here is a summary of the major siding problems and their repair.

Table 11

PREVENTION OF SIDING EMERGENCIES

Type of Siding	Damage	Repair
Clapboard	Warped board	Drive in as many common nails as necessary to straighten the board. Countersink nailheads, fill holes with wood filler, and cover with paint.
	Split board	Force the split carefully apart and apply a coating of waterproof wood glue. Drive the crack closed by hammering in one or two nails at an angle, closing the crack.
	Rotted board	Pry up the board above and slice through the nails over the area of rotted section with a hacksaw blade. Use a hacksaw to make vertical cuts in the section on each end of the damage. Chisel out the rotted area, measure, and cut a new length of board. Paint it on both sides and position it in place with nails. Countersink nailheads and caulk vertical cracks.
Wood shingle	Loose	Nail back into place, using aluminum or galvanized nails to prevent rusting.
	Badly split	Pry out chunks and remove the nails with a claw. Paint the new shingle and, when dry, install.
Asbestos shingle	Cracked, shattered	Replace. Break up the remains and remove chunks. Cut off nails with a hacksaw blade, lifting the shingle above carefully. Slip the new shingle into place. These are predrilled to accept nails.
Brick	Crumbled or cracking mortar in joints	Chop away loose mortar with a cold chisel. Brush out particles with a wire brush. Wet the cavity and pack mortar mix into the joint, bringing it out flush with the brick. Smooth with a pointing tool.
Masonry and stucco	Cracks	Cut out the crack with a cold chisel so that the bottom of the crack is larger than the surface opening. Brush out loose material. Wet the cavity, pack ready-mix mortar into the crack, and level it flush.

To replace a piece of clapboard siding, you should follow a procedure such as this:

1. Use a backsaw to cut the damaged sections vertically to overlap. A chisel will remove chunks of cut boards. Do not cut into tar paper.

2. Remove nails from the edge of the upper board to free cut lengths. To cut nails with a keyhole saw, lift the upper board with wedges.

3. Chisel out the ends of the cut length right up to the saw marks. Hold the chisel at an angle, to avoid splitting good section.

4. Wedge out the upper board. Patch tar paper; then insert the new board and nail it into place.

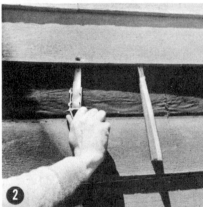

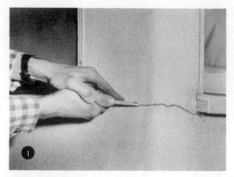

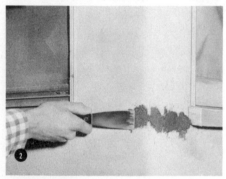

Repairing a hairline crack in stucco, you can do as follows.

1. Use a cold chisel to dig out all the loose cement; open the crack to about double its existing depth. Undercut the crack to provide a key or slot for the new cement to hold.

2. Wet the crack thoroughly with a brush or cloth, or use a hose. Fill the crack, using a putty knife, and overlap each side about 1 inch, smoothing cement into the existing surface.

3. If your stucco is colored, buy matching colored stucco, called "sand-finish," and dab a wet sponge in the material. Dab the material over the crack filler, applying in a circular motion.

4. This is the way the repaired crack should look. In 3 or 4 days the sand-finish will dry; it fades as much as 70 percent and should nearly match the old stucco finish.

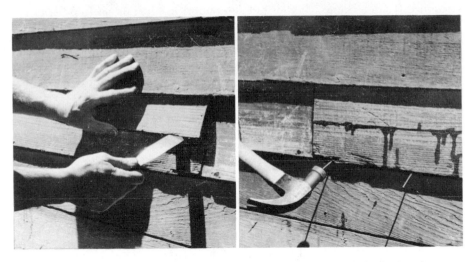

To mend a split board, pry out the loose portion and spread waterproof glue in the split. Drive nails in under the lower section, bending them up to force the split edges tightly together. Allow the glue to set hard; then remove the nails and plug the holes with wood putty.

How and Where to Caulk

There is one basic fact to remember about caulking compounds: use plenty in every crack and joint you find around your home. If you are not sure whether to caulk an area or not, caulk anyway. You cannot hurt anything. For specific places that need it, see the following check list.

Caulking Check List. Check caulked areas for crumbling compound. Recaulk as many of the following as you have on your house, if necessary:

1. Where the chimney meets roof shingles.
2. Between a dormer and roof shingles.
3. Between siding and window drip caps.
4. Between window sills and siding.
5. Between siding and an entrance overhang.
6. Between siding and door frames.
7. Between masonry steps, porches, patios, and the house foundation.
8. Between the underside of eaves and cable molding.
9. Between window frames and siding.
10. Between siding and a roof deck.
11. At corners formed by siding.
12. Between siding and vertical corner boards.

Caulk protects your home in two ways. It prevents heat loss during the winter and cuts down on draft; it prevents moisture from penetrating the structure. To determine whether old compound has lost its usefulness, probe it with a screwdriver. If flakes chip off, it's time to recaulk. Here's how.

Scrape away all old compound, first with a scraping tool and then with a wire brush. Wash down the joint with turpentine or paint thinner to dissolve remaining small particles and film, assuring a good adhesion surface for the new caulk. Lay down a wide bead of new caulk, making sure it covers the entire crack.

FOUNDATION PROBLEMS

You can easily fix small cracks in a foundation, but large structural cracks that run the entire height of the foundation and continue to increase in size should be examined by an expert, for they may indicate serious trouble. Small cracks should be repaired immediately to keep them from becoming larger and increasing the danger of water leakage.

Sealing cracks and splits requires the same basic technique for a variety of types, as well as locations. But crack lines have to be cleaned out, whether the crack is hairline or wide. Use a wire brush to dislodge and sweep clean the channel and the edges. If the channel is too deep for a wire brush, try a nail or a nail driven through a board, raking the channel several times to be certain that anything loose or crumbly is dislodged and removed.

Follow this step with a thorough soaking of the crack line and the channel, using a garden hose or a sponge which is sopping wet. Wet the surrounding area, too. Observe the water that flows away; if it contains bits and pieces of concrete or cement (or plant life), continue to irrigate the line until the waste water is clean.

The crack line is then patched with a mix: 1 part of mortar cement and 2 to 2½ parts of sand; add water to suit the repair. Foundation cracks are vertical; thus add only enough water to produce a thick consistency that will not run out of the crack.

Wide cracks are often caused by settling of the house. Another cause could be a hairline crack in which water entered and froze, expanding and forcing the crack wider. A wide foundation crack, whether in cinder or concrete block or poured concrete, is repaired in the same manner. However, in block-type construction, when the crack is wider than about ¼ inch, it may be necessary to remove and replace the entire block, since the crack may extend all the way through. We suggest, though, that the repair described here be applied first. If it does not hold, the block should then be replaced.

These steps will provide the tight, waterproof patch needed:

1. If the crack extends below ground level, dig down to the bottom of the crack. A neglected below-surface crack can widen to a point where water may begin leaking into the basement.

2. If jagged pieces are protruding from the edges of the crack, knock them off with a cold chisel and hammer. Do not widen the crack any more than necessary. Unlike a hairline crack, which is widened to give mortar a surface to which to adhere, there is already enough room here. Remove loose foreign matter and dirt with a stiff-bristled brush or wire brush.

3. Use a waterproof bonding agent to form the base of the repair and seal the crack. Work it well into and around the crack with a trowel or putty knife.

4. After the sealer dries, mix 3 parts of sand to 1 part of cement, or use a ready-mixed mortar. Apply the mix over the filled-in crack and smooth it with a trowel. Allow a few days for the mortar to dry. During the period, wet the area down about twice a day with a water-saturated sponge. This prevents the mortar from contracting and cracking as it dries.

5. When the mortar has dried, apply a final layer of bonding and waterproofing material; you can also use a tar preparation, such as ordinary roofing cement, or one of the relatively new silicone-base compounds. Spread this material over the patch for added strength and to prevent moisture from seeping in around the edges. Tar, of course, is black and is highly visible. Most waterproof bonding agents dry to about the same appearance as poured concrete and should be much less noticeable. The silicone-base compounds are clear materials when dry and are not readily noticed either. You can also paint over them. If a foundation crack extends through to the basement side, you can repair it in the same manner as an exterior crack. This will work sufficiently well for a poured concrete foundation. However, cinder or concrete blocks cracked all the way through may eventually have to be replaced.

Controlling Surface Water

If surface water is entering your basement, it usually reveals itself by stains on the wall starting at a level with the ground surface outside and gradually diminishing as the wall approaches the floor. Of course, sometimes surface water may trickle down and enter at low points on the wall, or even through the floor, in which case it is difficult to distinguish from ground water. But bear in mind that surface water can originate only in the overflow from puddles, streams, cisterns, or the like in your neighborhood—or from rainfall and thawing snow. Generally the water reaches your home by running down some slope. So if leak stains are more severe on the up-slope side of your basement, or if seepage occurs following periods of rain, suspect surface water. These cures are recommended:

1. If your house is on a well-defined slope, dig a ditch on the high side, 15 feet from the nearest wall and parallel to it. Make the ditch from 4 to 6 inches deep and have it extended at least 15 feet past both ends of the parallel wall. Seed the ditch with grass to help it hold its shape, limit erosion, and maintain good appearance. A ditch of this kind across each down slope approaching your home will often drain off surplus water effectively, leaving your cellar dry.

2. On either sloped or level ground, you can try building banks of earth against your walls, grading them so as to slope downward and away from the house. These, too, should be seeded to avoid erosion. Build such banks along each wall that leaks or shows the telltale stains of water seepage inside the cellar.

3. No precaution will keep your basement dry if your property does not have sufficient provision for disposing of rain water from your roof. Water entering the downspout from roof gutters and allowed to pour directly on the ground may ultimately find its way to foundations and cellar. Sometimes such water is permitted to fall on "splash blocks"; these prevent soil erosion under the downspout, but do little to prevent soaking of the ground near foundations. The ideal answer is a tile drain a few inches below ground surface, carrying rain water from your downspout to either a storm sewer or a dry well.

4. In the event that roof drainage is adequate but surface water still floods your cellar, the condition may be too severe to be corrected by a ditch or graded earth as outlined above. Or your house may be inconveniently situated for such measures. In such cases, your only recourse is to try the more drastic corrective steps usually reserved for combating ground water.

Ground Water Leakage

Ground water in the cellar often can be identified by leak stains low down on the wall. Suspect it, also, if the water enters through the floor itself or through the joint between the floor and wall. Persistent flooding generally results from ground rather than surface water. Since ground water originates in springs and seepage underground from nearby water sources, its course cannot be easily altered. At the same time, it can build up considerable pressure. Hence, it may prove difficult to correct.

There are three major methods for curing ground water penetration: laying a tile drain around the cellar, treating the outside wall surface, and treating the inside wall surface.

These methods, as already noted, can also come in handy to stop severe, puzzling surface water seepage when other cures fail.

Laying a Drain. This is the first method to consider. It happens to be one of the best all-round methods for preventing cellar dampness. However, it requires digging down next to the foundation to its full depth. This can be difficult, particularly where the ground is paved or it becomes necessary to dig under cellarless porches and wings.

Weigh the gravity of the dampness in your cellar against the cost and efforts of laying the drain. Mere moisture spots may be helped by cement-painting the interior. Flooding, on the other hand, requires heroic measures such as the drain. And if your house is located in a particularly low or damp spot, it becomes a virtual necessity. To build the drain, follow this procedure:

1. Dig a ditch all around your house to the depth of the footing on which the foundation rests. Makes the ditch wide enough for you to get into and work.

2. Deepen the ditch so as to make it slope downward about 1 inch per foot. Start deepening at the bottom of any one footing, and continue the slope downward around two sides of the house. Then start at the same footing and form the slope downward around the other two sides of the house.

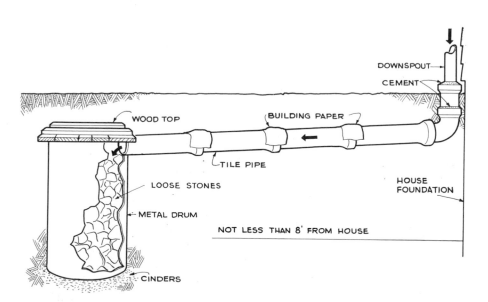

Typical dry-well arrangement.

3. Lay 4-inch unglazed clay tile drainpipe on a bed of coarse gravel at the bottom of the ditch, setting the pipe sections ¼ inch apart. This space permits water to enter at any point.

4. Cover the top and sides of the joint between sections with tarred building paper or copper-screen cloth.

5. Now test the system to make sure water flows through to the lowest point, no matter where you pour it in. Make necessary adjustments, using gravel to prop the tiles in the proper position.

6. When satisfied that the drain works properly, fill in the ditch with coarse gravel to within 1 foot of soil surface. Fill in the rest of the ditch with ordinary soil to ground level and plant grass or shrubs to resist surface water.

Once the drainage pipe is complete, the problem of where to conduct the surplus water must be disposed of. If a municipal storm sewer lies below the level of your pipe, it provides an ideal answer. If not, lead the water to a dry well, locating it at least 25 feet from the house, if possible. In either case, dig a ditch leading from the low point of the drain system to your disposal point and continuing the downward slope. In this ditch lay the tile end to end, and fill in with soil instead of expensive gravel.

Water from downspouts may be led into this drainage system by means of special tile. All materials needed can be bought from building supply dealers.

Exterior Wall Treatment. This method may be used in conjunction with laying a tile drain, since, like the latter, it requires digging a trench to the depth of the foundation. Here, again, weigh the expense and trouble against the benefits to be gained.

Wall treatment from the outside is more effective than treating inner walls, for it deflects water pressure instead of allowing it to push through to the inner surface. Thus, if any considerable water pressure is present— as in moist clay soil—or if the wall itself has rotted spots, exterior treatment may be necessary. Usually, the following treatment will suffice to water-proof:

1. Wash the walls with clean water, brush with a wire brush, and roughen the concrete surface by scouring with a hammer and chisel or coarse wire.

2. Fill the cracks with commercial ready-mixed patching mortar. If this is not available, use 1 part of waterproof cement and 1½ parts of sand, moistened to the consistency of damp earth and rammed in with a caulking tool.

3. Using a clean brush (an old paintbrush will do), cover the wall with "grout"—cement and water mixed to a milky consistency.

4. While grout is still wet—within an hour—apply a coat of mortar (1 part of cement, 3 parts of sand), mixed with a commercial waterproofing agent available from your dealer. Trowel this on to a ⅜-inch thickness, using a wooden float.

5. Roughen this coat with a wire brush or saw-tooth paddle, keeping it moist—and shaded, if possible—until it has set.

6. Apply a second coat, using the same mixture, again keeping it damp and shaded until hard.

When a basement is beset by really considerable volumes of water, as in marshy land or on ground near a spring, bituminous coatings are required over the cement. In such cases, keep the outer cement coat damp for three days. Then:

1. Cover with asphalt primer if you are going to coat with asphalt; tar primer if you intend to use tar.

2. Brush on hot asphalt or tar with a coarse brush or old floor mop to a thickness of ⅛ inch. To be on the safe side, apply a second coat after the first has begun to harden. Cold tars are also available, but are not as effective.

3. In the worst cases, alternate layers of asphalt or tar with layers of roofer's felt running horizontally, each strip overlapping the next one by 1 foot. As many as five felt layers are applied in the worst cases. This process is known as "membrane waterproofing."

There are, of course, efficient prepared mortar mixes, including waterproof ones, on the market today, to save you labor in treating exterior cellar walls. All you need do is add water. However, in the volume required to cover one or more walls with one or more coats, there are considerable savings in buying the components from a builders supply store and mixing them yourself.

As previously stated, basement dampness is curable by painting interior wall surfaces with waterproof cement coatings. Full details on interior basement wall treatments may be found in Chapter 6.

What to Do for Window Wells

During the winter months, a snow-clogged basement window well can cause water to seep into the cellar around the edge of the window when the snow begins to melt. In addition, it cuts down on the light in your cellar. To prevent this, nail a piece of clear plastic to the house right above the basement window. Extend the plastic to the ground at about a 45-degree angle and drive some pegs through the plastic into the ground to hold the

How to repair porch piers

1. A *partially* deteriorated post is rabbet-cut in the shape of a tenon; the form is for a base. Note the nails which help bond the wood to cement.

2. The post is asphalt-coated, and cement is poured. The beveled top facilitates water runoff.

3. The *totally* deteriorated base of a post should be completely cut off 2 inches above the rotted area.

4. Prepare the pedestal and slip it beneath the base of the shortened post; secure it with nails.

5. A rotted post in a concrete floor is rabbeted and finally reseated in the hole.

6. With the post asphalt-coated, the form is prepared for cement; edges are beveled. Note the nails.

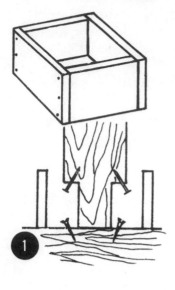

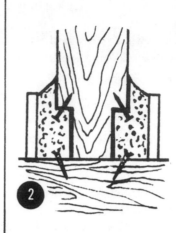

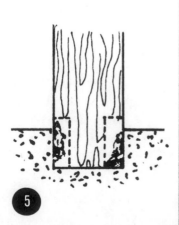

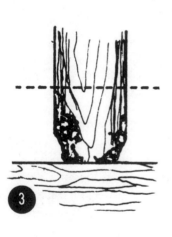

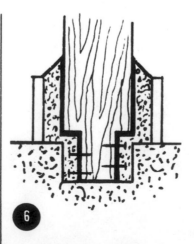

plastic in place. You can also keep the plastic in place by weighting it down with bricks, cinder blocks, or large stones. When it snows, the snow will land in the plastic, with most of it sliding off to the ground, rather than getting into the window well and clogging it. This is also a good measure to apply if your basement windows are flush with the ground and there is no window well. The plastic keeps snow from around the window, maintaining light in the cellar and keeping water from seeping in.

PORCHES AND STEPS

Often important structural members of the house are attacked by dry rot, and sudden collapse of sill and supports result. If these conditions exist in a foundation sill in your home, it is best to call in a contractor, but it's not difficult to repair wooden steps and porches.

Wood Porches

Rotted, cracked, and sagging porch floors indicate that repairs are in order for the joists that support the flooring. Get under the porch and you probably will find dry rot in one or more of the joists. If this damage is not extensive enough to warrant replacing the joists, they should be spliced with pieces of timber (not less than 5 feet long) of equal width and thickness. It is advisable to support the joist with a 4 x 4-inch post before cutting away the rotted section. Reinforcing is necessary also when an old joist is split and sagging. Do not cut the old joist in such cases. Prop it up, and splice a new section to it. A joist with only a small rotted spot along its top surface should have the damaged section sawed and chiseled out, and be reinforced with a piece of 2 x 4 or 2 x 6.

The piers which support a porch are usually out of sight, so out of mind. And, whether your porch has masonry or lumber posts, they should be inspected, too, for signs of damage and weakening. If an old pier has to be removed and replaced with a new one, the main consideration is an absolutely firm support of the porch. A screw-type jack is the support to use, but you must provide it with a firm base.

Broad boards and heavy timber can be used. Place them in a tier and put the jack on top. Raise the jack against the bottom of the porch, turning it up until the load rests on the jack instead of the pier. The porch should be raised about $\frac{1}{32}$ inch above the pier to allow removal of defective material. If you are working on a masonry pier, remove the defective pier and check its footing. If the footing is damaged, rip it up and make a new one, using 4 parts of gravel to $2\frac{1}{2}$ parts of sand and 1 part of cement. Then begin to rebuild the pier from the ground up.

If the new pier does not exactly fit beneath the sill, the space between can be filled with mortar or wooden wedges. Allow the masonry pier to set at least 24 hours before removing the jack and shifting the porch's weight to the pier.

Now, as for the posts which support porch roofs, there are two wood types. One type has the posts on a wood floor; the other has the posts set into concrete. To repair the wood-floor types, proceed as follows.

If the outside edges of the post have rotted near the bottom, necessitating reinforcement, rabbet-cut the post with a saw. The tenon must be at least half the thickness of the post. Drive several coated nails part way into the center or base and into the underside of the post. Start several large screws into the floor within the cutout area.

Make a form from ½-inch plywod to fit around the sides of the post. The form should be approximately 2 inches wider and longer than the size of the post. Coat the form with oil or grease to facilitate removal later. Coat the exposed wood with asphalt. Mix 1 part of cement and 2 parts of sand with water, and pack it into the form. Bevel the upper edge of the cement mix, allow the cement to harden, and remove the form. If most of the base of a post on a wood floor porch has rotted through, you have to cut across the post about 2 inches above the rotted area. Make a base from several pieces of wood, beveling the edges so it will shed water easily. Nail the pieces together with aluminum or coated nails that will not rust. Slip the base between the bottom of the post and wood floor of the porch. Nail it into position with coated finishing nails, and apply caulking or asphalt around the base to keep water out.

When a wood post set in concrete rots at the base, remove the rotted portion and cut the post to form rabbets for the new base. Drive several nails into the tenon portion of the post where the new base is to be added. The purpose of the nails is to hold the post securely in the new cement you pour in. Fashion a form for the concrete, setting it up as shown in previous sketches. Coat the exposed underpart of the post with asphalt, and pack in 1 part of cement to 2 parts of sand. Bevel the top of the concrete base so that water will not collect on edges.

The joint between the house and porch floor separates unless caulked well, and water seeps in. Boards contract, leaving gaps for moisture to penetrate to unpainted wood in tongue-and-groove joints and the undersides of the board. They then warp, twist, and separate. Caulking and paint on top preserves them; treatment with a preservative underneath helps, too.

Be sure to replace all rotted or badly cracked flooring immediately. If an entire board is gone, it should be replaced. To remove, split it lengthwise in several places and pry it out from the center toward the edges. Be careful not to damage the tongue and groove of adjacent boards. To set a new board in a tongue-and-groove floor, chisel off the bottom part of the grooved edge. The tongue of the new board can then be slipped into the groove of the adjoining board, and the grooved edge will fit over the tongue of the other adjoining board.

When only a small part of a floor board is defective, find the position of the nearest joists and draw pencil lines across the top of the floor to mark these. Then drill 1-inch holes in the corners between the pencil lines and the edges of the bad board. With a keyhole saw cut across the two pencil lines from hole to hole. The saw cuts should be almost flush with the inner edges of the joists. Split the defective board and pry it out. Nail 1 x 3-inch boards to the sides of the joists under the hole. Cut a new board to fit the opening. Remove the bottom part of the grooved edge. Then set it in and nail it in place.

Wooden Stairs

Outdoor wooden steps take a beating the year round. They should be checked over carefully for any signs of weakness or decay. First inspect the stringers—they are those sides that hold up the steps. In some cases, they are saw-tooth with the steps nailed across. In other cases they are merely straight with a step support nailed to it and the step nailed in between. If there are any cracks along the grain, these sides can be strengthened by bolting a 2 x 4 along the full length. Use bolts, as nails in old wood only split it further. Use ¼-inch carriage bolts spaced at 1-foot intervals. It's best to drill a $\frac{5}{16}$-inch hole through the side support and the 2 x 4. Then insert the bolt with a washer around the bolt head and another under the nut.

With those saw-toothed stringers, if the step support shows signs of weakness, remove the step first. Do this by tapping up lightly a little at a time on each end of the step. Next cut two pieces of wood to match the shape of the saw tooth, using 2-inch stock or a thickness to match that of the original stringer.

If the stringer is still in good shape, cut off the weakened saw tooth. Replace it by bolting the new piece. But if the stringer is supported by a 2 x 4, just add a new supporting angled piece to it in the same way. Then renail the step in position.

Maybe the steps need attention. Some may be worn unevenly in the center; if so, they can be turned over. But it may be necessary to visit the lumberyard to buy a replacement. If your steps are of the saw-tooth stringer type, it's easy to remove the step. Simply tap upward on each end, as noted before.

With the other type of step construction, where steps are nailed in between the side supports, the job is somewhat more exacting. The step, despite the side nails, is removed by tapping upward at each end. You have to hit a little harder, but the step will come out. After the step is removed, hammer the exposed nails back through the supports.

If the step supports attached to the stringers are worn, replace them. They pry up easily. Attach new ones with ¼-inch carriage bolts the same way as for the saw-tooth stringer supports. When replacing the steps, nail first to these step supports. Then drive nails through the stringers into the step.

An emergency measure on wood steps involves only removing a warped or split board and turning it over. The warp will become self-curing, and the split will draw together until complete replacement is possible.

If the railings become wobbly, secure them to the floor or columns with angle irons and screws.

Brick Porches and Steps

Loosened mortar is usually the first sign of trouble to come, and if left unattended, the porch (or stoop) and steps become dangerous and unsightly. An early repair is advised, using one of the two techniques described below.

There is nothing to replacing a single brick. First, chip away any remaining mortar with a cold chisel, meanwhile soaking the replacement brick in a pail of water. Hose down the stoop to flush out any mortar dust and to dampen the work area. Wipe away any puddles that collect on the surface to be worked.

Next, dust some Portland cement on the surface and, with a trowel, apply a batch of mortar equal in thickness to the original level. (Use a mortar mix, at 1 part of cement to 3 parts of screened sand; color with lampblack to match the old mortar.) Set the brick in place and tap it gently with the trowel handle until it settles flush with the other bricks; if the brick rides too high, remove the excess mortar and reset it. Finally, drop mortar in at the sides with the trowel and use a stick to pack it tightly. Produce a smooth joint with a flat, steel bar or pointing tool of your choice.

An excellent substitute for corner brick replacements is the cast masonry block, approximately 4 x 8 x 8. It is particularly suitable as an anchor for metal railings and is available at any builders supply store.

The block is mortared in the same manner as above, but you must, of course, remove two end bricks instead of one. If you are going to use it as an anchor for a railing, predrill the hole before installing the block and wait a few days after installation before inserting the rail post. If you forget to predrill for rail posts, allow the mortar to cure at least a week before drilling the block.

Concrete Porches and Steps

Concrete porches and steps should be treated like foundations—all cracks mended against frost breakage. Again, the important feature of this type of repair is to clean away all loose matter; then distinguish between vertical and horizontal work to be done.

Vertical repairs (as on the risers or sides) may be simple, thick patches on small chips, or larger patches involving scrap-board forms, as described earlier for chipped foundation corners. The do-it-yourselfer can patch at just about any angle, with the dual help of a slightly thickened patching material and/or a scrap board fitted to a space and braced to hold the concrete on the opposite side to dry.

Horizontal repairs are routine space fillers. The idea is to patch on a level with the surrounding step, filling all spaces and assuring a watertight seal.

Should water collect in a low spot, the floor can be leveled by either troweling on latex cement or chipping out concrete in the low spot to a depth of 1 inch and filling with mortar of one part of Portland cement to three parts of sand. (In the latter case, follow the technique described on page 111.) But, in such a repair, the patch will not match the surrounding surface unless you paint it; and do not forget that paint does not hold very well on concrete paving.

Iron Railings

Weak, shaky, and dangerous ornamental iron railings should be reinforced before an accident occurs. In most cases, the cause is not deterioration of the railing itself as much as weakening of the fasteners that hold it in place. This is especially true when the stoop is made of brick or concrete block. The bottom anchors may have weakened. They can be reinforced by packing in new mortar or pouring molten lead, if that was the original fastening material, until it is flush with the surface. Be sure to remove the old packing material first.

A shaky railing can also be reinforced by attaching the end firmly to the house wall with a heavy angle bracket. In brick or stone, use sleeve-type masonry anchors at least ½ inch in diameter. Set the anchors in holes drilled right into the wall. If the house is of frame construction rather than

A broken concrete step can be dangerous, particularly at night when lighting is poor. (Left top) Clean the area thoroughly with a stiff wire brush. (Right top) If a large section of step is to be built up, steel cut nails can be driven into the concrete to reinforce the new cement patch. (Left bottom) Forms to contain the fresh cement and support it until it sets can be made from scrap pieces of lumber and are held in place by stakes. (Right bottom) Be sure to wet the area before placing the fresh cement. Trowel off excess cement, making the surface flush with the top of the form.

masonry, be sure to fasten the wall end of the bracket to a solid framing member, not to siding alone which may not hold adequately.

WALKS AND DRIVES

Although walks and drives are not a part of the exterior surface of the house—and they seldom cause an emergency—you should know about their upkeep. Whether blacktop or concrete, any place that water can accumulate is a danger point, since this water will freeze and expand, cracking the masonry or asphalt. Then it goes deeper and repeats, and by spring the walk or drive is completely shattered.

Concrete. The first step in patching concrete sidewalks and driveways is to undercut the crack with a hammer and cold chisel. That is, the crack is enlarged so its bottom is wider than the top. This lets the patch lock in place. Wait about 45 minutes to let the cement set a bit; then smooth it with a steel float. If a rougher texture is desired, use a wood float—a wood block—with a circular motion. Cure the cement; keep it damp for a few days to assure a properly hardened patch. Curing is particularly important when temperatures are 75°F. or more, because evaporation will rapidly suck moisture from it and it will dry soft. To retain moisture, cover the repaired spot with an old blanket or burlap bag and wet it twice a day for several days.

Concrete slabs may in time develop any number of defects, notably bulges, depressions, and up-turned corners. And this may be due to one or a combination of two usual occurrences: tree roots pushing against the slab, and compacting or sinking of the earth beneath it.

For example, where two slabs are forced up at their edges, forming a wide inverted V, you may have a massive root-removal job facing you. If the slabs are severely cracked, you also may have to break them up and pour completely new sections. But when the slab sticks up at one corner only, it is possible to reset it properly by lifting the slab, clearing out space, laying a concrete cushion, and lowering it back into place. Use a long pinch bar in combination with sturdy wood wedges to raise the slab out of the way and examine the subsurface. Very likely, the culprit will be a tree root which has to be removed; your best bet here is a hatchet, chopping the root at both exposed ends. Then spread an inch-thick layer of thinly mixed cement and slowly lower the slab into place over the wet mortar. As you lower, check the level of the slab; if you need more substance in the mix, sprinkle small stones onto the surface where the slab dips.

Slabs which have cracked into two pieces and formed dips that collect puddles after rainfalls can be repaired with the same concrete cushion technique. Sometimes you can substitute a thin layer of gravel only. Either way, the two pieces are easily realigned with a pinch bar and the cracks patched with cement.

When any defect is minor, you can, of course, either fill the depression level with the sidewalk or chip off slight buckles and smooth up the rough spots. This does not correct the basic cause if it happens to be a root or ground shift, but will do for the time being.

Blacktop. Repairing a blacktop driveway involves less effort than a concrete one. A ready-to-use, cold patching material is available in various quantities. After brushing dirt and loose material out of the crack or hole, shovel in some gravel if the hole is large. Tamp it with the end of a 2 x 4 and fill the hole with asphalt patching material. Work the asphalt thoroughly with a shovel to remove air pockets, then tamp with the 2 x 4 until the asphalt is compacted. You repair a small hole the same way, but you do not need gravel.

Flagstone Walks. Flagstones will heave or lift during winter's freezes. Some settle back in the spring, but others will remain displaced. A close inspection will also show that the mortar between these flags will have cracked and split. Areas that heaved and resettled will also have damaged mortar.

In severe cases of unseating, it's best to take up a whole section of flags, discard the old, broken mortar, and reset the flags. In milder cases of lifting, all you have to do is remove all loose bits of cement between the flags, retain solid mortar which is not separated from the flagstones, and patch the spaces—first being sure the flags are level.

To avoid spotting or staining by cement, spray the edges of the flags with a silicone spray or brush on lubricating oil. After the mortaring job, this will allow you to clean away easily any overfill that is spread on the flagstones. Trowel on a prepared mortar mix from the hardware store, first wetting the grooves between the flags thoroughly. Cure for about three or four days thereafter, sprinkling lightly with water twice a day.

CHAPTER 6

Door, Window, and Interior Surface Emergencies

Many of the problems and difficulties discussed in this chapter cannot be classified as real emergencies needing *immediate* attention. However, if they are not taken care of in a reasonable period of time, these troubles could lead to real emergencies.

DOOR PROBLEMS

Few door problems can be classified as emergencies. The exception is a door that freezes shut. In storms or bad weather, make certain you can get in and out of your home at all times, just in case of an emergency. Therefore, if freezing rains or snow cause a door to bind shut, take immediate action. Get out through another door or window. Pour boiling water over the ice while someone inside the house is pulling on the door. If the temperature is very low, this will not work. Instead, use a blowtorch, moving it about and not playing on any one spot too long. Play the flame at the joint where the door and frame meet. Remember, the torch can be held several inches away and still melt ice.

Actually no one really pays any attention to a door as long as it works smoothly, but when it starts to stick or resists being closed, the door becomes a source of annoyance and a menace to comfort. But door ailments are cured easily, once you pinpoint the trouble spots.

One of the best ways to determine the cause of your door problem is to stand on the side of the door that is away from the stop—so the door closes in, away from you. Now, note the width of the cracks on either side of the closed door. If the crack is very narrow and the door is sticking or binding on the hinged side (called the hinge stile), but the crack is wide

113

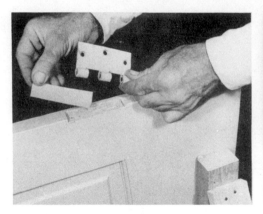 

(Left) Placing a cardboard shim under the hinge leaf may stop sticking. (Right) One way to correct a sag in a door is to reset the top hinge into a deeper mortise.

on the opposite side (called the lock stile), this tells you that the hinges are set too deeply and need shimming up.

If, however, the width of the crack on the hinge stile is wide, but the crack at the lock stile is narrow (where the door is sticking), this tells you the hinges are not set deeply enough. Perhaps all that is needed is a tightening of the hinge screws, which may have become loose. But if the screws will not tighten, the holes have probably become enlarged, preventing a tight-fitting hinge. For a remedy, try a longer screw; if this does not work, the door will have to come off for further repairs.

Most doors ride on butt hinges which consist of two leaves, one attached to the door (called the gain) and the other attached to the jamb. The two are connected with a pin. Usually, the pin can be knocked out by striking the underside or flange of the pinhead with a screwdriver or hammer. If this does not work, insert a thin nail in the small hole at the bottom of the hinge and tap it up with a hammer. With the pin removed, you can separate the gain and jamb hinges, lifting the door from the frame.

Remove the screws from the hinge that refuses to tighten. Fill the enlarged screw holes with a wood filler, allowing it to dry overnight. After that, the hinge can be reset firmly, as if over new wood. Another method is to insert wood matchsticks into the oversize hole.

Now, what if the hinge screws are all right but the door still sticks, with the space between door and jamb at the hinge-stile side wide enough to permit undercutting of the hinge mortises? You undercut, very carefully, with a chisel. Often a very small cut of both top and bottom hinge mortises is all that is needed to keep the door from rubbing against the frame. It really does not matter if you make the cut in the gain mortises on the door or in the hinge mortises in the jamb. However, do not vary the position of the cut; if you chisel out the top hinge mortise on the jamb, make sure you chisel out the bottom hinge mortise on the jamb. Never switch to the gain mortises unless the cut becomes so deep that the hinge goes below the surface of the wood. If this is the case, you should take a little off the gain mortises on both the top and the bottom of the door as well as a little off the hinge mortises on the top and bottom of the jamb.

Repairing the door by chiseling out a mortise is a trial-and-error procedure, at best. Perhaps only a slight undercut on one mortise is all that is needed. If so, after you have done a little chiseling, replace the door and see whether it closes properly. No more cutting may be needed.

Upon examination of a door, suppose you find it sticking at the hinge-stile side, with the space between lock stile and jamb wide enough to permit shimming of the hinges. Cut some cardboard shims to the size of the jamb hinge, punching in holes that line up with the holes in the hinges.

Begin by placing one shim beneath the top or bottom hinge—or both top and bottom hinges. If sticking persists, try another shim beneath one or both hinges. If, however, the *full length* of the hinge stile is binding against the jamb, both hinges have to be shimmed. Many times this second cardboard shim provides a trifle too much thickness, causing the door to push against the jamb on the lock stile. If this is the case, cut *paper* shims for the second, third, or fourth shims.

Badly adjusted hinges are not always the cause of the door problem. Moisture may have caused the door to swell against the jamb on both lock- and hinge-stile sides. The way to determine this is to close the door and check the width of the cracks on each side. If both cracks are very narrow, sticking at any point, your only recourse is to reduce the over-all dimensions of the door.

There are two ways to do this. You can plane the door, or you can sand it, planing being faster but more dangerous because of possible excess stock removal, and sanding being slower but safer because of better control of stock removal. Often, the complete door will not need shaving. A comparatively small section only may have to be planed or sanded, so inspect the cracks carefully, noting only those areas that bind. In stock-reducing a door, professionals recommend that the hinge-stile side be shaved. This may necessitate deepening of the hinge-gain mortise later if the leaf is not flush with the surface of the wood when it is repositioned. However, this seldom happens because wood usually expands in the center or at the top or bottom of the door—not in the mortise.

Plane from the edge of the door to the center, as planing from the center out could cause the edge to split. Always set the plane blade for a very thin cut. And do not remove too much stock before replacing the door in position for testing. A surprisingly slight removal may cure the problem.

If the door binds at the bottom against the threshold, either the threshold is warped or damaged or the door is sagging. Sagging, of course, can be quickly corrected by readjusting, but if this does not work, the door will have to be trimmed to shape. Planing the bottom (and the top, for that matter) of a door is a difficult job. Wood will easily splinter when planed against the grain, possibly marring the door face. For this reason, it's much better to use sandpaper. A damaged threshold must be replaced.

Doors frequently warp when one side is exposed to moisture and the other side is kept relatively dry. The wet side swells and the dry side shrinks, pulling the door out of shape. Another cause of door warpage is the absence of protective paint on the top and bottom edges, because unpainted edges soak up any and all moisture. As a practice, always make sure that these top and bottom edges are well painted.

There are a few procedures you can try in an attempt to straighten out a warped door. First, lay the door in the hot sun and let it dry out. It may straighten itself. If this does not work, lay the door across two supports with the warped or bulge side up. Place about 50 pounds of weight on top, allowing it to remain for at least 24 hours before checking for correction.

If this remedy fails, you can try to pull the door into shape with wire and turnbuckles. Place the turnbuckles on the top and bottom of the door, connect them with wire, and set a 2 x 4 bridge beneath the wire on the bulge side. Twist the turnbuckles until the wire is tight, the force being placed on the bridge and, subsequently, against the bulge. As the door slowly straightens, take up the slack on the wire.

Another type of door damage occurs when the door frame settles, no longer fitting the door. Cracks in the plaster or plasterboard around the frame are usually a sign of this condition. Because it's difficult to square a door frame without completely dismantling it, you should attempt to alter the door to the out-of-kilter frame. This is best done by shaving the door and/or resetting the hinges.

Binding of heavy doors is usually corrected by adding a third hinge at the center to relieve the strain. The hinge should be of the same kind as the originals, set into carefully cut mortises, which can be marked and cut without removing the door.

A common condition that causes annoyance occurs when the strike plate is not in proper adjustment. If the clearance is too light, the door must be slammed to latch. If there is too much clearance, the door will rattle or vibrate. Examine the strike plate closely while you open and close the door several times. The latch should be at the exact level of the tongue; if too high or low, the hinges may need shimming. Possibly the screws have become loose and allowed the strike plate to drop slightly in its mortise. New screws should correct this.

If the latch locks only when the door is pressed tightly, this can be relieved simply by enlarging the plate opening with a file to give more clearance. Remove the plate and lock it in a vise for uniform filing. Another cause of poor latching is a plate recessed too deeply in the mortise; usually, it can be brought out by shimming with a thin piece of wood. If a door rattles, the plate is probably too far forward and does not hold the door against its stop moldings. This may also be the result of filing the bar too deeply. Occasionally the cause is stripping of the plate screws so the plate is not held tightly. It is difficult to move the plate further back because the new and old screw holes would be so close together; in that case, you can chisel out a section of frame and replace it with a new wood insert. Before you go this far, however, try to get a new strike plate that will cover the area.

Splintered or Worn Threshold

Worn and splintered thresholds are unsightly and dangerous, yet easily replaced. Thresholds (often called "saddles," and sometimes "carpet strips" when installed under doors in interior walls) usually are made of rough maple or oak. Care should be used in removing them to avoid harming the finish of the adjacent floor.

Removal can be accomplished by splitting the threshold with a cold chisel or a heavy wood chisel driven into the center top section. The pieces may be removed by prying them up with a wrecking bar. Insert the flat edge of the bar into the crack in the threshold and put a block of wood under the heel of the bar for extra leverage if necessary. Of course, the old nails must be pulled from the floor before making a replacement.

Although specified by the width of the doorways for which they are intended, stock thresholds (available from lumber dealers) are made long enough to permit extension of an inch or more along the face of the door casings. Begin fitting a threshold by centering its length across the door casings and measuring for all cutouts.

After the cutouts are made, you are ready to push the threshold into place. The fit should be snug, but do not force the strip. If it is too tight, sand the edges of the cutouts, using a block to hold the sandpaper. Before nailing the threshold, slope the ends of the projecting shoulders which fit against the door casings, and saw them, too. Use 6- or 8-penny nails for fastening the threshold to the floor. Wax the nails with a piece of candle or push them into a bar of laundry soap before attempting to drive them, or maple and oak may cause them to bend. (It is often wise to predrill the threshold with holes slightly smaller than the nails to prevent them from bending.) First drive a nail on a slope through each of the projecting shoulders and into the base of the door casings. Now drive six nails into the threshold and into the floor. Do not drive nails through the center section of the threshold or it will probably split. Put all nails through the shoulders. Set the nailheads below the surface of the wood with a nail punch and fill the holes with plastic wood. Finish the threshold as desired.

Accordion Doors

If an accordion-type door operates stiffly, clean the overhead track and coat it very lightly with a lubricant such as Vaseline. Should the latch jamb touch at the top but not at the bottom, unscrew the door from the opposite jamb. Then loosen the screws in the overhead track except the last one before the latch jamb. Starting at the opposite jamb, insert wood shims under the track until the door hangs parallel with the latch jamb. Then screw the track tightly in place. For appearance' sake, the long wedge-shaped crack between the track and the top jamb can be filled with a wood molding.

On the other hand, when the latch jamb touches at the bottom but not at the top, loosen all the screws in the overhead track except the last one before the opposite jamb. Shim the track down, as above, until the door hangs parallel with the latch jamb.

Sliding Doors

When sliding doors, either wood or glass, move stiffly, clean out their tracks with a vacuum cleaner; then make sure there is nothing in the track. Then cover the inside of the tracks with a light film of lubricant.

If a sliding wood door becomes warped, there is little that can be done other than preventing the door from binding against the frame or other doors by installing door guides on the floor. Of course, if a door repeatedly jumps off its track and it appears to be straight and hanging correctly, the problem could be the size of the roller wheels in the track. If they are less than 1 inch in diameter, it may be wise to install a new track with larger wheels.

Should water enter under the track of exterior glass sliding doors, force caulking compound under it. If this does not stop the leak, call professional help.

Swinging Doors

If a swinging door acts stiffly, take the cover plates off from both sides of the hinge at the bottom of the door. Remove all dust and dirt from the mechanism and apply powdered graphite to the spring and pivot. Then work the door back and forth until it swings freely.

Should the door strike the jamb, check whether the hinge and the pivot at the top of the door can be moved closer to the hinge jamb. If they cannot be moved, the swinging edge of the door must be carefully planed down *slightly*.

Screen-Storm Doors

If the door closer cannot be adjusted to function properly, the unit may be mounted on the jamb too far from the door. If so, reset the mounting bracket as close as possible to the door. If the closer is mounted at the top of the door, you may find that it works better when relocated near the middle, where its pull is more efficiently distributed.

In hydraulic closers, a source of trouble may be oil leakage from the cylinder at the washer seal, evidenced by drip marks on the floor or screen. Replacing the unit with a new closer is the best bet in this instance.

Warped, twisted doors and damaged hinges are most often the result of being blown open—repeatedly—in a strong wind. Bent hinges, of course, must be replaced so that the door hangs plumb. If it still hangs askew, the corners out of square, chances are one or more corner joints are separated. Working with metal doors, particularly aluminum, there is an inside corner fitting which may have cracked under the pressure of a sudden whipping movement. This will necessitate removing the door, reassembling the rails at the corners, replacing the corner brace, and reinstalling the door.

The fit of the door at the sill is another important check to make. With aluminum and steel doors, an adjustment is no problem: a series of screws along the base of the door permits raising or lowering a sliding neoprene gasket or channel. Adjust with a screwdriver, inspect the door in a closed position, and adjust again, if necessary.

If the storm door is of wood, it may be repaired as described earlier. Nevertheless, one wooden storm door repair is *sag*, a condition which cannot be corrected by resetting hinges. The door must be made square. The first step in this repair is to measure the sag—the largest open space between the top of the door and the door frame. Then remove the door and measure off the amount of sag on the hinge side of the door at the top. Using a straightedge, scribe a line from the end of the door to the mark; that is, from the sag to the mark which represents the amount of sag. Use this same technique for the door bottom, if necessary.

Saw off the top edge of the door along the scribed line. Next, glue and nail a wooden spacer strip to the top of the door, corresponding in size to the door frame. When you rehang the door, probably it will not close, so you will have to shave off a fraction of the spacer.

Often, the bottom rail of a wooden storm door becomes separated—a break, not a sag. To repair this damage, increase the separation slightly and insert glue on the dowel pins holding the bottom rail to the door. Clamp tightly and, as an added reinforcement, screw a metal brace against the joint. You can often cover the damaged section with an attractive brass or plastic kick plate, attached with roundhead screws.

Stile splitting is a problem with wood storm-screen doors. To repair it, spread the split and apply plastic epoxy cement. Clamp the frame by entwining the door with wire and taking up the slack on the wire by twisting a screwdriver in it. Or, you can buy a turnbuckle, screw it to the door, and tighten. This can be left in place; it helps prevent warping and further stile splitting.

If you wish to reinforce the area after the glue has hardened (although with a turnbuckle it's not absolutely necessary), drill several pilot holes, driving in a few long, thin screws across the break. Of course, you should make sure the hinges are firmly set and that the glass or screen is in good condition. More on their repair can be found later in this chapter.

Garage Door Care

Heavy garage doors can work as smoothly and easily as any door in the house if they are properly lubricated and adjusted. Neglect can result in doors that are hard to open, damage to the special roller bearings, and costly service calls.

Sectional-type overhead doors have a special hinge with extending shafts on which small wheels ride inside a channel. The hinges hold the door sections together and, because of the weight, are subject to considerable strain. Hinges of this type have oil holes for lubrication. The track rollers ride on ball bearings and also must be oiled periodically to avoid wear and jamming. Some doors have long tension springs; others have cables which wrap around a spring-actuated shaft. In most cases the springs need no lubrication, but the mounting brackets and spring shafts should be oiled occasionally. In addition, the door-locking hardware (in most cases a long bar that slides into a retainer housing) should be greased for easy operation.

The swing-up type of door has either balancing springs or weights. Moving parts should be oiled about every three months. This is true also of the hinges on standard side-swing wood doors. Oil is easiest to apply, particularly with a squirt gun, but many door servicemen use grease because it lasts longer.

Door Locks

It's not surprising that door locks act up occasionally, considering the use they get. To offset wear and maintain smooth operation, periodically remove them from their seat and test for good working order. Before replacing them, lubricate with graphite powder. Once reinstalled, test for a smooth spring-latch action, noting that the latch engages the plate without unnecessary pressure on the door.

If you have to give the door an extra push in order to hear the latch click, a slight repositioning of the strike plate (usually forward) will correct this annoyance.

Then, too, there is always the possibility of worn keys. Or a key may not have been cut properly when it was duplicated. To be absolutely sure on this score, take out the lock cylinder and ask a locksmith to cut a new master key, following the cylinder's contours. After this, you can have duplicates made, using the new master.

When the lock and key become provoking by getting stuck or broken, you may need to make only a slight adjustment to put them back into smooth working order. The following are the most common lock emergencies and the ways to overcome them.

Table 12

LOCK EMERGENCIES

Problem	Cause	Cure	How to Prevent
Lock frozen—can't get the key into the cylinder.	Moisture in the lock expands when frozen, thus binding free movement of the cylinder.	Warm the key; insert in the cylinder gradually; alcohol on the key will speed the process.	Keep the inside dry; best to spray with graphite; or use fine typewriter oil, but not ordinary lubricating oil.

Table 12 (Continued)

Problem	Cause	Cure	How to Prevent
Bolt stuck—the key turns, but the bolt will not move open or closed.	Door out of line puts pressure on the bolt.	Check the door alignment; see pages 113–117 for details on how to cure faulty doors.	Check the door alignment regularly, especially when it shows signs of jamming.
	Bolt blocked by paint over the end.	Scrape clean with a knife; use paint remover to assure full removal of paint.	Use extra care when painting the edge of a door to avoid going over the bolt or plate.
Key binds—goes into cylinder but will not turn.	Improper mounting so that the cylinder is out of line with the lock housing.	Remove the lock; check all parts to see that they are aligned.	Make certain to follow instructions when installing a new lock; use the templates or pattern included with the lock by the manufacturer.
	Cylinder in upside down; tumbler springs will not work properly.	Remove the cylinder; replace it in proper position.	
	Poor duplicate key fails to line up tumblers inside of cylinder.	Use the original key to check whether door works; have a duplicate key checked by locksmith.	Do not buy poor-quality blanks for duplicate keys; stick to top names.
	Outside elements have affected the metal inside of cylinder or housing.	Remove the cylinder; a new one undoubtedly will be needed.	Make a cover to fit over the cylinder; use thin coated metal; cut to any decorative shape.
Key breaks—part of the key remains inside the cylinder.	In 9 out of 10 cases, the key was not in all the way before it was turned.	Remove the cylinder; use a long, fine pin to push key out from shaft end. Or slide a long crochet hook along top of cylinder; lower hook over end of key and pull it out. If no spare key is available, the tip of a screwdriver can be used to open or close the lock if cylinder is turned properly.	Lubricate the cylinder with graphite; insert the key fully before turning.
	Wrong key used; did not line up tumblers and therefore cracked when turned.		Mark keys for easy identification; better yet, have one key to work all locks.

How to Release a Frozen Lock. Wind-driven snow or rain on the bitterest days may freeze the locks on your car, causing all kinds of delay and inconvenience—with you on the outside looking in. For this important reason, make it a point to have an aerosol can of deicer handy in the garage or under the hood. First spray the outside, test with the key, and spray again, if necessary; you may have to spray the key also, working it in and out of the lock until the tumblers unbind and the key turns. A squirt of antifreeze in the slot for good measure will assure continued operation for some time to come.

If you have no spray, heat the tip of the key with a match or lighter (several times, if necessary), forcing it into the slot. If the lock still will not turn, pour some lighter fluid or antifreeze on the key, repeating the forcing action.

WINDOW TROUBLES

Having put up with the sticking, binding, and banging of ailing windows from time to time, you will be happy to know that most if not all of these defects can be corrected immediately and effortlessly, probably with a minor adjustment only. For the trouble usually has to do with the opening/closing mechanisms (that is, metal slides or rotor gears) and not necessarily the wood frame or sash, as many a homeowner might easily suppose.

Sliding Mechanisms That Don't. Double-hung windows are of two types: those which are removable from the frame and those which cannot be removed. And because horizontal-sliding windows are nothing more than double-hung windows turned sideways, have similar mechanisms, and are usually removable, they can be treated in the same way you would work on the double-hung types.

The key to proper adjustment of windows with metal slides is the *bow*, as follows. Turning the adjusting screw clockwise loosens the pressure on the window, whereas turning the screw counterclockwise increases the pressure. These screws are found in only one track; its mate contains the spring mechanism. The top and bottom screws (far left and far right, if a horizontal sliding unit) are always turned in more than the center screw, thus producing a slight bow which holds the window firmly, wherever you position it. You will know that a horizontal-sliding type is adjusted when it slides easily and shows no play as you test it by exerting upward pressure against the unit.

Nonremovable double-hung windows that operate on aluminum track require a different adjustment. Springs behind the channels seldom lose tension, but when they do—indicated at first by creeping of either window —simply crimp the flexible aluminum lip in or out along the channel's length. This can be done with a screwdriver.

In and Out of Square. Installed properly, these newer, double-hung windows should never go out of square. But when they do—or you think they do—there are checks and procedures to be carefully followed.

First, never mistake a window that is loose in its channels for a unit that is out of square. So be sure to try an adjustment before doing anything else. But a window that *is* out of square often has a definite, tilted look—the back or top window and the front or bottom window, when both are raised, appear slanted—make no mistake about it.

Correcting an out-of-square window requires patience and judgment. The easiest way, of course, is to carefully plane the window sash on both sides, replacing and removing the units until an easy fit is restored (you may also have to plane the top of the back window and the bottom of the front window to achieve flush closings). This is no problem with removable windows. Not so with the nonremovable types, as you then have a masterful repair job on your hands. This is what to do.

To begin with, remove the three trim pieces that encircle the window— the two side pieces and the top piece that butt against the aluminum channel. Remove the head stop—the underside trim piece at the top of the frame. Now, examine the channels, removing all fasteners that anchor them to the casing. They are usually stapled at the factory, so it's an easy matter to pull every staple you find. This done, bring the front and back windows together, grab them at their top and bottom rails, and pull out the window and channels as one piece. Finally, slide the windows from the channels.

Plane the sides, as noted earlier, and reassemble. Or, if channels have to be replaced, the windows are simply inserted into the new units and everything is put back into place in the frame. You do not, however, have to use staples unless you wish to, as small nails will do as well.

Windows that slide with difficulty in aluminum tracks may be binding between track and sash despite a perfect adjustment. This is caused by a lack of lubricant and/or by dirt and grit accumulations in the track. So as a regular part of your window maintenance (and before attempting any adjustment), thoroughly brush out the tracks and lightly lubricate the channel on both sides, using a paste wax, paraffin, or an all-purpose aerosol spray lubricant. In most areas of the country, brush and lubricate twice a year. In salt-water areas, lubricate more often to fight oxidation, a condition which, unfortunately, cannot be prevented. Even anodized aluminum will oxidize in time, so be on guard. As soon as you notice any traces, remove them with 2/0 steel wool. There are a number of aerosol lubricants available containing either Teflon or silicone, and they work remarkably well.

Sticking wooden window sashes can sometimes be loosened by rubbing paraffin or silicone formula white grease stick along the sides and stops where the window slides. Apply the lubricant and run the sash up and down. If the sash will not budge, you can take it out for special treatment. First, remove the stop strip with a broad-bladed putty knife or chisel, prying slowly to avoid damaging the strip. Then you can swing the sash out as you would open a door. But you should be warned that you may have to remove the interior molding trim as well, which may slightly disfigure the walls, necessitating repainting the room (you cannot make touch-ups that do not show). If you do remove the sash, bake the moisture from the wood with a heat lamp or home movie lights. Test to see whether the sash slides freely. If it does, seal the sides with shellac thinned 50 percent with alcohol. If not, sand the sides slowly, testing for fit as you work, and finish these raw edges with five or six coats of wood preservative for good sealing.

For Older Windows. Older double-hung models are still with us, and the only real complaint we have about these faithful units is a broken sash cord. When a cord breaks, you can keep the window open by using a stick of wood forced under the sash. But replacing a broken sash cord can be easy. Little skill is required, and you can do it with only a hammer and screwdriver. However, use of the right tool makes the job not only easier on you but easier on the woodwork. In place of a screwdriver, get a floor chisel of the kind suggested for treating stuck windows.

Before any new cord, upper or lower, can be installed, the lower sash must be taken out of the window frame. The first job, then, is to pry off the flat wooden molding on the side of the frame. This is called the window "stop," and it holds the lower sash in place. You need remove the stop only on the side where the cord is broken. Begin prying with the chisel at the bottom of the stop and work up. The chisel is recommended here since it's almost impossible to pry with a screwdriver without marring the wood. If you must use a screwdriver, the best method is to open the window and begin to pry from the outside of the house. In this way, any marks made on the wood will be concealed when the window is reassembled. Once the first few inches are loose, the rest of the stop can be pried off from the inside without damage. With this molding off, you will find that the sash easily lifts out of its groove.

If it is a lower window sash cord that has broken—and usually it is— notice, then, how the other, unbroken cord is attached to the sash, for you will want to attach a new cord in the same way. And, while not an

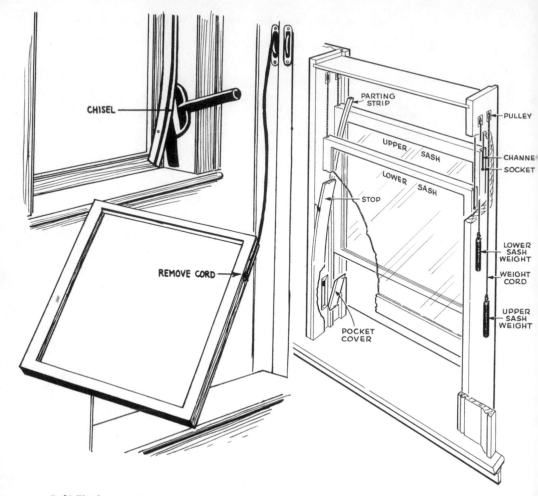

CHISEL

REMOVE CORD

PARTING STRIP

PULLEY

UPPER SASH

CHANNEL

SOCKET

LOWER SASH

STOP

LOWER SASH WEIGHT

WEIGHT CORD

UPPER SASH WEIGHT

POCKET COVER

(Left) The lower sash slips right out of the frame after the inside stop is pried off. To take out the upper sash, remove the parting strip as well as the stop. (Right) In older-type windows, removal of the pocket cover is necessary to recover the fallen sash weight and tie on a new cord.

absolute must, you will find it easier and safer to detach the unbroken cord and stand the sash in a safe place while you continue to work. Now that the window stop and sash have been removed, you will find that you have exposed the oblong-shaped pocket cover. Take out the screws and pry off the cover. Lift out the sash weight which has fallen to the bottom of the pocket, and cut off the old cord. You are now ready to install the new cord.

The idea, of course, is to pass the new cord over the pulley and down through the frame to the opening made by the pocket cover; but new sash cord curls so that it is almost impossible to do this. The best way to get the cord through is with a guideline. Attach a small weight—a nail will do—to a thin string. Feed the weighted end over the pulley. When you can reach the nail through the pocket cover, attach the other end of the string to the sash cord, pull the sash cord through, and cut off the guideline. Tie the cord securely to the sash weight and put the weight back in the pocket. Next, place the sash on the window sill. Pull the new cord until the weight is at the top of the window against the pulley. Now, measuring the cord against the sash, cut the cord off 3 inches below the socket in the sash. Tie a knot in the end of the cord and insert the knot in the socket, but make sure that your knot fits entirely into the socket. Now attach the other cord, if you have removed it, and place the sash back in its grooves. Raise and lower the sash several times to be sure the new cord is of the right length. The weight should not hit the pulley when the sash is closed nor rest on the bottom of the pocket when the sash is up. If everything is correct, lift out the sash and replace the pocket cover. Put the sash back in position and replace the window stop.

In prying off the stop, the nails may have pulled out of the stop. Remove these from the frame. If the nails came out with the stop, do not drive them out, as this will damage the finish. Instead, pull them through—the nail-heads are small and will pull through easily—with the claw end of the hammer. Fasten the stop in place with new nails, sinking the heads slightly and filling the holes with plastic wood; then touch up with paint.

To replace an upper sash cord, remove the lower sash as explained above. Then pry out the narrow molding, called the "parting strip," which separates the upper and lower sashes. Pliers are handy here. Grasp the strip at the bottom and pull sharply. The strip will usually come free of its groove. If the strip sticks, take a sharp knife and cut the paint seal on each side of the strip. Then proceed as with the lower sash.

When Rotor Gears Balk. The major cause of damage to rotor-geared windows is misuse of the gearbox. For example, when a window is locked shut, someone may inadvertently turn the crank to open the window, the force breaking off a tooth of the gear. Many times, too, people develop the habit of cranking the window shut *beyond* the closing; that is, after it is shut, they continue to crank an extra half-revolution or so, putting unnecessary strain on the gears. These abuses shorten the effective working life of gearboxes, necessitating replacements occasionally, especially at heavy-use windows. Here is how to install a new unit.

Remove all the screws holding the gearbox to the window sash, including the retaining screw (if there is one) which holds the box to the frame. Go outside and unscrew the activating arm—a part of the gearbox assembly—from the lever that is attached to the window. You will notice that the screw which joins the arm and lever is fitted with a small cotter clamp on the take-up side. Be sure to save it for reassembly of the linkage. Having done this, slip out the gearbox and arm as a unit, replacing the new box and arm in precisely reverse order.

Now, with a casement window, for example, the activating arm setup is different, fitting directly into a slide mechanism. The arm is moved by cranking the gears and, in turn, it actuates the slide mechanism which moves the window. Therefore, when you remove the gearbox, the activating arm will come with it in one action—so do not be surprised.

Awning window sash comes in for a lot of punishment because many homeowners have the habit, when house painting, of placing their ladder against the open sash. And, of course, there's always the possibility of pane replacements. In either case, you will need to take out the sash for repairs. To do this, remove the screws from the metal arms holding the sash on both sides and simply slide the sash off for the work you have to do. Replace the unit in reverse order.

If the casement window catch does not lock into place effortlessly, as it should, file away any burrs that appear on the metal tongue. Thereafter, the catch will not snag. Some casement windows do not close tightly and cause drafts which are annoying, if not costly. Ordinarily a professional mechanic can correct this condition by bending the frame where it may be warped or damaged. An alternative do-it-yourself method is to line the casement with special neoprene gaskets, thus firmly sealing all metal-to-metal contacts regardless of whether they are warped or not.

Top- and bottom-hinged windows are spared the usual mechanical difficulties because of their simplicity. The sash will, however, react to exposure and moisture, necessitating planing and adjustment, probably only once in its lifetime. Just follow the general outline described earlier.

Broken Windows

Accidents *do* happen, and a broken window is usually the result of an accident, except in cartoons. Aside from aiming football- or snowball-throwing children in a different direction, not much can be done as a preventive.

As an emergency treatment, keep on hand a stock of vinyl plastic sheeting with which you can construct an emergency storm sash. This material is also available in kit form, some with adhesive to apply to window casing, or with edging slats to be tacked up. Two such emergency windows, one inside and one outside, will serve as well as a glass replacement.

Tack this plastic sheeting over the window to the frame; double over all edges for added strength; tack the top up first, then the sides, and finally the bottom; use a tack every 8 to 12 inches, making sure there are no gaps in the plastic sheeting between tacks. But if you cannot get to the outside of the window—maybe it's on the second floor—do the second best thing. Cut the plastic sheeting with scissors or a knife to fit over the pane that is broken. Use Scotch tape or masking tape and seal the plastic sheeting over the sash—the part of the window that slides up and down. Adhering this sheeting to the wood will help keep most of the water out. Better put some towels along the window sill, just in case any of the rain drips through.

Other materials can be used also, of course. A piece of corrugated cardboard cut to the proper dimensions is a good emergency stopgap, too, or hang an old blanket over the entire window. It may block out daylight, but it will also resist wind and rain.

Replacing a Broken Windowpane. Though care is required, replacing a broken windowpane is not difficult. All you need to make the replacement is putty, a putty knife, an old chisel or screwdriver, and a glass cutter. If you prefer not to cut the replacement glass—though there is no reason why you cannot—you can purchase it in the exact size needed.

If the pane is cracked but still in place, remove the old putty with a putty knife or chisel, taking care not to cut the frame. If the putty is very hard, pass a soldering iron or propane torch over it quickly, and scrape it away while still soft. Then remove the glazier's points—the little triangular metal cleats holding the glass in place—with pliers or a screwdriver, and take out the pane.

When the pane is shattered, remove the fragments first, wearing gloves for safety. Take out putty and points, using the same method as described above.

Measure the opening for the size of the new pane, being sure to include the rabbeted sections of the frame on which the glass rests; then subtract ⅛ inch from the length and width so there will be space allowed for possible contraction of the frame.

When cutting glass, use a quality cutter and work on a surface padded with newspaper or a blanket. Clean the glass thoroughly and scribe the cutting line on the underside with crayon. A common mistake is to scribe on the cutting side; then the wax interferes with the cutting action. Before making the cut, put a single drop of light oil on the cutter wheel. Use a straightedge for a guide, and start the cut $\frac{1}{16}$ inch inside the far edge of the glass, holding the cutter between the first and second fingers, using the thumb for support, and at a right angle to the glass. Draw the cutter toward you with a firm, constant pressure until you have passed the near edge.

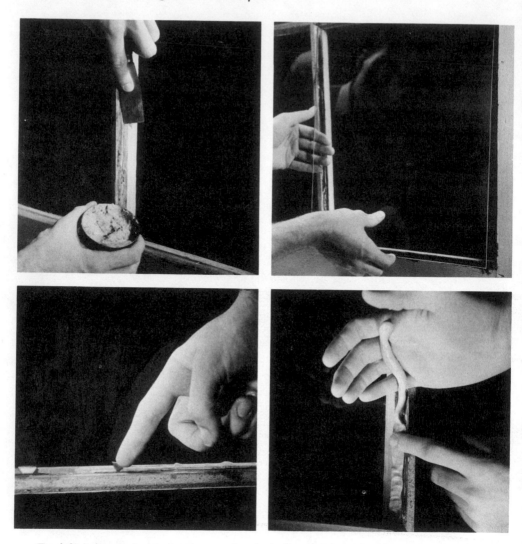

(Top left) Before replacing the glass, apply a bed of putty over the linseed oil. Apply a layer about $\frac{1}{16}$ inch thick. This cushions the glass against future shocks and keeps out air.
(Top right) To preclude easy breakage, set in the glass with the concave side inward. You can spot the concave side by sighting along the edge of the sheet. Press in firmly until it meets the layer of putty along all edges. (Bottom left) Glazier's points should be inserted about every 4 inches. Start them with your fingers and then drive them in about halfway with a chisel (or the driving tool sometimes supplied with them). Slide the chisel along the surface of the pane to prevent breakage of the glass. (Bottom right) Before applying putty, make sure it is of the consistency of dry, thick dough. If you are using old putty, add some linseed oil and knead the mixture on a piece of glass. When ready, roll the putty into pencil-size strips. Start at a corner and lay the strips end to end around the glass. To complete the job, smooth and bevel the putty with a putty knife.

Handled properly, the cutter produces a continuous, even sound as it scores. To remove excess, use the ball end of the cutter to tap the underside of the glass near the score line on the excess side. This will start a split along the line. Or, working on a padded surface, place the straightedge under the glass, about ½ inch from and parallel to the score line on the pane side, and snap off the excess cleanly with firm pressure. If necessary to make cuts that will intersect, remove the excess after each cut. Since "feel" is all-important in cutting glass, it is advisable to make a practice cut on scrap glass first.

Before installing new glass, dust the window rabbets clean; then brush them with linseed oil to preserve the putty and protect the wood against rot. Apply a bead of putty worked to a doughlike consistency about ⅛ inch thick to the rabbets to make a seal. If you have hard putty on hand, you can make it workable by adding linseed oil, then kneading.

Press the glass into position and use a chisel to tap glazier's points into the wood about 4 inches apart, just far enough in so they will hold the glass. Now apply a seal of putty where the glass meets the frame by first rolling it into a strip a bit thicker than a pencil and pressing it into place with the fingers, then smoothing with the putty knife to produce a bevel. An alternative method is to put the putty on in small amounts with the knife, then smooth it. Immediately after applying the putty, brush on house paint to preserve it. The paint film seals the putty, letting it stay pliable; then it can expand and contract with the window frame.

Metal window frames in basements are very easy to work with when replacing glass panes. First of all, the frame itself can be detached for convenience and the work accomplished under less cramped conditions. The materials should consist of a glazing compound (a nonhardening type of putty), a putty knife, a chisel to chip away old putty, a wire brush to clean the frame of bits and particles, and the replacement glass. Use the old retaining clips which help keep the glass in place, although they are not absolutely necessary. With the old glass removed and the frame clean and dry, lay a bead of putty all the way round (prepacked putty is quite pliable, but in colder weather may need warming in the hands for best results). Press the new glass into the bead of putty, followed by the clips (there are slots in the frame for them) and the finish layer of putty. For appearance, you may want to effect a neat beveled putty line between the glass and the frame. This is easily accomplished by smoothing the putty with a putty knife held at an angle. The new putty can be painted immediately.

Storm-Screen Windows

In the case of aluminum storm windows, look at the bottom of the channels. You should find two or three small holes called "weep holes" which allow condensation that may form inside the storm window to drip out, preventing rotting of sills over a period of time. Always keep these little holes clear of obstructions. And if none are there in the first place, drill two or three, using a $\frac{1}{16}$-inch bit.

Aluminum storm windows have a vinyl molding around the perimeter of the glass which should always be firmly in place. If it is not, air can leak in past the glass. So if this weatherstrip-type molding has come loose, remove it completely, dab on some plastic epoxy cement (put some on the metal seat, too), and press it back firmly into place.

To remove broken glass, slip a putty knife beneath each vinyl strip edging the glass. Lift a small section, grasp it with your fingers, and simply pull the vinyl from its seat. Remove the broken glass, taking care, of course, not to cut yourself. You may want to wear work gloves to prevent this possibility. Carefully measure the length and width of the opening from channel to channel. Now, have a glazier cut a pane of glass to size; he will cut it slightly smaller, as previously described.

Place the glass in the frame. Reinsertion of the vinyl strips is easier if you first brush soapy water around the channels and onto the reverse side of the vinyl. Simply press the vinyl into its channel seat by hand. If you hit a tight spot, do not press too hard. Use the edge of a putty knife to get the vinyl into its seat. Be especially careful when you get to the edges of the window, which are its weakest points. It's best to use a putty knife here.

Wooden Storm Sash. Wooden storm windows offer more of a maintenance problem than those made of aluminum. They need painting, preferably every year, to give them maximum protection against the weather. So now is as good a time as any—but not before checking the hangers to make sure they are secure. Some of the old, rusted hardware can be replaced with corrosion-resistant hangers. You will probably have to use oversized screws to hold the new hangers, or else fill the old holes.

Joints may have taken a beating, too. If they have started to separate, attach metal corner braces, drawing the joints firmly together. Check the putty around the glass, and if it is crumbling, remove it and replenish with fresh glazing compound.

Generally, it is not advisable to reset wood storm sash in hot weather, as there is a tendency for wood to expand and bind. In cooler weather, however, storm sash may shrink and fit perfectly or need just a bit of planing.

If your wood storm sash is badly abused, beyond practical repair, think of purchasing new ones—aluminum, this time. They offer fewer maintenance problems.

Aluminum Window Screens. These should be prepared by following the same procedure for the frame as described for aluminum storm windows. An added consideration is the screening itself. A screen that has a small break or puncture, but is otherwise in good condition, can be repaired neatly and quickly with a patch.

Use scissors to trim the break so that its sides are straight. Cut a patch from an old screen (or you can buy a small packet of screen patches) to a size that overlaps the break about ½ inch on all sides. Strip off two cross wires from each side of the patch, place the ends against a block of wood, and bend all the wires at right angles. Now place the patch, from the inside of the house, so that the bent wires go through the original screen. Back up the patch with the wood block while you tap the bent wires flat with a mallet, holding the patch neatly in place.

Screening that has rusted through at the corners should be completely replaced. If the screening has bulged out at the center or is sagging, you may be able to tighten it by resetting the retainer tacks.

In metal frames—either steel or aluminum—the screening is held in place with thin splines pressed into grooves along the frame members. Pry up these splines to remove the screening. Some types of steel frames have a single tubular retainer that fits the channel all round and is removed the same way by starting at one end.

To install the new screening, lay the frame on a flat, firm surface. Set the screening over the frame and press in the spline at one side. It's quite easy to get the rest locked in tautly by folding the screening over each spline before it is driven in—but avoid making it too tight, as the thin wires will break under excessive pressure. Screens must fit snugly in the window channels. Any spaces at the sides can be sealed with flexible self-adhesive window stripping available at hardware stores, or you can build up the wood frames with additional thin strips, nailed in place.

In a wood frame, remove the thin molding strips that cover the sides. Lift the molding carefully with a chisel so it will not split (though you can use new molding if this happens) and pull out the tacks or staples. To reset, attach the screening firmly along one side—you will find it easiest and most effective to do this with a staple gun—pulling tightly while you tack the other side down. Finally, smooth down and staple the two ends. Replace the moldings.

Combination storm-screen windows may give some sticking trouble because the latch locks will not have been used for a couple of months. You may note that in sliding the screen section up and out of the way, the release catch will fight you; and when you do succeed in pulling it back, it refuses to snap forward into locking position again. The same balking may be true of the glass-storm window section, as you try to lower it into winter position. Depending on manufacture, these finger-operated latches function in a variety of ways, but all need frequent oiling (or squirts of graphite) for best results. While you are about it, check the small slots in the channels, to be sure they are not crimped, preventing the latches from entering.

Venetian Blind Repair

Broken tapes are the most common emergency with Venetian blinds. When these occur, take the blind down and remove the raising cords. Then slide out the slats and remove the tapes (which are tacked to the top and bottom boards in wood blinds; clamped in place in metal blinds). Buy new tapes at a department or variety store. Cut them to the right length and attach them to the top of the blind. Then rehang the blind, slide the slats into the tapes, and attach the tapes to the bottom board. Knot cords at one end and slip the other end up through the bottom board, the slats, and the top board. Then run the cords over the pulleys and down through the hole in which the cord catch is located. Adjust tension on cords so that the blind does not tilt when raised.

If you have snapped or bent a Venetian blind slat, you can fix it in minutes. A few taps with a light hammer will remove the end cap from the bottom bar. Then remove the slat from the bar. You will see that the cord holding the slats is passed through metal clips at each end of the bar and knotted on the underside. Slide the clips out of the bar, undo the knots, and remove the bar and slats. If the replacement slat is not a perfect color match, install it at the top of the blind where it will not be conspicuous. (If your blind has no end caps on the bottom bar, pry out the tacks or staples that secure the tape ends to the bar. The cord can then be untied and the slats removed.)

In the case of a wooden slat that breaks, it can be repaired if the break runs with the grain. Coat the edges with epoxy glue and press together. Then with epoxy glue stick a patch cut from thin aluminum or a tin can to the back of the slat over the joint. Clamp with C clamps until dry. If the break is across the grain, a repair is unwise.

A metal Venetian slat that is bent can be straightened by hand and with pliers (cover the jaws of the pliers with adhesive tape so you do not mar the finish on the slat). If you cannot repair the slat, it's possible that you may not need to buy a new slat. Blind tapes stretch to a surprising degree after hanging a long time. If the blind is resting on the window sill, replace the damaged slat with one from another part of the blind. Then shorten the tape and reassemble.

Should the cord catch not hold and the blind sag, take down the Venetian blind, scrape away the rust from the catch, and oil it. When the blind is down, it's a good idea to clean and oil other moving parts, too.

Window Shades

Window shades can cause trouble. For example, if a shade will not wind up properly, pull it down about two-thirds. Then remove the roller from the brackets and roll up the shade by hand. When you replace the roller in its brackets, the shade should roll up properly, but if it does not, repeat the process.

Should the shade snap up violently when raised, raise it to the top. Remove the roller from its brackets and unroll the shade by hand half its length. Then replace it in the brackets. If the shade is still too tight, repeat the procedure until loose.

If the shade will not catch when rolled down, take the roller from its brackets. Then clean and oil the ratchets on the flat rotating pin. When the bindings are broken on bamboo or split wood shades, unroll them on the floor and remove the broken bindings. Cut a new cotton cord about three times the length of the shade and fold it in two equal lengths. Loop it around the bottom wood strip and tie it with a square knot; then loop it around the next strip and tie, and so on to the top of the shade.

FIRST AID TO FLOORS

Hardwood floors that are kept clean and well waxed add distinct beauty to a home. Yet, when they sag or creak they can be a real nuisance—and possibly a danger.

Floors Can Weaken

A well-built floor is rigid, giving no vibration. In time, however, the floor may start to vibrate underfoot in certain spots and lose its rigidity. There are a number of ways to correct this.

1. Most homes have one or more girders running the width or length of the house which support the joists and are, in turn, supported by columns or posts. If the floors above this girder are vibrating, loose, or sagging, it may

(Left) A sure way to stop floor sag caused by a heavy object: reinforce the joist with an adjustable steel floor jack. (Right) Here is another way to reinforce floors. Cut stock of the same size as the joists. Force it between the joists as shown here; then toenail the piece all the way round.

mean that the posts are settling. The sag can be corrected by driving metal wedges between the top of the post and the girder.

2. Where floors are not above a girder or post, you may be able to stop sagging by driving a 2 x 4 or 2 x 6 brace between the joists snugly against the subfloor. Toenail the brace to the joists at each end. Then, for a solid repair, drive finishing nails down through the floor from above into the brace. Countersink the nails and fill the holes with wood putty. Cover with varnish.

3. If the brace method does not work, you will have to erect a post to support the weakened area. Posts can be of 4 x 4 timbers, or you can purchase adjustable metal supports, called "jack posts" or "Lally columns." Place the post under the joist below the sagging area. The base of the post should be placed on a concrete block to spread the load, since the basement floor is not usually strong enough to carry the weight. If the floor cracks when the jack is lifting, back off on the jack and chop a hole in the basement floor. Dig down about 12 inches; then pour concrete to provide a foundation for the post.

4. If a floor above a finished ceiling is sagging, you will have to rip out the ceiling to get at the joists and repair the sag. It's a tough job, but there is no alternative. Luckily, a floor that is soundly constructed will seldom sag or vibrate.

Creaking Floors

The most common cause of squeaks in hardwood floors is the movement of one flooring strip against another, natural shrinkage having taken its toll in time despite the best original installation. If it is quickly traceable, isolated to one spot, a little powdered graphite or liquid soap forced between the strips will eliminate the noise, if not the cause.

It's possible, however, for the whole floor to develop multiple squeaks, in which case your best bet is to seal the floor. This is accomplished by brushing penetrating floor sealer *with* the grain, working the liquid into the joints. Let it set for a few minutes; then wipe off the excess *across* the grain. Next day, apply a floor finish of your choice *across* the wood's grain, followed in the end by light strokes *with* the grain. Like the graphite-and-soap method described before, this sealer treatment does not remedy the basic cause of squeaks, but at the same time neither are you necessarily neglectful of an ailing floor. To be sure, read on.

Another major cause of floor squeaks is subflooring which has dried out and pulled away from the joists. If the squeak is on the first floor, the repair is easy. Listen from below while someone walks overhead. Pinpointing the noisy spot, drive a shim or two between the subfloor and the joist. A wood shingle is ideal for this purpose, as it's tapered. Be smart and coat the shim with glue before wedging it into place.

Still another noisemaker, although you would never guess it, is the bridging strip. You probably know them as those crisscrossed supports nailed between the floor joists. When two of these bridging strips rub against each other, at the intersection of the X, you have a squeak. Therefore, take a saw and pass it between all adjacent strips to be sure there is a gap. If they are touching, saw a space between the two.

Make sure the individual bridging strips are tightly emplaced. If you can move them at all by hand, hammer some nails through the support and into the joist.

Warped or loose floor strips not only make noise but cause vibration as well, so they will have to be secured to the subfloor. A warped board is obvious, but a loose one may be tricky to detect. The best bet, again, is to go into the basement while someone walks overhead.

Having located the squeak, drill a pilot hole through the subflooring and into the hardwood, stopping short of the surface. Drive home a No. 10 1-inch or 1¼-inch roundhead screw while someone above keeps his weight over the weak spot. This done, you may have to add three or four more screws, on 4-inch centers, to finally silence the squeak.

All the repairs thus far are relatively convenient because they are in the basement, working on an exposed subfloor. Squelching squeaks on the second floor is more or less difficult. Because you cannot get to the subflooring, you have to work on the surface, driving additional nails into the flooring strips. Your only problem will be locating the joists (where subflooring separates, causing squeaks), if you cannot sound them out by tapping. A popular method is to use a magnet on a string, moving it along the floor strips. When you feel the magnet tug, you know you are over a concentration of nails in the joist. Drill a small pilot hole through the floor at an angle, into the joist, and follow with finishing nails, countersunk. Ringed-type dry-wall nails are best because of their holding power. Fill the holes with wood putty and dab with varnish or shellac.

Cracked Floor Joist

A cracked floor joist can be a dangerous defect and should be attended to at once. Get an adjustable Lally column or jack post at a builders supply store and place it under the cracked beam. Turn the screw jack at the top of the steel column and slowly jack up the cracked beam until it is at its normal horizontal position. The next thing to do is to find the cause of the crack. Is there a concentration of weight, like a piano or some other very heavy object, directly above the crack in the beam? Can the weight be moved or at least spread? If there is no especially heavy weight above the beam, it could be that there was a crack in it from the beginning that became worse with normal expansion and contraction.

Set a new joist alongside the cracked one and bolt the two together or spike them together with 3¼-inch nails. The new joist should be of the same size as the old one, and its ends, like those of the original beam, should rest on the foundation. Once the new "splint" is in place, you can remove the steel Lally column.

Damage to Finished Wood Flooring

Warped boards, particularly wider ones, can be flattened by wetting them with an old towel which has been thoroughly soaked in warm water, then setting countersunk screws or screw nails through their outer edges into the subfloor. Another method is to sand down the raised board.

Boards with cracks along the grain may be repaired by forcing glue into the cracks with a putty knife. This treatment stops the cracks from lengthening. Use a glue-and-sawdust mixture when the opening is wider than ¹⁄₁₆ inch. Do not attempt to fill the cracks without cleaning them out thoroughly. Grease or dirt will keep the filler from adhering to the wood. Green

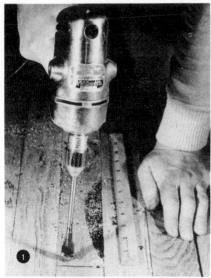

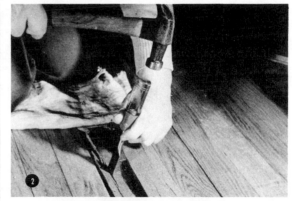

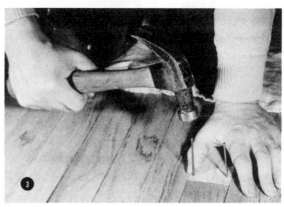

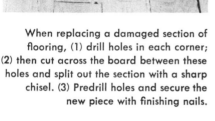

When replacing a damaged section of flooring, (1) drill holes in each corner; (2) then cut across the board between these holes and split out the section with a sharp chisel. (3) Predrill holes and secure the new piece with finishing nails.

or wet boards used in a new floor often shrink and separate as the wood dries. Any such openings should be filled with glue and sawdust, plastic wood, or wood putty.

Floor areas just inside doorways tend to become ground down and filled with grit. Scrub these areas with steel wool to remove spots. Then apply a plastic finish, which is tougher and holds up better than shellac or varnish.

Deep marks, such as cigarette burns, dents from furniture and glides, and gouges from dropped objects, can be removed with a curved chisel or knife. The hole should be filled with plastic wood chosen to match the flooring. After the plastic wood has dried, sand it smooth, shellac, and wax.

Discolorations from rubber heels, casters, crayons, and such can be removed by rubbing briskly with a cloth moistened with solvent or turpentine. Although this treatment may remove some of the finish, it can be touched up easily. Scrub the floor with steel wool and then coat the area with clear shellac. Complete this job of renovating by waxing after the shellac has dried thoroughly. Discolorations due to uneven exposure to sunlight, or stains that penetrated through the finish into the wood itself, can be removed by first taking off all the old wax and then the finish. Next, bleach the stain by using a commercial bleach. Most bleaches have an acid base which is applied first, then a neutralizer. Follow the directions on the label of the bleach you buy. When applying shellac to the floor, dilute it at least 50 percent with denatured alcohol and brush it on along the grain. Two coats are usually sufficient.

Linoleum Repair

A damaged portion may be replaced if you have saved some remnants from the time the linoleum was first installed, or at least if you are able to locate a matching scrap at some sympathetic flooring dealer's showroom. If matching your particular design or pattern is out of the question, all is not necessarily lost. For if the damaged spot is centrally or symmetrically located, you can patch in a contrasting diamond-shaped tile, as if deliberately planned. Next to sinks, of course, anticipating further wear to the right and left, you can install a large, long, rectangular patch—a sort of runner—which will look quite natural and be of real service.

Having resolved these problems, you can get down to it. If you are matching materials, cut a straight-sided (not necessarily square) patch somewhat larger than the worn area. To cut, use a linoleum knife or wallboard-trimming knife (scissors, least of all), making absolutely sure the slice is straight down, not beveled. For best results, use a steel ruler or straightedge held firmly against the cut line to guide the blade.

Using the cut patch as a template, place or position it over the worn area, matching the design continuation. When ready, hold it firmly with one hand and make two light cuts on each of the sides, keeping the blade snug against the patch's edges. Put the patch to one side, and, guided by the light scoring, make the final cuts down to and through the felt paper beneath (again, use the steel ruler as a sure guide). Remove the worn section and clean out the opening. Test-fit the patch for snugness.

Do not worry about an uneven surface under the patch, as the linoleum paste will provide a smooth, level base when hardened. Therefore, fill in more than enough paste and press the patch into place, flush with the floor surface. A rolling pin is great for this step. Wipe off excess paste that oozes out from the cut lines and allow the recommended drying time.

Very small holes in linoleum can be filled by pulverizing a piece of linoleum of the same color. Mix the powdered linoleum with spar varnish to make a thick paste, which is pressed into the hole with a putty knife and left to dry. The best way to powder linoleum is with a rasp or coarse sanding disk.

Replacing Damaged Floor Tiles

When replacing damaged resilient floor tile, it's often difficult to buy one that matches. It's always good practice to buy a few extras when installing a new floor for future repairs. If you cannot get the replacements, a good-looking repair can be made with tiles of a contrasting color to form a design.

First remove the damaged tile, taking care not to damage adjacent tiles. Heat does it. For taking up vinyl-asbestos or asphalt tile, the best thing is a rented electric heating plate, but use this only for extensive repair. Or you can use a torch, taking care to keep the flame moving, or a household iron at its hottest setting. If you use an iron, place a wet rag over the tile to prevent the iron from sticking. As you heat the tile, pry along the seams with a putty knife. Or cut off a corner of the tile and apply heat; the tile usually curls up and can be pried free fairly easily.

To remove vinyl, rubber, or linoleum tile, you do not need heat. Run a curved linoleum knife deeply along the seams to free the tile there; then cut it out with a hammer and chisel, working from the center outward to avoid damaging the edges of adjacent tiles. After removal of any type of tile, cut down high spots with a chisel and fill in low areas with wood putty to provide a level surface for replacements.

It's likely that the old adhesive will be sticky enough to hold the new tile. If not, scrape away as much of it as you can and apply new according to the manufacturer's directions for your type of tile. With the adhesive down, press the tile in place, using a short piece of dowel or a roller to assure good contact, especially along the edges.

More on the repair of floor coverings can be found in Chapter 7.

Removing Stains from Floors

The following table suggests methods for removal of stains from floors. Try the methods in sequence, as they are listed in the three columns of the table, progressing to the next proposed method only if the first one listed does not work. For example: In removing ink from an asphalt tile floor, try (1) synthetic liquid detergent and warm water. If this will not work, try (16) ink remover; if this will not work, try (4) oxalic acid in water; and so on.

Make a small test first to determine whether a particular method will work. Begin at the outer edges and work toward the middle to prevent the spread of the stain. When the method requires a poultice, apply it about ½ inch thick. Poultices, in drying, absorb moisture that has penetrated the stain and draw the stain out with the moisture.

Table 13

STAIN REMOVAL—FLOORS

Stain	Resilient Tile[a]	Wood or Cork	Nonresilient Floors[b]
Alcoholic beverages	1, 10, 4	1, 10, 4	1, 10, 5
Blood	11, 12	11, 12	11, 32
Candy	1 and 3	1 and 3	33
Chocolate	6	6	6
Coffee	7, 8, 9	7, 34, 9	7, 34, 9
Dyes	13, 14, 9	13, 14, 9	13, 5, 9
Fruit	2, 4	2, 4	2 and 15
Grease or oil	1	29	30
Ink	1, 16, 4, 17	1, 16, 4, 17	1, 21
Iodine	18, 19, 20	18, 19, 20	18, 19, 20
Lipstick	1 and 3, 4	1 and 3, 4	1 and 3, 5
Paint	1 and 3	4	31
Rust	22	22	22
Soft Drinks	4	4	5
Soot	23, 1 and 3	23, 1 and 3	23, 1 and 3
Tar	24, 25, 26	24, 25, 26	24, 25, 26
Tobacco	2, 7, 5, 9	2, 7, 5, 9	2, 7, 5, 9, 28
Urine	9, 5	9, 5	9, 5
Varsol	35	35	35

[a] *Resilient Tile Materials:* Asphalt, rubber, vinyl, and linoleum.
[b] *Nonresilient Materials:* Terrazzo, marble and travertine, ceramic and quarry tile, and concrete.

Key:
   (1) Synthetic liquid detergent and warm water.
   (2) Synthetic powdered detergent and water water.
   (3) Grade 00 steel wool.
  *(4) Tablespoon of oxalic acid in pint of water.
  *(5) Absorbent cloth soaked in hydrogen peroxide laid directly over the stain; an ammonia-saturated cloth on top of this.
  *(6) Use ammoniated alcohol: 9 parts of denatured alcohol and 1 part of stronger ammonia (26 percent).
   (7) Saturate an absorbent cloth with solution of 1 part of glycerine and 3 parts of water and lay it over the spot.
  *(8) Apply a poultice made of 1 part of chlorinated lime and 3 parts of washing soda and calcium carbonate. Allow to stand until dry. *Do not use on linoleum.* For linoleum use a poultice of hydrogen peroxide and whiting.
   (9) Poultice of abrasive powder and hot water.
 *(10) Follow step (1) with denatured alcohol if necessary.
  (11) Try cold, clear water first; then add a few drops of ammonia.

   Note: * Wear chemical-resistant gloves when working with these materials. Remember always to pour acids *into* water. Be careful of splashing acid-based fluids.

*(12) For old stains try 2 ounces of salt and 2 drams of formic acid in a pint of water. Soak the stain for an hour; then rinse and blot up with an absorbent cloth.

*(13) Try a chlorine bleaching agent.

 (14) Apply a solution of 1 tablespoon of permanganate of potash to 1 pint of water. When dry, apply a solution of 1 tablespoon of oxalic acid to 1 pint of water.

 (15) If a rough spot results, rub with powdered pumice stone under a block of wood.

 (16) Ink remover.

 (17) If a brown stain remains, treat as a rust stain.

*(18) Apply ammonia.

*(19) If the stain is old or deep, apply an ammonia-saturated cloth.

*(20) Poultice of denatured alcohol and calcium carbonate.

*(21) Poultice of 2 tablespoons of sodium perborate in 1 pint of water mixed into a paste of calcium carbonate.

 (22) Poultice of calcium carbonate mixed with 1 part of sodium citrate crystals to 6 parts of water added to an equal portion of glycerine. Allow to stand two to three days.

 (23) Cover with salt or rub in calcium carbonate and rub off. Wash with synthetic detergent and water.

 (24) Poultice of synthetic powdered detergent and whiting.

 (25) Stoddard solvent (Varsol) on any floor *except* asphalt and rubber.

 (26) Freeze to brittleness with dry ice. Scrape off.

 (27) Lemon juice in water.

 (28) Equal parts of alcohol and glycerine.

 (29) Pour kerosene on the spot. Soak for 5 minutes. Wipe dry with a clean cloth. Wash with synthetic liquid detergent and water.

 (30) Pour Stoddard solvent (Varsol) on the spot. Rub with a clean, soft cloth.

 (31) One pound of synthetic powdered detergent in 1 gallon of water. Scrub and rinse with clear water.

 (32) Wet the spot with lukewarm water and sprinkle with powdered malt. Let stand an hour and rinse.

 (33) Use a synthetic scrubbing pad and synthetic detergent.

 (34) Poultice of hydrogen peroxide and calcium carbonate.

 (35) Poultice of synthetic powdered detergent.

STAIRS CAN BE A PROBLEM

A squeaking, creaking staircase is a potential danger spot if neglected. The trouble is often due to a loose tread. When the stairs are used, the tread touches the top of the riser (the vertical board intended to support the tread), and spooky sound effects result. If inspection shows that the tread is not firmly attached to the riser, repair may be carried out in either of two ways.

Where the underside of the staircase is accessible, repairs are best made from underneath. If the tread and riser were originally butted together, a wood cleat should be glued and nailed to the inner face of the riser. The top edge of the cleat must be flush with the top of the riser. The job is completed by driving wood screws through the cleat upward into the underside of the tread. If desired, finishing nails may be driven downward through the step into the riser, but usually the cleat-and-screw method is sufficient.

If the tread fits loosely into the stringer (the grooved board that supports the ends of the treads on both sides of the stairway), a few hammer blows will drive in the wedges that anchor the tread in its groove. It's not unusual for the bottom of the riser to work away from the tread. The remedy is to drive wood screws through the riser into the edge of the tread.

If the staircase has been built with dado rather than butt joints, a loose tread can be repaired by driving small wooden wedges into the dado from the underside. Coat them with wood glue before driving. In stubborn cases, it may be necessary to have a helper stand on the step, using his weight to bring it down into position while the wedges are driven. Where the staircase is enclosed, use glue and finishing nails to secure the tread to the riser. If there is a molding under the edge of the tread, it will have to be pried away so that glue can be applied.

A loosened handrail can be braced by simply tightening or replacing the wall-bracket screws. They must, of course, be solidly anchored in a wall stud or used with heavy plugs, if the wall is masonry. At the top of the stairs, where the handrail end may be attached to the wall, a few long finishing nails can be used for reinforcement; if necessary, break out the plaster and see to it that the rail end is well seated against a solid support.

At the bottom, where the rail posts are set into the steps, the peg may be loose. If so, an extra nail will help. Or the newel post may be completely detached from the end frame. Correct this by working some glue into the back and tighten the post with screws, countersunk and plugged with matching grain.

Two simple methods of stopping creaking stairs.

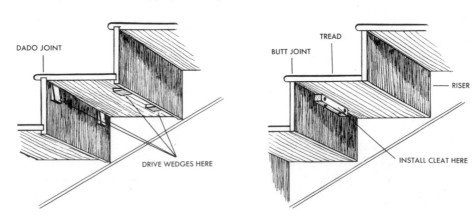

DADO JOINT

DRIVE WEDGES HERE

TREAD

BUTT JOINT

RISER

INSTALL CLEAT HERE

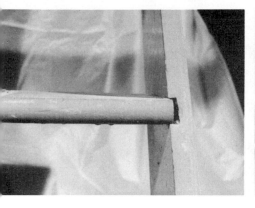

(Left) This step is dangerously close to slipping out of the supporting groove. The stair rail has warped with age, causing the separation, but it is otherwise sound and repairable.
Locations under selected steps are drilled and fitted with 3-foot-long threaded rod; the size used here is $\frac{5}{16}$-inch diameter. "Step" washers (flat washers, large plus small, as needed) are used with two nuts for a secure setting. (Right) The repair is finished when the rod is tensed enough to close the gap at the step-to-rail connection. Do not apply more tension to the inner nuts than is necessary to close the separation. Then, with two wrenches, bind the outer nut against the inner one at each end.

DAMAGED WALLS AND CEILINGS

Practically every homeowner must sometime face the project of repairing plaster or plasterboard walls. Damage here may be from accidental or natural causes.

Repairing Plasterboard

When repairing plasterboard, use the joint cement which is made specially for plasterboard; it is available in package or tube at your hardware or builders supply store. Spackle can be used, but it dries much faster and, if you have a big job to do, you may find yourself with a pan of hardened spackle. Joint cement shrinks when it dries, so do not paint over it immediately after application; when the cement shrinks, the damage will reappear. Let the cement set for the time recommended and then reapply.

The most common type of damage to a dry wall is popped nails. To repair, drive in the protruding nails with a punch and hammer; then mix joint cement as recommended on the package and cover the area with a layer of this. Let it dry at least 3 hours. Then apply a second layer of cement, using a putty knife to smooth it off flush with the wall.

When too much pressure is applied to plasterboard, a section is likely to "give," producing an ugly crack. Since such walls are hollow, there is no way to supply support behind the broken section. If the crack is small, you can avoid replacing an entire panel of the material by removing only the damaged area. Drill a hole in the plasterboard large enough for the insertion of a keyhole saw, and cut a rectangle (1) around the full extent of the crack and the weakened material. Cut scrap plywood to a size that will overlap this opening at least ½ inch on each side. Center this piece over the opening and drill pilot holes through each corner and the plasterboard beneath. Hook a heavy wire through a larger hole drilled in the center of the plywood and slip the piece through the opening (2). Draw it snug against the back face of the wallboard, aligning the pilot holes, and drive screws through the wall to secure it. Cut a new piece of dry-wall material to fit the opening and fasten it to the plywood with screws. Apply spackle (3) to fill cracks and cover screwheads; then sand the patch smooth and paint it to match the surrounding wall.

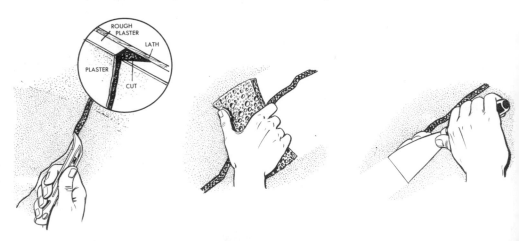

For small holes and cracks, use a spackling compound and apply with a broad knife held flat against the wall. (Left) Use a special crack-cutting tool—or a beer-can opener—to remove all particles from the crack's opening. (Center) After brushing out dust, wet the inside and both edges of the crack before applying the spackling compound or filler. (Right) Pack the filler into the crack with crisscross strokes; smooth the surface by dragging the knife slowly, permitting the patch to dry to a hard finish; then sand with medium-grit paper to remove any surface defects.

Another common type of damage to plasterboard is a hairline crack caused by settling of the house. This is easily repaired. First widen the crack to give the patching cement a place to take hold. About the best "tool" for widening hairline cracks is a beer-can opener—you have better control over this implement than over a chisel or screwdriver. Place the point of the tool in the crack and pull with a heavy enough hand to widen the crack appreciably. Clean out all loose material with a brush or rag and apply joint cement. Let it dry for several hours; then apply another coat, smoothing it with a putty knife.

To repair a long, wide gash in plasterboard, you need joint tape. First fill the gash with a liberal amount of joint cement. Take a strip of perforated tape, long enough to cover the gash, and place it over the filled area. Pull the putty knife over the tape, applying pressure. Excess cement from the gash below will ooze out through the perforations in the tape. Let the repair set for a day; then finish it off with another layer of joint cement, taking care to remove any excess. If this shrinks, a third coat may be necessary after the second dries.

A hole in plasterboard up to about 3 inches in diameter can be repaired by first stuffing some wads of fiberglass insulation into the hole. Cover this with plenty of joint cement. Let it set for at least 24 hours; then apply another coat, using enough cement to overlap the wall. Use a straightedge board to smooth over the patch flush with the wall.

For larger holes, use a compass saw or a sharp knife to cut out the damaged section of plasterboard back to the studs on either side. Nail another piece of plasterboard to the studs and cover the joints with tape and cement as above.

Patching Plaster Walls

Plaster is a mixture of lime, a binder, water, sand, and sometimes a fiber. It is applied in two or more coats over wood, gypsum, or metal lath at the base of the wall. When repairing plaster, use a mixture of half spackle and half plaster of Paris to assure a hard, permanent repair.

Small, fine cracks in plaster are repaired the same as is this type of crack in plasterboard. Widen the crack with a beer-can opener and apply a layer of the mixture. Let dry for an hour or so (this mixture will dry much more quickly than joint cement) and apply another layer, smoothing the repair with a putty knife so that it's even with the rest of the wall.

To repair a large hole in a plaster wall, first clean out all loose plaster pieces and dust from the area until the lath is exposed. Apply a mixture of brown coat (a combination of 3 parts of cleaned and screened sand, 1 part of prepared gypsum plaster, and water) to within $\frac{1}{16}$ inch of the surface of the wall. Let the brown coat dry for a few days. Then dampen the area with water and apply a second coat of spackle and plaster of Paris compound. Let this dry and, if necessary, apply another coat. Use a straightedge board to smooth the final coat even with the wall.

Ceiling cracks and separation are treated much the same way as wall cracks. But the handyman may be called upon for a little artistic innovation as well. The problem is with dappled plaster ceilings. Patching the crack conventionally leaves a visible repair line—a smooth path in the dappling. Blending or dappling the crack line is desirable.

When a ceiling receives water damage—from a leaky roof or an overflowing bathroom fixture—the stain will not go away by itself, nor will a soaked and sagging ceiling return to normal, even though the cause is gone. First of all, remove all the damaged plaster and the lath beneath if that, too, is damaged. Insert the blade of a trowel under the edges of the old plaster and pry off all *loose* portions while holding the palm of one hand up against the area near the trowel. Let it drop easily, for plaster is heavy. Cut off the old plaster so a square or rectangle, bounded on two sides by ceiling joists, is left to fasten in the patch or patches. Nail furring strips onto the exposed joists thick enough to bring the plasterboard, if that is your patching material, even with the old plaster.

Plasterboard should be nailed to the furring strips at intervals of 8 to 12 inches along all sides. Drive the $1\frac{1}{2}$-inch shingle nails flush with the surface of the board; then punch them slightly below the surface with a nail set. The edges of the plasterboard must come to within $\frac{1}{2}$ inch or less of the old plaster. Undercut the edges of both old plaster and new plasterboard so the crack will form a V with the narrow end exposed.

This V joint is then filled with prepared plaster mixed according to directions. When buying plaster from a hardware store, also purchase enough joint tape to bond the joints and prevent cracking. Bear in mind that only enough water should be added to keep the plaster from becoming too stiff to work into the joint, yet not too much so that the plaster drips from the crack. If you use plaster of Paris, add a tablespoon of vinegar to prevent too-rapid hardening. Spackling will not harden as rapidly.

Fill the joints by pressing the filler material into place with a small trowel. This tool will be found very useful in smoothing the plaster even with the surface of the old plaster. Once this is done, lay the tape along the joint so that it laps over both old and new work. Press it into the fresh material; then trowel a thin coating of plaster over the tape, feathering it to a fine edge on both sides. When the plaster has set a few minutes, brush it lightly with a soft wet brush. Do not neglect to use this tape at all corners when making plaster repairs.

Do not try to paint the new ceiling for at least two to three weeks after the repair is complete. Plaster takes a long time to dry thoroughly enough so that paint will not peel and flake off. Remember, too, that if your ceiling or the space between roof rafters was filled with rock wool or other fluffy insulation material, it probably became wet from the leak and must be removed and replaced. If this is neglected, all your work may have been finished too soon and may have to be done over.

Acoustical tile on a ceiling sometimes becomes loose or bulging. When the tile is applied on plaster, nail it back, using cement-coated nails or ceiling-tile adhesive. If the tile is applied to wood furring strips, nail back to the strips with flathead nails. Countersink the nailheads and cover with spackle.

Ceramic Tiles

The ceramic tiles used for the walls and floors of bathrooms and kitchens are laid in a concrete base and attached to it by means of a thin cement mortar. When individual tiles become loose and fall out, it is usually due to the fact that they were not installed correctly. Tiles can be cemented into place by means of a special plastic cement made for this purpose, which can be purchased at most hardware stores.

Apply a liberal amount of plastic adhesive to the back of the tile. The adhesive, packaged in a tube, comes in two forms. The white variety is nonwaterproof; the black type is waterproof. Both dry quickly, so press the tile into position as soon as the adhesive is applied. Excess cement that oozes out must be wiped off immediately. Use cleaning fluid to remove black adhesive; water will clean off the white type.

Drive four wooden wedges into the space around the tile for accurate alignment. Then place a board over the tile and tap lightly until the new tile is flush. If necessary, add or remove adhesive for accurate seating. After a few minutes, pull out the wedges and apply white tile caulking-in-a-tube around the tile. For a neat job, indent the caulking with a putty knife. An alternative method is to allow the cement to dry; then force conventional grout into the spaces.

To replace a damaged ceramic tile, cut out the broken tile with a cold chisel and light hammer blows. Care is needed to avoid damage to adjacent tiles. Remove the old cement with a knife or chisel. If necessary, the new tile may be cut to size with a glass cutter and the edge smoothed with a file. If a curved cut is needed, make small crisscross cuts inside the section to be removed. Then carefully break off small pieces of the waste, using pliers.

Metal or plastic tiles can be handled in the same fashion as ceramic.

BASEMENT MOISTURE

Dampness in basements can be separated into two distinct classes: (1) the basement shows dampness by odor or mildew, but has no water seepage; and (2) actual seepage of water exists through walls, floors, windows, or backing up of sewage. The first group is, by far, the more numerous, and the solution is easier. A more difficult, but not incurable, problem exists when water actually enters the basement. This may be very slight, just enough so that the wall feels "wet" at times, or it may be a veritable deluge under certain conditions.

Checking Musty Odors and Mildew. This is the simplest type of basement dampness problem to solve. First, you should make certain that there is no water penetration. Wait until after a heavy rainstorm and then inspect the understructure of the house for any signs of water penetration. If there is none, you can solve this dampness problem in one or more of the following ways.

1. In very many cases, merely finishing the basement walls with the necessary stud framing and walls and covering the floor with asphalt tiles will provide a possible cure for cellar dampness.

2. Cover sweating pipes which create moisture in the basement with felt tape and special preformed tubes or with pipe wrap-around material. Cover all exposed surfaces except actual control wheels and stems of valves.

3. Increase ventilation in the basement. Keep a window open and add louvers or use a ventilating fan. In the winter, heating the basement will lessen the difference in temperature between the basement and the rest of the house, thus avoiding condensation of household moisture on colder basement walls.

4. In some areas, the air is extremely humid, and condensation cannot be controlled by either of the methods above. In that case, it is necessary to reduce the moisture content of the air with special chemicals or with an electric dehumidifier.

5. Check outside drainage to keep water away from the outside of the basement walls. See water runoff outside the home, page 99.

Fixing Cracks in Basement Walls. If there is water seeping into the basement, look for cracks in poured concrete, loose or crumbling mortar between cement block and brick walls, openings around pipes and electrical conduits, window openings, and cracks in the floor.

1. Small openings around pipes or electrical conduits coming into the cellar should be stuffed with oakum, then filled with caulking compound.

2. Larger holes around these pipes and holes in the wall should be filled with a concrete mix. For how-to details, see page 103.

3. Check your windows; they are often the greatest cause of leaks into the basement. The joint between the window frame and concrete foundation should be filled with concrete.

4. The wall-floor joint is another major trouble spot. If there is water seepage, chop the concrete away at this joint, forming an opening about 1 to 2 inches wide and about 4 inches deep. Fill with waterproof cement and extend this waterproofing material about 2 inches above floor level. Add a cove of waterproof cement to seal this wall-floor joint.

Waterproofing Walls on the Inside. If a wall is free of visible cracks or other defects, but actual moisture is present, solve your problem with a waterproofing compound. The various prepared "paint-on" coatings for concrete and masonry surfaces, all of which claim a certain amount of waterproofing action, can be applied according to the manufacturer's directions on the package. Also, new rubberized coatings and a copper-bearing hard cement are available for waterproofing, along with other compounds which have been standard for many years. These prepared coatings and mixes are available in many colors and usually require two coats.

Do not expect miracles of them. Where exterior water pressure is considerable, or where the cellar walls are in bad shape, they may give only limited relief. But they do have the advantage of affording this relief in the easiest and quickest way; that is, through bonding to interior wall surfaces that are convenient to reach. Weigh the inconvenience of outer wall treatment against the comparative ease of the inner wall method, and you may decide in favor of it despite its admitted limitations.

To get maximum damp-proofing action, before applying the coatings pretreat your cellar walls as follows.

1. Remove dust and dirt by brushing.

2. Remove efflorescence (mineral salt crust), or previous coatings of whitewash, or flaking or scaling cement paint, if any, by scrubbing with a wire brush. Warm water helps remove whitewash.

3. Remove old oil or water paint with commercial paint remover or a

solution of 2 pounds of trisodium phosphate to 1 gallon of water, using a scraper, wire brush, or steel wool after the paint has softened.

4. Clean the wall with a solution of 2 parts of muriatic acid to 10 parts of water, washing off the solution with clean water and a bristle brush after the acid stops foaming. Wear gloves, goggles, and old clothes while working.

5. Fill cracks, chipping away rotten cement to a depth of 2 inches and packing with commercial patching cement mortar. If you are applying a mortar-mix type of compound rather than a paint-on coating, score the walls first with a wire brush. Such roughening makes for a better bond.

Floors which seep water through slight cracks or rotted spots can often be cured simply by chipping away the faulty areas and filling with patching mortar or commercial waterproof mixes. Floors which leak badly must be relaid or covered with waterproof topping. Because of the considerable labor involved, many homeowners would prefer to call in a contractor to do the job. But you can save up to two or three hundred dollars, even in average-sized homes, by doing the job yourself, and it requires no skill whatsoever. The steps are:

1. Remove any previous coatings and clean the floor, as you would in treating walls.

2. Fill cracks with patching mortar. Chip away rotten concrete and patch with the same mortar.

3. Roughen with a wire brush or chisel.

4. Apply a "grout" coat of cement and water.

5. Cover the floor with concrete 2 inches thick, using ready-mixed concrete, or preparing your own mixture of 1 part of Portland cement, 2 parts of sand, 4 parts of gravel.

6. One inch below the surface of this concrete layer, lay 14-gauge lightweight steel-wire mesh.

When this new floor hardens, it generally proves impervious to water. But in cases where large volumes or heavy pressures of water attack the floor, it may be better to substitute the "membrane waterproofing" system instead.

To do this, clean and patch the old floor as indicated above. Apply hot asphalt or tar with an old floor mop. Atop this coating, lay roofer's felt, allowing each strip to overlap its neighbor by at least 1 foot. Then apply a second coating of asphalt or tar and a second layer of felt. Above this, after the coatings have hardened, add a 2-inch-thick layer of concrete.

In homes built above subterranean springs, or where the sewer periodically backflows, a sump pump is a vital addition. The pump and motor should have a capacity equal to the greatest possible flow of water you may encounter. Installation of such a pump should be left to experts.

Seepage of water through walls and floors may also be prevented by exterior basement waterproofing and water runoff. Details on this may be found in Chapter 5.

CHAPTER 7

Emergencies and Household Furnishings

True, household furnishing emergencies are generally not a matter of life or death. But household furnishings are a major investment, and once a stain occurs, it requires immediate action.

FURNITURE PROBLEMS

Major furniture repairs can be largely eliminated by making frequent inspections to detect weak spots, wear, and minor scratches or breaks and taking care of them before they become serious.

First Aid to Wood Furniture Surfaces

When furniture accumulates scratches and other blemishes, only complete refinishing can be guaranteed to restore the original appearance. Before going to the expense of a professional job, or before starting this laborious task yourself, try some first aid. These treatments are suggested by our technical experts and other furniture authorities. Remember that there are many different types of finishes on various kinds of wood, so no one remedy can be a cure-all for every problem.

Minor Scratches and Blemishes. When the blemish has not penetrated the finish on the wood, a simple application of wax will sometimes hide the mark. If not, try applying the paste wax with 3/0 steel wool, rubbing gently with the grain; then polish. If the blemish still shows, there are some other tips to try, but first remove the wax (which prevents absorption of coloring matter). Rub the area with a cloth saturated with naphtha; then wipe it dry with a clean cloth.

Nut meats, linseed oil. The oil from a Brazil nut, black walnut, or butternut may provide enough coloring to hide a minor scratch. Break the nut meat in half and rub well into the blemish. Rubbing the mark with linseed oil may help, also, but do not use crude oil; this could soften the finish on the wood.

Coloring crayon, wax sticks. Try coloring the blemish with brown crayon. Or use wax sticks made specially for furniture in wood tones. They are softer than ordinary crayon and easier to work with. Fill the scratch with wax and rub in well with your finger. Wipe with a soft, dry cloth.

Shoe polish. Use paste shoe polish in the brown shade for walnut, the cordovan shade for mahogany, and the tan shade for light finishes. Apply with a cotton-tipped toothpick, rubbing carefully on the blemish; then buff dry. If the color is darker than the wood tone, erase with naphtha. Black paste shoe polish can be used to touch up scratches on black-lacquered wood. Remember that the polish will provide a shine when it is buffed, so the repaired area could be noticeable if the furniture has a dull finish.

Iodine. To conceal scratches on red-finished mahogany, use new iodine; for brown or cherry mahogany, iodine that has turned dark brown with age. For maple, dilute tincture of iodine about 50 percent with denatured alcohol.

Rottenstone and oil. Get an ounce of rottenstone from a paint or hardware store and keep it in an old salt shaker. Put a few drops of lubricating or salad oil on the blemish and shake on enough rottenstone to make a paste. Rub briskly with the grain of the wood, using a clean, soft cloth. Wipe frequently in order to compare and match the gloss of the damaged area with the original finish.

Medium Scratches and Blemishes. When damage is too conspicuous to be hidden by simple remedies, try this more professional method. First clean with naphtha to remove all wax or oil.

Step 1—Stain. Get ¼ pint of oil stain of the proper color. Do not use spirit stain; this could soften the finish on the wood. For light wood dilute ¼ teaspoon of stain with a few drops of naphtha or turpentine; mix them in the cover of the stain can. Apply with a small brush or cotton-tipped toothpick, wiping with a cloth and reapplying until the stain matches the original finish. Let dry at least 12 hours.

Step 2—Seal. Fill the scratch with white or orange shellac to seal in the stain, using a toothpick or fine water-color brush. (On some maple, orange shellac will match the shade of the wood and step 1 can be eliminated.) Let dry at least 4 hours. Repeat until the scratch is filled, allowing 4-hour drying time between treatments.

Step 3—Sand. To even off the surface, sand with very fine sandpaper

(8/0) or the fine side of an emery board. Bend the board about an inch from the end. Rub lightly with the grain of the wood until the scratch is even with the finish.

Step 4—Rub down. Finish by rubbing with rottenstone and oil, as described above. Use paste wax for a final polish and subsequent protection.

Severe Burns and Blemishes. The deeper the damage on wood finishes, the more difficult the treatment. The following method requires care and patience, but it may save complete refinishing by a professional.

Step 1—Clean. Scrape the blemish clean with a sharp knife or razor blade (taped for safe handling). Remove all loose dirt or charred wood, and clean with naphtha on a cotton-tipped toothpick.

Step 2—Prepare. Smooth the damaged area with 3/0 steel wool wrapped around the point of a wooden skewer or orange stick. Clean as before. Then rub with the grain of the wood, using 6/0 or 7/0 sandpaper or fine emery board.

Step 3—Stain. Follow the directions in step 1 under *Medium Scratches and Blemishes.*

Step 4—Fill. Fill the damaged area with stick shellac to match the wood finish. (This is preferred to plastic wood, which may damage lacquer.) Heat a spatula with an alcohol flame or electric burner. Do not use gas or a candle; soot may discolor the shellac. Have the blade just hot enough to melt the shellac. Scrape off a bit and press it into the blemish with the edge of the blade. Repeat until filled.

Step 5—Level. Heat the blade of the spatula, wipe it clean, and scrape across the patch to level. Shave off excess shellac with a razor blade.

Steps 6 and 7—Sand and rub down. Follow steps 3 and 4 under *Medium Scratches and Blemishes.*

If the surface is so damaged that neither of the procedures above is practical, cover the entire surface with plywood or tempered hardboard cemented down with woodworking glue or a contact-type cement. First, remove the finish and sand the old surface until it is smooth and free of irregularities. Cut the edges of the covering flush with the old top edge. If the old edge is marred, use a thin wood banding of the same finish and wood as the original surface. Make sure the top edge of the banding is flush with or very slightly under the surface level of the new top. Make the banding wide enough to cover both the old edge and surface material. A tempered hardboard surface need not be finished unless it is desired to change the color.

White Spots—Cause Unknown. Many white spots or rings on wood furniture can be removed, but the success of the treatment depends on the amount of damage and the cause. Try these tips:

1. Rub the blemish with cigarette or cigar ashes, using cloth dipped in lubricating oil, vegetable shortening, lard, or salad oil. Wipe off immediately and rewax.

2. Rub rottenstone or table salt on the blemish with cloth dipped in any of the lubricants listed in *method 1* above.

3. For varnish or shellac (do not use on lacquer), dampen a cloth with spirits of camphor or essence of peppermint and daub on the spot. Do not wipe; let dry undisturbed at least 30 minutes. Rub down with rottenstone and oil.

4. With a cloth, rub on a thick paste of 3/F powdered pumice and linseed oil. Use a cloth wet with naphtha to wipe the surface, stopping often for inspection. Finish with a rubdown of rottenstone and oil.

Alcohol Spots. Perfumes, medicines, and beverages containing alcohol can quickly cause irreparable damage because alcohol has a tendency to dissolve any finish. Always wipe up spills as quickly as possible. If the finish has been protected with wax, there may be no spot. If there is one, try these suggestions:

1. Rub with a finger dipped in paste wax, silver polish, linseed oil, or moistened cigar ash. Rewax.

2. On some finishes a quick application of ammonia will do the trick. Put a few drops on a damp cloth and rub the spot. Follow immediately with an application of wax.

3. For alcohol spots on which treatment has been delayed, a more complicated remedy is necessary. Mix rottenstone into a creamy paste with a few drops of linseed oil and salad oil. Apply the paste to the spot with a soft cloth, rubbing with the grain of the wood. If necessary, substitute 3/F powdered pumice for rottenstone. (Pumice is a harder abrasive.) Finish with rottenstone treatment.

Heat Marks. White blemishes caused by heat are usually very difficult to remove without complete refinishing. If the damage has not penetrated too deeply into the finish, the following suggestions may prove effective.

1. Stroke the spot lightly with a cloth moistened with camphorated oil. Do not use a linty cloth, as fuzz may stick to the wood. Wipe immediately with a clean cloth. If rough, rub with 3/0 steel wool dipped in paste wax or lubricating oil.

2. Try rottenstone and oil treatment (page 155).

3. Try *method 3* under *White Spots—Cause Unknown.*

Watermarks. Marks or rings from wet glasses, vases, or plants are common on tables, especially if these surfaces have not been waxed. Wax cannot prevent damage when liquids are allowed to stand on the finish indefinitely. However, it will keep them from being absorbed immediately, thus giving you time to wipe up the liquid before it harms the finish. If watermarks appear, here are some tips to try.

1. Apply paste wax with 3/0 steel wool.

2. Place a clean, thick blotter over the ring and press with a warm (not hot) iron. Repeat until the ring disappears.

3. Try rottenstone and oil treatment.

4. Try camphorated oil (*method 1* under *Heat Marks*).

Ink Stains. If the finish is worn or damaged so unsealed wood is exposed, ink stain will penetrate deeply and will be almost impossible to remove. When the finish has been protected with wax, ink often can be blotted up immediately without leaving a spot. If a mark does show, try the following.

1. Pat the spot with a damp cloth. Do not rub, but keep turning the cloth to a clean area. Repeat as many times as necessary.

2. Rub down with rottenstone and oil.

Paint Stains. Paint can be removed as follows.

1. If the paint is fresh, remove with a cloth saturated with wood cleaner or rub with 3/0 steel wool dipped in a floor-wax cleaner.

2. For old paint stains, cover spots with linseed oil and let stand until the paint is softened. Wipe with a cloth wet with linseed oil. Remove the paint with rottenstone and oil.

Other Problem Stains. You may be faced with the following.

Nail-polish stains. If the surface has been waxed, polish may not have penetrated into the finish. Try rubbing with fine (3/0) steel wool dipped in a floor-wax cleaner.

Candle wax. Hold an ice cube on the wax for a few seconds to harden it, but wipe up melted ice immediately. Crumble off as much wax as can be removed with the fingers; then scrape gently with a dull knife. Rub briskly with a cloth saturated with a wood cleaner or floor-wax cleaner, wiping dry with a clean cloth. Repeat until the mark disappears.

Milk spots. When milk or foods containing milk or cream (ice cream, custard, and so on) are allowed to remain on furniture, the effect of the lactic acid is like that of a mild paint or varnish remover. Therefore, always wipe up this spilled food as quickly as possible. If spots show, clean with a liquid cleaner. Then follow the tips under *Alcohol Spots*.

Yellow spots on light wood. The aging of bleached or blond furniture is accompanied by a change in color. With time, the chemicals used to bleach out the natural wood color begin to lose their effect. The wood darkens so gradually you are not aware of it until you purchase a new piece of the same shade. When light furniture is exposed to direct sunlight, however, the change may occur in a few days and can result in ugly yellow spots. Nothing can be done to remove these yellow spots or change of color.

Paper sticking to surface. Saturate the paper with lightweight oil. Let stand; then rub lightly with steel wool. Wipe the surface clean with a dry cloth.

Foggy appearance. If a highly polished surface grows foggy, rub it with a cloth dipped in vinegar solution (1 tablespoonful of vinegar to 1 quart of water). Rub with the grain until the surface is thoroughly dry.

Veneered Surfaces

Minor Defects. Use stick shellac to repair minor defects in veneered surfaces.

Defective Areas. If the damage is confined to a small area, repair it as follows.

1. Select a patch slightly larger than the damaged section. (New veneer can usually be purchased at wood craftsman shops and some lumberyards.) Apply three or four small spots of glue to the damaged area, press the patch over the glue, and allow it to set.

2. With a sharp knife held vertically, cut through both patch and the damaged veneer. This cut need not follow a rectangle; it is better to taper it to a point at each end.

3. Detach the patch and clean out the damaged veneer within the cut area. Apply glue, insert the patch, and place a weight on it. Remove excess glue from the surface and allow the repair to set.

If veneer corners are chipped, salvage pieces if possible, or try to match the wood with patches. Glue them into place with a good furniture glue. Cover with cloth and press under a heavy weight for 2 or 3 days. Touch up the joint between old and new with shellac. If bare wood is still exposed, touch up with oil stain before application of the shellac.

Locks and Catches

Minor shrinkage or warping can make door locks and catches fail to work properly. To correct this condition, shift strike plates or adjust hinge positions.

Drawers

Sticking drawers can be freed by sanding or planing the sides or bottom. Apply powdered soapstone to relieve minor sticking. A slight readjustment of the drawer guides may eliminate a great deal of work on a warped drawer. If glue joints at corners show signs of loosening, repair them with glue blocks, preferably triangular or quarter-round in cross section, to prevent dovetail corners from breaking. Do not repair loose corners with brads; they may split the wood and do not equal glue blocks for strength.

Fastenings and Attachments

Enlarged Screw and Nail Holes. Screw or nail holes often become enlarged, with resultant loosening of hinges, strike plates, latches, handles, and similar fittings. Fill such holes with composition wood or a soft wood plug. Replace the fittings and fasten securely.

Wear around Fittings. If wood surfaces around a fitting become seriously worn, remove the fitting, inlay a new piece of wood in the worn area, and refasten the fitting. If this is not practicable, relocate the fitting. Use the following method to relocate butt hinges for doors or lids.

1. Mortise the door or lid to a depth equal to the double hinge thickness. This eliminates the second mortise and reduces the chance of an error in marking or mortising.

2. Fasten hinges on the door or lid. Cut off one screw just long enough to project about $\frac{1}{16}$ inch through the hinge when it is closed and the screw is in place. File a point on this stub and set it in the hinge.

3. Set the door or lid in position and press the hinge against the frame. Drill a screw hole in the frame at the point marked by the stub screw. Then fasten the hinges to the frame.

Miscellaneous Repairs

Splits or Cracks. Repair lengthwise splits or cracks extending entirely through a member by forcing glue into the crack and then applying pressure to close it. Maintain pressure until the glue is dry.

Warped Tops. Replace warped tops. To increase stability, use a glued-up board instead of a solid one.

Regluing Furniture

Furniture usually comes apart because of dampness in the atmosphere or in the wood itself; because moisture gets into the joints when the piece is washed and this dissolves the glue; because in a dry, hot atmosphere, wood shrinks and glue dries out; or because one part is not plumb with the rest of the piece or does not fit properly, and the strain breaks the glue.

The parts to be reglued should be completely free from the old glue, paint, and other surface covering; the wood should be dry; the parts to be glued should be close-fitting, with all surfaces touching each other; and they should be held together tightly until dry (about 1 to 24 hours, depending on the type of glue). The adhesive should be applied according to its manufacturer's directions.

RUGS AND CARPETS

Spots and stains are, of course, inevitable, but will prove harmless if treated at once. The first step is to blot up as much as possible with clean blotting paper or absorbent cloth. Do this carefully to avoid spreading the stain. The following table lists the most common types of stains and the treatment for removal. If soap and water are used, be careful not to get the rug too wet. Soak up as much of the water as you can and brush the pile erect while it is still damp. Exercise caution when using carbon tetrachloride. Work only in a well-ventilated room and keep the bottle closed when not pouring.

Table 14
HOW TO REMOVE STAINS FROM RUGS AND CARPETS

Animal stains	Sponge with a solution of $\frac{1}{4}$ cup of salt to 1 pint of water and follow with a solution of 1 part of ammonia to 20 parts of water. When using ammonia be sure to keep a window open, as the fumes are quite strong. It is also wise to wear rubber gloves to protect your skin.
Blood	Sponge with a cloth dampened with cold water. This method is not always effective, but is about the best you can do. It will generally lighten the stain so that it is almost invisible.
Candle wax	*Do not treat this stain at once.* Allow wax to harden on rug. Then scrape it off with a dull knife or spatula.
Candy (lollipop, sourball, etc.)	Sponge with warm water and brush the pile erect while damp.
Chewing gum	Sponge the area with lighter fluid. This will soften the gum so that it can then be scraped up with a dull knife.
Chocolate	Scrape off the excess. Sponge with soap and warm water.
Cocktails	Sponge immediately with a cloth dampened with mild soapsuds. Rinse with clear water. Stains from cocktails made with fruit juice or wine are extremely difficult to remove and are best left for professional treatment.
Coffee and tea —Clear —with Cream	Sponge with lukewarm water. If the spot remains, use mild soapsuds and then rinse with clear water. Sponge with carbon tetrachloride.

Table 14 (Continued)

Grease or oil	Dampen a cloth with benzine. Sponge lightly over the spot. When dry, brush up the nap. Benzine is highly inflammable and should be used with great caution.
Ink	Some of the nonpermanent inks react well to applications of lukewarm water. If this is not effective, sponging with milk sometimes works. Follow the milk application by sponging with carbon tetrachloride. India ink stains cannot be removed, and this ink should not be used where there is the danger of staining a carpet or rug.
Mud	Allow to dry thoroughly. When caked, it may be brushed off with a stiff brush or broom.

Carpet and Rug Repair

Burns are the number one emergency repair problem of carpets and rugs. A process known as "burling" is used to repair such areas where this occurs. It may be done in one of two ways.

One way is to replace the damaged or missing tufts with tufts picked here and there from the selvage or taken from a matching piece of carpet. Use a small-sized, curved upholstery needle threaded with carpet thread and catch the needle under a yarn of the carpet foundation. Fasten the thread at the start by taking two or three short stitches, one on top of the other, in the foundation material. Make a loop in the thread by pulling the last stitch only partway through. Put three or four loose tufts into the loop of thread. Hold these tufts in place with the thumb and forefinger and pull the thread tight to anchor the tufts in place. Continue until the bare spot is completely filled.

The other way to burl is to fill in the bare spot with loops of yarn, which are then clipped and sheared. For this method, use either a long darning needle or a curved upholstery needle threaded with carpet yarn or a coarse, harsh knitting yarn, as nearly like that in the carpet as you can get. Slip the needle under a crosswise yarn in the carpet foundation. Draw the yarn partway through, leaving a loop about ¼ inch to ⅜ inch long. After you have made several loops close together, clip them. Continue—clipping loops as you make them—until the worn spot is filled. Then shear the new tufts even with the rest of the pile.

To flatten the new pile slightly and to take off some of the newness of the yarn, steam-press it lightly. To do this, cover the mended spot with a damp cloth, set a medium-hot iron down gently, lift it and set it down again. (*Caution:* Do not bear down heavily and do not push back and forth.) Using an iron that is too hot or pressing until the yarn is completely dry makes the wool shiny, hard, and matted. When you are through steam-pressing, brush against the lay of the pile with a clothesbrush or whisk broom.

Mending a Tear. When a tear in a carpet or rug has not frayed too much, darn the edges together. With a large darning needle and carpet thread, weave in and out from the underside. Keep the loose ends of yarn on the wrong side while you are darning; then clip them to about ½ inch in length. Spread the ends evenly so as to prevent a bump; pin a strip of carpet binding over the darned place, on the wrong side; and sew the edges of the binding to the back of the carpet.

OTHER PROBLEM SURFACES

There are surface materials in and around the home that can cause problems. While few could be called emergencies, they should be taken care of as soon as possible.

Wallpaper Need Not Be a Problem

There are on the market today many different types of wallpaper, including such types as roller prints, screen prints, engraved, lithographed, plus plain and embossed papers. These fall into three categories: water-resistant, water-sensitive, and plastic.

Many of the papers manufactured today are guaranteed washable. If you are not sure whether or not your paper is washable, try dabbing at an inconspicuous spot with a damp cloth. If the paper promptly soaks up the water and remains damp, it is not washable. Once you have established that your paper is washable, cleaning it is not a great problem. For ordinary soilage or surface dirt on washable paper, dissolve a nonabrasive type of washing powder in lukewarm water. Immerse a cloth or sponge in this solution and wash the entire surface with long, free strokes. For best results, begin at the baseboard and work ceilingward. When beginning each new area, start in the clean area. (Unless full sections of the wall are washed, the difference may be noticeable because of the film remaining on unwashed portions.) Do not scrub—do not soak—you are dealing with paper, not iron! Rinse the paper thoroughly with clear water. For particularly soiled areas, you can use a prepared cleaner, following the manufacturer's instructions. A clean cloth dipped in dry borax and rubbed lightly over soiled parts is frequently effective.

When dealing with nonwashable papers, great care must be exercised in cleaning. It's not an easy job and requires a great deal of time and, even more important, patience. One of the most successful cleaners on the market today is a doughlike preparation similar to putty. This is available at wallpaper dealers and hardware and department stores. Draw the cleaner steadily *but lightly* over the wall, lifting at the end of each stroke. Since the surface of this cleaner picks up dirt, the mass should be constantly kneaded to expose a fresh portion for use. It is best to rub in one direction, to avoid a streaky effect. After cleaning the wallpaper, brush the walls and baseboard to remove any crumbs of cleaner that may cling to them. If the paper is only slightly soiled, a simple household remedy of semistale bread will suffice. Remove bread crusts and rub large pieces of bread from ceiling to floor in wide, sweeping strokes, overlapping cleaned portions. As the bread becomes soiled, fold it under to a clean section. Engraved or lithographed papers are only partially water-resistant and should be cleaned with a putty or dough-type cleaner.

A number of the newer wallpapers are plastic-coated. This process keeps them pretty free from stains and grease. Soap and water are safely used on these papers; they can be washed as frequently as necessary with very gratifying results.

After all your warnings, little Johnny marks up the wall with crayon or spills over the inkstand, completely splattering the wall. Or maybe a visitor leans a pomaded hairdo against your living room paper. All common enough happenings, but doubly exasperating if you do not know what to do about them. Your chances for removing spots and stains from wallpaper are greatly increased if you act quickly. Time is against you. If you wait too long, you may find that any treatment powerful enough to remove the stain will also remove the paper. Spot and stain removal is a very delicate job and must be done carefully, although promptly. It is not always possible to remove all traces of the damage, but repeated treatments may lighten it so that it is almost invisible.

Ink Stains. The first step in ink removal is to blot up quickly, being careful not to spread the stain. There are then two alternatives which may be used. One is to apply absorbent powder (plain starch or powdered chalk), brushing it off as fast as it takes up the ink. Repeat until no more ink is taken up. Ink eradicators may also be used, but must be applied very cautiously. The harsh chemical may tend to remove part of the pattern, but if the spot is small, the paper can be touched up with poster paint, which can be purchased in a variety of colors.

Crayon Marks. Dampen a soft, clean cloth with carbon tetrachloride. Although this chemical is nonflammable, certain precautions should be followed. Use only in small quantities, and work in a well-ventilated room.

Keep the bottle stopped up while working. Sponge the stain lightly; *do not rub.* If a ring appears after sponging, apply a poultice of dry cleaning powder and carbon tetrachloride. Allow to dry and then brush off.

Grease Spots. The preferred method makes use of a thick paste of fuller's earth and benzine or carbon tetrachloride, applied sparingly over the spot. Let it remain until thoroughly dry and then brush off. Repeat the treatment if necessary. Spots may also be removed by holding a clean white blotter over the stain with a hot iron. Hold in place for several minutes. The blotter will soak up more of the grease.

Water Stains. Occasionally wallpaper becomes discolored with an ugly brown stain caused by the seepage of water. This usually occurs around windows or under eaves. A fuller's earth poultice, as used for grease spots, will generally remove this type of stain.

We would like to voice a word of *caution* at this point. Certain colors "bleed," that is, run into one another, when carbon tetrachloride is applied. Since it is impossible to determine this by merely looking at the paper, it is suggested that all applications of this solvent be tested before use. You can do this by lightly dabbing a spot behind a piece of furniture or in an inconspicuous corner. If your paper is of the type that bleeds, use one of the other methods described.

Removing Concrete Stains

Chances are that your patio, walks, and other concrete surfaces will accumulate a number of stains during the summer season. Some of these will be due to grease spattered from the barbecue; others will be due to oils and other spilled liquids. In addition, metal furniture or other metal objects standing out in the rain may have left ugly rust stains.

All these stains can be removed quickly and easily by brushing a thick mixture of salt and lemon juice into the stained area. After a few minutes, rinse this off with clean water. For stubborn stains, a few applications may be necessary. If the stain still persists, try rubbing in benzine or another grease solvent with a stiff brush. As a last resort for the most stubborn stains, whether rust, grease, or oil, try the following treatment.

Dissolve 1 part of sodium citrate (available in drugstores) in 6 parts of water and combine with powdered whiting (available in paint and hardware stores) to form a thick paste. Spread a thick coating over the stain and allow it to stand for several days to a week. During this time, keep the paste moist by adding sodium citrate solution to it, or replace the dried-out paste with fresh paste. When the time comes to remove the paste, it can be washed off with clean water.

Smoke Smudges. Fireplaces have gone rugged these days. Masses of brick, cut stone, and fieldstone rise directly from fire chamber to ceiling without a mantel. So when a puff of smoke comes out and up, it smears quite a large area with grime. Getting a few layers of this off a porous stone surface is not easy with ordinary soap and water.

First try a steel-wire brush, used dry. Better still, use the wheel type that attaches to an electric drill. If neither of these does the job properly, get a can of mechanic's hand soap—a thick pasty material loaded with mild abrasive—and use this with the wire brush. Rinse with clear water and a sponge at once. Repeat until the stains are gone.

Discolored Porcelain. If the ordinary household cleaner will not eliminate discolored spots on porcelain sinks, bowls, and bathtubs, rub carbon tetrachloride (available in hardware stores) vigorously over the stain. Make certain to use this in a well-ventilated room. Rinse with clear water.

If the stain persists, use a strong solution of oxalic acid (which can be bought in any hardware store). Mix 1 part of oxalic acid to 8 parts of water and scrub the stain with a brush or small mop. After the stain disappears, wash thoroughly with clear water.

Tile Stains. When the joints between ceramic or plastic tile become extremely dirty and stained so that no amount of scrubbing seems to get them clean, the problem can often be solved by using either a common laundry bleach or a little ordinary kerosene, rather than the usual cleaning agents. Scrub on vigorously with a small, stiff-bristled brush such as an old toothbrush. Allow the bleach (if used) to soak on the surface for several minutes. Rinse thoroughly and repeat if necessary.

Refinishing Marred Metal Surfaces

Refinishing the surface of an appliance which has been scratched or otherwise marred is one job many homeowners avoid. Surprisingly, it's not difficult, and the result is worth the effort.

Helping to simplify the job are aerosol spray cans of primer, finish, and blending coats, which appliance distributors sell or which you can buy from a paint dealer who sells to automotive paint shops. If you can secure the code number of the finish on your appliance from the store who sold it to you, so much the better. Ask the paint dealer for the color by this code. If not, you will have to match the color by eye. Also, make sure the primer, finish paint, and blending coat you buy are lacquers, not enamels. In this case, it is difficult to blend the enamel with the old finish, and your work may be wasted because enamels darken with age.

To refinish a marred surface on any appliance surface—refrigerator, dishwasher, freezer, washer, or clothes dryer:

1. Wash the finish thoroughly with strong detergent and hot water.

2. Sand the scarred area to bare metal with a block covered with No. 360 wetted sandpaper. Hand-held sandpaper will leave marks on the surface. Sand with a circular motion and dip the paper into water frequently. When the surface is smooth, wipe dry.

3. Mask chrome trim with tape, and larger areas with newspaper. You do not want to hit these with overspray.

4. If there are signs of rust, you must apply a primer. If not, you can apply the finish coats. Use white primer if the appliance is light in color, gray primer if dark.

5. The secret of an invisible patch is correct technique; unless finish coats are properly applied, your work will be largely wasted. If this is your first attempt at spray painting, it's suggested you practice on a piece of waste hardboard or other smooth surface; a large tin can, cut lengthwise and flattened, is good if you use primer first. The procedure is the same for all coats—primer, finish, and blender. Spray in short bursts, moving the nozzle back and forth smoothly and fairly rapidly. The nozzle should be about 8 to 10 inches from the work. Never start spraying directly at the work. Instead, aim the nozzle at a piece of scrap cardboard held to the side, then sweep across to the work.

6. If primer is used, give it at least 10 minutes to dry. Sand lightly with No. 360 wetted sandpaper until smooth.

7. Apply the finish coat. Make just one pass with the can. "One pass" means one sweep across and one sweep back. Let the paint dry. Then make another pass and let dry. You may have to do this four or five times to cover, but spraying must be done this way to assure proper blending and to avoid running. You have applied a sufficient number of finish coats when the paint dries with a gloss. The refinished surface will be more or less in a round shape, and will not match the old finish precisely. Now it's time for the blending coat which alleviates this condition.

8. Spray the blending coat in a straight-across motion, to cover about 4 inches more than the spot. Let dry for about 30 minutes; then treat lightly with rubbing compound similar to powdered pumice to remove dirt and lint, if any. Rub with a gentle circular motion. Wipe off the compound with a clean cloth.

CHAPTER 8

Other Home Emergencies

There are many miscellaneous emergencies around the home that cannot be grouped under the general headings of the preceding chapters. We have consequently gathered them together here.

ELECTRIC POWER FAILURE

One never expects a power failure or looks forward to the unpleasant experiences that follow, but it occurs in thousands of homes every year. And when electric power fails, you will discover how dependent you are on it. But power failure is a mere inconvenience compared to what may happen if the cause is a fallen electrical line. In such an emergency, immediately call the power company, but do not wait for them to come and fix the trouble before taking steps to protect passers-by. It may be a while before a serviceman arrives, especially if roads are snow-clogged and icy. Make a warning sign out of a large piece of white cardboard; print the letters boldly and with black crayon. Such a sign could read: "CAUTION! KEEP AWAY! LIVE WIRE!" Then tack the sign to a stake and drive the stake into the ground a good distance from the wire. Face the sign toward the most likely avenue of approach to the risk area. If the wire has fallen across a walk, it may be necessary to fashion two signs, placing them on both sides of the wire facing in opposite directions to warn pedestrians approaching from either side.

If possible, blockade the danger area. One way is to encircle the area with cinder block. Another way is to drive stakes into the ground around the downed wire and rope the area off, much the same as you would rope off newly sown lawn. Another protective measure you should take, particularly if the wire comes down close to evening and will remain down overnight, is to circle the danger area with warning lights. You could use flares, although most types do not burn for extended periods. It is better to use a

168

couple of kerosene lanterns, which will not burn out quickly and the flames of which are protected from the wind. Light the lanterns and place them where they cannot be missed by pedestrians.

When power fails, there are important considerations to keep in mind. Immediately disconnect all appliances that run continually on electricity, such as refrigerators, home freezers, furnace blowers or forced air systems, and electric pumps of water systems. This is done to safeguard those appliances when the power is restored. When power is turned on after a failure, it is often initiated at half the usual voltage. Your appliances are built to run at full voltage. This means that if they were connected their motors would work faster, trying to draw the missing voltage. The result could be a burned-up appliance motor if the half voltage continues for an extended period. To keep informed of the status of electric power, keep a lamp turned on in some conspicuous area of the house. When the power comes back on at half voltage, the lamp's bulb glows dimly. Keep appliances disconnected. You can connect them again when the lamp's bulb glows normally bright.

As for using appliances during a power failure, avoid unnecessary opening and closing of refrigerators and freezers. The cold these have stored up before the power failure is usually sufficient to keep food preserved for at least 36 hours. If your water supply comes from a well, there is no way for that well's pump to draw water during a power failure. Thus, use as little water as possible until power returns at its normal voltage.

Of course, a power failure in cold weather hits you harder than at any other time if you have an oil burner or radiant heating system. Aside from this discomfort and the absence of light, loss of heat may freeze water pipes in the basement if power is not restored for several hours. If you have a fireplace, keep it going. It will prevent a too-sharp temperature drop in a moderately widespread area and is adequate for personal comfort at close quarters. If you do not have a gas range, you can manage a pretty fair "cookout" in picnic style—or, take the grate from a barbecue pit, support it with bricks in the hearth, and you can prepare some robust potted meals, using the old iron kettle. In lieu of or in addition, you can use a hibachi stove or portable barbecue grill, providing it is set close to an open window to allow smoke to escape.

Do not forget propane camp stoves or Sterno stoves, either. Even a propane soldering kit can be pressed into service by improvising a range using the same grate setup.

Whenever outside temperatures remain consistently below zero, you can save freezer foodstuffs by placing the contents outdoors next to the house, always on the shaded side. Refrigerator contents, of course, do not require as extreme outside temperatures, and spoilage is less imminent.

An alternate method to outside storage involves acquiring dry ice and packing the freezer with it. Use it in the refrigerator, too. Thereafter, check temperatures occasionally, assuring all foods are fully protected. Incidentally, if your water supply comes from a pump-operated well, you may have to rely on melted and filtered snow and ice for your water.

There is nothing you can do about your heating system if electricity fails and you have an oil burner, since electrical power is needed right at the burner's electrodes. You will have to wait it out. But most modern, gas-operated systems have a self-energizing arrangement. That is, the burner will continue to function normally and automatically in the event of a power breakdown. (However, forced hot water systems which rely on an electrically operated pump for circulating hot water, and forced air systems with electrically operated blowers, are not self-energizing. Their burners depend for their function on an electrical impulse from the thermostat.)

You have to get the main gas burner going if you are going to get some heat into the house. This can only be done, though, if the burner has a manual control. Look for a switch or button on the gas line feeding the burner which allows manual operation of the gas supply to the burner. If there is no such control, there is no way of getting gas to the main burner. *Whatever you do, do not try to light the burner with a match.* There is a great deal of gas fed to that main burner, and it often flares when ignited. To use the control, just press or turn it until the main burner lights. The initial flame is provided by the pilot.

Next step, in a forced hot water system, is to open the flow valve on the water feed line and shut off the pump motor. This allows heated water to be gravity-fed through the system. Of course, there will not be as much heat as when the pump is operating, but there will be some.

In a forced air system, remove the filter (or filters if there is more than one) and shut off the blower motor. Warm air will be gravity-fed to the registers—again, not much, but better than none at all. Now, this is important. With your furnace operating on manual control, you must guard against a build-up of pressure and temperature inside the furnace. If there's a "throttle" on the gas line which permits you to raise and lower the flame as you can on a kitchen range, lower the flame for 10 minutes, every half hour or so, to allow the furnace to cool. If there is not a throttle, shut it off with the manual control for 10 minutes every half hour. Once electricity is restored, make sure the manual controls are turned off, to return the system to normal automatic operation.

Aside from the comfort factor, the house must be kept above freezing temperatures in order to protect the plumbing and heating system from serious damage—particularly, water pipes that run past basement windows. Therefore, one of the newer space heaters (oil- or propane-fired) should be kept operating in the basement near the boiler (if a steam or hot water heating plant) or in the area of water pipes. (*Special note:* Kerosene space heaters should be vented to the outdoors; if this is not possible, crack a window about 1 inch for adequate ventilation of the fumes.)

To further battle the possibility of a freeze-up, obtain a couple of gallons of auto antifreeze, similar to the economical methanol type. Pour about 8 ounces into each bathroom bowl and 2 to 3 ounces into each sink drain, repeating the treatment after each use. Some experts say that an alternative, effective way to prevent line freeze-ups is to keep water flowing rapidly from the highest faucet in the house.

If you are going to leave the house for a day or more and freeze-ups threaten, it's an excellent precaution to drain the house water lines. First, open all the taps; then drain the water from the lowest faucet, usually at the boiler or basement laundry washer. Having drained both hot and cold lines, pour antifreeze, as noted, into each sink, bowl, and tank. Do not forget to operate the dishwasher and laundry washer a few minutes, forcing water already in the units to be pumped out.

One way to overcome any power loss is with an auxiliary generator. Connected to the house lines through a switch that simultaneously cuts the outside power source, a specially installed indicator light at the house meter or circuit box signals when city power has been restored.

SNOW EMERGENCIES

A snowed-in home may have a picture-book quality, but the charm of it all ends there. Walkways have to be cleared, and the driveway must be free. Snowplow blades that attach to garden tractors do a good job, but for top maneuverability and efficiency, a snow thrower (or snow blower) is the fast answer. But someday during the winter, after a snowfall, you will uncover that snow blower in the corner of the garage, roll it out into the biting cold, prime the carburetor, and attempt to start the machine—only to have it balk. An hour later, distressed and disgusted, you will reach for the shovel.

To prevent this, first take your engine into the basement or garage and warm it; it's possible you cannot spin the engine fast enough to fire because the oil is too heavy. So, in the future, in extremely cold climates, use SAE 5 oil. In average cold weather, use SAE 10.

Make certain the magneto is functioning properly. Remove the spark plug, reconnect the wire to the plug, and ground the plug base against the engine; as long as you do not touch the electrodes, you can perform that test safely with the plug in your hand. Crank the engine normally. A vivid, blue spark should snap loudly across the gap, indicating that the plug is operative. Just to be sure, clean it and properly space the gap, if needed.

If the spark is good, check the gas. The tank may be empty and/or full of rust; the gas may not be turned on, or the carburetor may not be choking. You need to choke almost 150 percent in cold weather; it's not likely an engine will flood when it's cold, so you will need what appears to be an excessive amount of fuel to get started.

If, after these points are checked, the engine still remains stubbornly silent, have it gone over by a local service agency. One important note about ethers and windup starters: authorities say that the use of ethers to start a cold engine is too dangerous and that windup starters are not really effective in low temperatures.

Next year, or as soon as possible, follow this maintenance check.

1. Clean out dust and dirt, removing all debris from the rotor and drive chains.

2. Unscrew the spark plug, cleaning and adjusting the electrode and gap as recommended by the manufacturer.

3. Fill the gas tank with fresh fuel (never use last season's gasoline), and change crankcase oil.

4. For models with rotating ejection chutes, lubricate the base with a heavy grease or petroleum jelly and wax the inside of the chute and rotor housing.

5. Tighten all nuts, bolts, and screws.

6. Oil the snow thrower at all points shown in the manufacturer's instruction book.

If you belong to the great fraternity of the blistered palms and aching biceps—those without a snow thrower—you can give yourself a break at least to the extent of using the proper tools for the job. For example, a wide-bladed sheet-metal shovel is fine for light snow because of its large capacity. But when the snow is wet enough to be sticky, or more than a foot thick, this type of shovel picks up a load too heavy for most people to lift easily. For such work use a shovel with a narrow, straight blade—a coal shovel will do if you have one, though a longer-handled shovel is easier on your back. Above all, never handicap yourself by trying to use a garden spade for removing snow. Always remember that lubricating the shovel bottom keeps snow from sticking to it and makes scraping easier. Lubricate by rubbing the bottom with (1) a candle, (2) jelly-jar paraffin, or (3) paste floor wax.

One thing to bear in mind is that falling icicles each year kill a not inconsiderable number of persons. With pole or rake, knock off any icicles dangling where they may do damage if they break loose.

As for ice on steps, walks, and driveways, this, too, takes an avoidable annual toll of accidents. Often you can prevent ice formation if at the beginning of a snow, sleet, or winter rainstorm you liberally sprinkle rock salt —the kind used in ice-cream freezers—on your walks, drives, and steps. Calcium chloride, however, is even more effective. Available from drug supply houses, farm feed-and-supply stores, many building materials dealers, and hardware stores, these chemicals lower the freezing point of water, thus acting as melting agents.

Even after ice has formed, sufficient salt or calcium chloride will take all the stubbornness out of it, making it soggy and easy to clear away, unless the temperature is really arctic. One thing to avoid, when using these substances, is getting them on your lawns. Calcium chloride, in particular, is poisonous to growing things. Try not to let chemicals or salt remain on your concrete any longer than necessary, too, as they tend to damage the surface. Flush the surfaces with water on the first warm day that comes along.

Despite all you can do, inevitably there will be times when ice does form solidly, especially during or after sleet storms. On these occasions, you will need a special (but inexpensive) tool for chopping it away. Available at all hardware stores, it does a far better job than a shovel and is much less trouble to handle. Of course, sometimes it is inconvenient to clear the ice off your walks and the pavement in front of the house. When this happens, do not forget to sprinkle the ice well with sand or ashes to form a nonskid surface. This seems a precaution almost too elementary to mention; yet thousands of successful damage suits are lodged every year against homeowners who neglect it. And, quite aside from your legal liability, it's no fun to slip on your own front walk and break an arm.

Snow or ice piled on flat roofs—such as decks over garages or porches— puts a quite needless burden on roofing and supports. At the same time, the freezing and thawing action may crack the roofing material. So shovel it off at your first opportunity.

The weight of snow or icicles sometimes breaks off tree branches. If you own trees you value, make a simple forked pusher to shake them clean.

With all that snow piled up at entries, moisture together with extreme temperatures may swell door frames and thresholds, holding the door fast. An infrared heater placed at the frame should dry and contract the wood enough to permit opening and closing.

If an outdoor drainpipe is frozen, make a strong salt solution—2 handfuls of table salt in a gallon of boiling water—and pour it *slowly* into the drain. Remove the cover or grille, if any, and as ice melts, break it up with a sharpened stake. This must be handled gently to avoid damage to drainpipe.

FLOODS AND THEIR PROBLEMS

Floods are a natural and inevitable part of life along the rivers of our country. Some floods are seasonal, as when winter or spring rains and melting snows drain down narrow tributaries and fill river basins with too much water, too quickly. Others are sudden, the result of heavy precipitation. These are flash floods, raging torrents which rip through river beds after heavy rains, surge over their banks, and sweep everything before them.

The transformation of a tranquil river into a destructive flood occurs hundreds of times each year, in every part of the United States. Every year, some 75,000 Americans are driven from their homes by floods; on the average, eighty persons are killed annually. These destructive overflows have caused property damage in some years estimated at more than $1 billion. Floods also are great wasters of water—and water is a priceless national resource.

Whether the flood is seasonal or a flash flood, whether the flood warning is received weeks or hours before the flood crest strikes the town, proper action is the key to keeping damage to a minimum. Here's what should be done.

Before the Flood

1. Keep on hand materials like sandbags, plywood, plastic sheeting, and lumber.

2. Install check valves in building sewer traps, to prevent flood water from backing up in sewer drains.

3. Arrange for auxiliary electrical supplies for hospitals and other operations which are critically affected by power failure.

4. Keep first-aid supplies at hand.

5. Keep your automobile fueled; if electric power is cut off, filling stations may not be able to operate pumps for several days.

6. Keep a stock of food which requires little cooking and no refrigeration; electric power may be interrupted.

7. Keep a portable radio, emergency cooking equipment, lights, and flashlights in working order.

When You Receive a Flood Warning

1. Store drinking water in clean bathtubs and in various containers. Water service may be interrupted.

2. If forced to leave your home, and if time permits, move essential items to safe ground or upper stories; fill tanks to keep them from floating away; grease immovable machinery.

3. Move to a safe area before access is cut off by flood water.

During the Flood

1. Avoid areas subject to sudden flooding.

2. Do not attempt to cross a flowing stream where water is above your knees.

3. Do not attempt to drive over a flooded road—you can be stranded and trapped.

After the Flood

1. Do not use fresh food that has come in contact with flood waters.

2. Test drinking water for potability; wells should be pumped out and the water tested before drinking.

3. Seek necessary medical care at the nearest hospital. Food, clothing, shelter, and first aid are available at Red Cross shelters.

4. Do not visit the disaster area; your presence may hamper rescue and other emergency operations.

5. Do not handle live electrical equipment in wet areas; electrical equipment should be checked and dried before returning to service.

6. Use flashlights, not lanterns or torches, to examine buildings; flammables may be inside.

7. Report broken utility lines to appropriate authorities.

8. During any flood emergency, stay tuned to your radio or television station. Information from the Weather Bureau and civil emergency forces may save your life.

Salvaging after a Flood

After every disaster, there is a period of seeming hopelessness; then comes the question, "What can be done about it?" In most cases, surveying the situation discloses that all is not lost. There is much that can be salvaged.

The loss in dollars can be materially reduced even though the loss in work hours cannot be calculated. To aid in that first survey of damage, look outside the house for these things.

1. Upturned walks, broken masonry, walls, patios, rubble washed onto your property—all form the basis for rebuilding. Use this for footings under new walks, driveways, piers, walls, stairs, and porches. Plan first; then move each chunk just once to the new location to save time and labor.

2. Uprooted trees and shrubs are rarely damaged if salvaged soon after the flood. Replant, cover exposed roots, prop up securely; then turn your hand to more important things.

3. Wood steps and porches may be shifted by high waters. Check carefully for safety. If torn loose, dismantle and salvage materials for rebuilding. Wet wood, stored and air-dried, is as good as new material.

4. Lawns that have been buried under more than 1 inch of silt will die. The others will benefit from the flood unless it is salt water. The flood-borne silt is often more valuable than purchased topsoil.

5. Septic systems cease to work once the ground is flooded. Your drains are out of service until the ground is dry. You can speed things by having the septic tank emptied professionally; then introduce bacterial stimulants.

Your basement takes the worst of the flood damage. Furnace, electric power system, sump pumps (if any), and drains are all affected. So, too, are unsealed wells under the house. Cleanup follows these lines:

1. Pump water from the basement with a gasoline-powered sump pump, or have it done.

2. Have your furnace overhauled by a qualified serviceman. This calls for skilled hands and special tools.

3. Restore electric power only after the system is checked by your power supply company. BX cables and conduits may be waterlogged and useless.

4. Have your well pumped out by a firm equipped with heavy pumping equipment. Your pump may not reach the bottom of the well. Then have the water checked by a laboratory for traces of contamination by flood-borne bacteria.

5. Flood deposit and water damage are serious. (But you can spread silt over lawns and gardens if it is not salt-contaminated.) Wood furniture can be air-dried, then refinished, unless warped beyond recognition. Plaster which has been water-soaked is a total loss and must be removed and replaced. Where basement walls have been finished with wood, the panels must come down to check foundations and to dry out materials in and behind the wall. Salvage wood panels by careful removal.

6. Loosened floor tiles may be gathered up, the adhesive removed with rubber-cement solvent, and relaid. But the floor must be checked carefully for signs of injury due to underfloor water pressures.

SURVIVAL IN AN EARTHQUAKE

Many earth scientists in this country and abroad are focusing their studies on the search for means of predicting impending earthquakes, but, as yet, an accurate prediction of the time and place of such an event cannot be made. From past experience, however, one can assume that earthquakes will continue to harass mankind and that they will occur most frequently in the areas where they have been relatively common in the past. In the United States, earthquakes can be expected to occur most frequently in the western states, particularly in Alaska, California, Washington, Oregon, Nevada, Utah, and Montana. The danger, however, is not confined to any one part of the country; major earthquakes have occurred at widely scattered locations.

The actual movement of the ground in an earthquake is seldom the direct cause of death or injury. Most casualties result from falling objects and debris because the shocks can shake, damage, or demolish buildings and other structures. There are, however, many actions that you can take to reduce the dangers from earthquakes to yourself, your family, and others.

Before an Earthquake Occurs

1. Check your home for earthquake hazards. Bolt down or provide other strong support for water heaters and other gas appliances, since fire damage can result from broken gas lines and appliance connections. Use flexible connections wherever possible. Place large and heavy objects on the lower shelves. Securely fasten shelves to walls. Brace or anchor high or top-heavy objects.

2. Hold occasional home earthquake drills to provide your family with the knowledge to avoid injury and panic during an earthquake.

3. Teach responsible members of your family how to turn off electricity, gas, and water at the main switch and valves. Check with your local utilities office for instructions.

4. Provide for responsible members of your family to receive basic first-aid instruction, because medical facilities may be overloaded immediately after a severe earthquake. Call your local Red Cross or civil defense director for information about classes.

5. Keep a flashlight and a battery-powered transistor radio in the home, ready for use at all times.

6. Keep immunizations up to date for all family members.

7. Conduct calm family discussions about earthquakes and other possible disasters. Do not tell frightening stories about disasters. Also think about what you should do if an earthquake strikes when you are at home; driving your car; at work; in a store, a public hall, a theater, or a stadium; visiting friends; or involved in any of your other regular activities. Your planning may enable you to act calmly and constructively in an emergency.

During an Earthquake

1. Remain calm. Think through the consequences of any action you take. Try to calm and reassure others.

2. If indoors, watch for falling plaster, bricks, light fixtures, and other objects. Watch out for high bookcases, china cabinets, shelves, and other furniture which might slide or topple. Stay away from windows, mirrors, and chimneys. If in danger, get under a table, desk, or bed; in a corner away from windows; or in a strong doorway. Encourage others to follow your example. Usually it is best not to run outside.

3. If in a high-rise office building, get under a desk. Do not dash for exits, since stairways may be broken and jammed with people. Power for elevators may fail.

4. If in a crowded store, do not rush for a doorway, since hundreds may have the same idea. If you must leave the building, choose your exit as carefully as possible.

5. If outside, avoid high buildings, walls, power poles, and other objects that could fall. Do not run through streets. If possible, move to an open area away from all hazards. If in an automobile, stop in the safest place available, preferably an open area.

After an Earthquake

1. Check for injuries in your family and neighborhood. Do not attempt to move seriously injured persons unless they are in immediate danger of further injury.

2. Check for fires or fire hazards.

3. Wear shoes in all areas near debris or broken glass.

4. Check utility lines and appliances for damage. If gas leaks exist, shut off the main gas valve. Shut off electrical power if there is damage to your house wiring. Report damage to the appropriate utility companies and

follow their instructions. Do not use matches, lighters, or open-flame appliances until you are sure no gas leaks exist. Do not operate electrical switches or appliances if gas leaks are suspected. This creates sparks which can ignite gas from broken lines.

5. Do not touch downed power lines or objects in contact with the downed wires.

6. Immediately clean up spilled medicines, drugs, and other potentially harmful materials.

7. If water is off, emergency water may be obtained from water heaters, toilet tanks, melted ice cubes, and canned vegetables.

8. Check to see that sewage lines are intact before permitting continued flushing of toilets.

9. Do not eat or drink anything from open containers near shattered glass. Liquids may be strained through a clean handkerchief or cloth if danger of glass contamination exists.

10. If power is off, check your freezer and plan meals to use up foods which will spoil quickly.

11. Use outdoor charcoal broilers for emergency cooking.

12. Do not use your telephone except for genuine emergency calls. Turn on your radio for damage reports and information.

13. Check your chimney over its entire length for cracks and damage, particularly in the attic and at the roof line. Unnoticed damage could lead to a fire. The initial check should be made from a distance. Approach chimneys with caution.

14. Check closets and storage shelf areas. Open closet and cupboard doors carefully and watch for objects falling from shelves.

15. Do not spread rumors. They often do great harm following disasters.

16. Do not go sightseeing immediately, particularly in beach and water-front areas where seismic sea waves could strike. Keep the street clear for passage of emergency vehicles.

17. Be prepared for additional earthquake shocks called "aftershocks." Although most of these are smaller than the main shock, some may be large enough to cause additional damage.

18. Respond to requests for help from police, fire-fighting, civil defense, and relief organizations, but do not go into damaged areas unless your help has been requested. Cooperate fully with public-safety officials. In some areas, you may be arrested for getting in the way of disaster operations.

There are no rules that can eliminate all earthquake danger. However, damage and injury can be greatly reduced by following the simple rules given above.

TORNADOES AND WHAT TO DO

Of all the winds that sweep this planet's surface, tornadoes are the most violent. Their time on earth is short, and their destructive paths are rather small. But the march of these short-lived, local storms through populated areas leaves a path of terrible destruction. In seconds, a tornado can transform a thriving street into a ruin, and hope into despair.

Tornadoes occur in many parts of the world and in all fifty states. But no area is more favorable to their formation than the continental plains of North America, and no season is free of them. Normally, the number of tornadoes is at its lowest in the United States during December and January and at its peak in May. The months of greatest total frequency are April, May, and June. In February, when tornado frequency begins to increase, the center of maximum frequency lies over the central Gulf states. Then, during March, this center moves eastward to the southeast Atlantic states, where tornado frequency reaches a peak in April. During May, the center of maximum frequency moves to the southern plains states and, in June, northward to the northern plains and Great Lakes area as far east as western New York State. The reason for this drift is the increasing penetration of warm, moist air while contrasting cool, dry air still surges in from the north and northwest; tornadoes are generated with greatest frequency where these air masses wage their wars. Thus, when the Gulf states are substantially "occupied" by warm air systems after May, there is no cold air intrusion to speak of, and tornado frequency drops. This is the case across the nation after June. Winter cooling permits fewer and fewer encounters between warm and overriding cold systems, and tornado frequency returns to its lowest level by December.

During the period 1953–1970, an average of 631 tornadoes per year occurred in the United States, about half of them during three months— April, May, and June. For the same period, the annual average number of tornado days—days on which one or more tornadoes were reported—was 158. Average annual frequency by states for this period ranges from 109 tornadoes in Texas to less than 3 in most of the northeastern and far western states.

Tornado *watches* are the first alerting message between the National Severe Storms Forecast Center and areas potentially threatened by tornadoes. They specify the area covered by the watch and establish a period of time during which tornado probabilities are expected to be dangerously high. Watches are teletyped directly to local offices of the Weather Bureau and disseminated by those offices to the general public via radio and television stations in and around endangered areas. Law enforcement officers, emergency forces, volunteer storm reporters, and other cooperating personnel are also alerted by the watches, and they relay the alert to others in the watch area.

Tornado watches are not tornado warnings. They are issued to alert persons to the possibility of tornado development in a specified area, for a specified period of time. Until a tornado warning is issued, persons in watch areas should *not* interrupt their normal routines except to watch for threatening weather.

Tornado *warnings* are issued when a tornado has actually been sighted in the area or indicated by radar. In many cases, warnings are made possible through the cooperation of public-spirited persons who notify the nearest Weather Bureau office or community warning center when a tornado is sighted. Warnings indicate the location of the tornado at the time of detection, the area through which it is expected to move, and the time period during which the tornado will move through the area warned. When a tornado warning is issued, persons in the path of the storm should take immediate safety precautions.

Before a tornado strikes, seek inside shelter, preferably in a tornado cellar or the basement of your home. In the latter case, seek shelter under a sturdy workbench or heavy table if possible. In a home with no basement, take cover under heavy furniture in the central part of the house. Keep some windows open, but stay away from them.

Once the tornado passes, follow the applicable steps given for *After an Earthquake.* Of course, in parts of the country where tornadoes are comparatively frequent, a form of shelter is vital for protection from tornadoes. The shelter may never be needed; but during a tornado emergency, it can be worth many times the effort and cost of preparing it. One of the safest tornado shelters is an underground excavation, known as a storm cellar.

When possible, the storm, or tornado, cellar should be located outside and near the residence, but not so close that falling walls or debris could block the exit. If there is a rise in the ground, the cellar may be dug into it to make use of the rise for protection. The cellar should not be connected in any way with house drains, cesspools, or sewer and gas pipes. The size of the shelter depends on the number of persons to be accommodated and the storage needs. A structure 8 feet long by 6 feet wide and 7 feet high will protect eight people for a short time and provide limited storage space. Reinforced concrete is the best material for a tornado shelter. Other suitable building materials include split logs, 2-inch planks (treated with creosote and covered with tar paper), cinder block, hollow tile, and brick. The roof should be covered with a 3-foot mound of well-pounded dirt, sloped to divert surface water. The entrance door should be of heavy construction, hinged to open inward. The floor should slope to a drainage outlet if the terrain permits. If not, a dry well can be dug. An outside drain is better, because it will aid ventilation. A vertical ventilating shaft about 1 foot square can extend from near the floor level through the ceiling. This can be converted into an emergency escape hatch if the opening through the ceiling is made 2 feet square and the 1-foot shaft below is made easily removable. Slat gratings of heavy wood on the floor also will improve air circulation.

A lantern and tools—crowbar, pick, shovel, hammer, pliers, screwdriver —should be stored in the cellar to ensure escape if cellar exits are blocked by debris. Stored metal tools should be greased to prevent rusting.

HURRICANES AND THEIR DESTRUCTIVENESS

Compared to the great cyclonic storm systems of the temperate zone in the Pacific Ocean area, hurricanes are of moderate size, and their worst winds do not approach tornado velocities. Still, their broad spiral base may dominate weather over thousands of square miles and from the earth's surface into the lower stratosphere. Their winds may reach 200 miles per hour, and their life span is measured in days or weeks, not minutes or hours. No other atmospheric disturbance combines duration, size, and violence more destructively.

The following are safety rules that will help you save your life and the lives of others when hurricanes strike.

During the Hurricane Season

1. Enter each hurricane season prepared. Every June through November, maintain your supply of boards, tools, batteries, nonperishable foods, and the other equipment you will need when a hurricane strikes your town.

2. When you hear the first tropical cyclone advisory, listen for future messages; this will prepare you for a hurricane emergency well in advance of the issuance of watches and warnings.

3. When your area is covered by a hurricane watch, continue normal activities, but stay tuned to radio or television for all Weather Bureau advisories. Remember: a hurricane *watch* means possible danger within 24 hours; if the danger materializes, a hurricane *warning* will be issued. Meanwhile, keep alert. Ignore rumors.

When a Hurricane Warning Is Received

1. Keep calm until the emergency has ended.

2. Plan your time before the storm arrives and avoid the last-minute hurry which might leave you marooned or unprepared.

3. Leave low-lying areas that may be swept by high tides or storm waves.

4. Moor your boat securely before the storm arrives, or evacuate it to a designated safe area. When your boat is moored, leave it, and do not return, once the wind and waves are up.

5. Board up windows or protect them with storm shutters or tape. Danger to small windows is mainly from wind-driven debris. Larger windows may be broken by wind pressure.

6. Secure outdoor objects that might be blown away or uprooted. Garbage cans, garden tools, toys, signs, porch furniture, and a number of other harmless items become missiles of destruction in hurricane winds. Anchor them or store them inside before the storm strikes.

7. Store drinking water in clean bathtubs, jugs, bottles, and cooking utensils; your town's water supply may be contaminated by flooding or damaged by hurricane floods.

8. Check your battery-powered equipment. Your radio may be your only link with the world outside the hurricane, and emergency cooking facilities, lights, and flashlights will be essential if utilities are interrupted.

9. Keep your car fueled. Service stations may be inoperable for several days after the storm strikes, due to flooding or interrupted electrical power.

10. Stay at home, if it is sturdy and on high ground. If it is not, move to a designated shelter, and stay there until the storm is over.

11. Remain indoors during the hurricane. Travel is extremely dangerous when winds and tides are whipping through your area.

12. Monitor the storm's position through Weather Bureau advisories.

13. Beware the eye of the hurricane. If the calm storm center passes directly overhead, there will be a lull in the wind lasting from a few minutes to half an hour or more. Stay in a safe place unless emergency repairs are absolutely necessary. But remember: at the other side of the eye, the winds rise very rapidly to hurricane force, coming from the opposite direction.

When the Hurricane Has Passed

1. Avoid loose or dangling wires, and report them immediately to your power company or the nearest law enforcement officer.

2. Seek necessary medical care at Red Cross disaster stations or hospitals.

3. Stay out of disaster areas. Unless you are qualified to help, your presence may hamper first-aid and rescue work.

4. Drive carefully along debris-filled streets. Roads may be undermined and may collapse under the weight of a car. Slides along cuts are also a hazard.

5. Report broken sewer or water mains to the water department.

6. Prevent fires. Lowered water pressure may make fire fighting difficult.

7. Check refrigerated food for spoilage if power has been off during the storm.

Remember that hurricanes moving inland can cause severe flooding. Stay away from riverbanks and streams, and follow the advice given on page 174 if a flood should occur.

IN CASE OF FIRE

Any discussion of protection against fire should begin with the best way of preventing a fire from getting started. The following suggestions are intended as a general guide for the prevention of fire in the home.

1. Keep matches out of the reach of young children. Teach children the dangers of playing with fire.

2. Do not throw away cigars, cigarettes, and matches without first making sure they are extinguished.

3. Do not allow accumulations of combustible waste materials in or near the house. Without them fires from carelessly discarded materials would be less frequent.

4. Keep chimneys and stovepipes clean, with all joints and connections tight. Provide separate metal cans for ashes and rubbish. Never mix the two.

5. Place substantial fire-resistant guards in front of all woodwork close to sources of heat.

6. Keep greasy and oily rags in tightly closed, preferably metal containers provided for the purpose.

7. Avoid the filling of lighted kerosene and gasoline lamps. Avoid the use of kerosene to start fires in stoves and the like.

8. Do not use gasoline, naphtha, or benzine for cleaning unless proper precautionary measures are taken. You may wish to choose some of the safer solutions now obtainable and use these, in any considerable quantity, only out of doors and during the day.

9. Keep all open flames away from gas leaks. Explosive mixtures of

gas and air are quickly formed in enclosed places, and they need only a lighted match or a spark to cause disastrous results.

10. Avoid hanging curtains and other draperies near gas jets or other open flames. Remember that the draft from nearby windows may cause fires to spread and make them difficult to extinguish.

11. Use decorative wax candles with caution. Each year some deaths of children and adults are due to placing candles on Christmas trees or using them near flammable materials.

12. Avoid placing articles made of celluloid, pyralin, xylonite, fiberoid, viscoloid, and similar materials, such as combs, toilet articles and so on, on or near sources of heat, as they are very likely to catch fire. Also remember that articles of these materials should not be worn in the hair, as they may readily catch fire and seriously burn the wearer.

13. Permit only experienced persons to install or repair electrical fittings and appliances.

14. Never leave unattended heating appliances, particularly kitchen ranges and stoves, toasters, waffle irons, or other equipment of a similar nature.

15. Make sure that when you burn refuse you do so out of doors in a metal container well away from any building. Also be sure that when you leave you have extinguished all smoldering embers.

Fire Extinguishers

Fire-fighting equipment for the ordinary dwelling will usually be limited, by practical considerations, to portable hand apparatus. Principal reliance for extinguishing fires which have gained any appreciable headway must, of course, be placed on outside aid. When a fire occurs, the fire department, if one is available, should always be summoned *without* delay.

It is true, however, that most household fires start from a small beginning and in the majority of cases can be readily extinguished before they have gained headway and before any considerable damage has been done or risk of personal injury has developed, if the proper means is right at hand and can be promptly applied. The immediate application of a little water or the use of blankets may readily extinguish a small blaze which might otherwise develop into a disastrous fire. A partially filled pail of water may often be used effectively. A broom can be used to apply the water in a finely divided state, which is often satisfactory for extinguishing a fire, and it also may be used to bring within reach burning draperies or to beat out a small blaze. An ordinary garden hose with a nozzle, kept where it can be quickly attached to a water faucet, is also an effective fire-extinguishing device for the area over which its length will permit its application. But water should not be used to combat oil, grease, or electrical fires.

There are on the market portable hand extinguishers which are specially designed for first-aid fire fighting, the effectiveness of which has been demonstrated by years of experience. They are much more effective than improvised means and have the added advantage that, since they are intended for one purpose only, they can be kept in assigned places where they will be available when needed. It is, therefore, distinctly worth while to have one or more good portable fire extinguishers in every household.

In providing first-aid fire-fighting devices for the protection of the household, it is of prime importance that the devices purchased be reliable and designed and constructed in accordance with recognized standards with regard to safety and performance, such as are defined in federal specifications or those set up by the Underwriters' Laboratories, or other recognized authorities. Since it's usually not feasible for the householder to make adequate examination and tests, he will have to rely on the results of tests and approval made by others, as evidenced by inspection labels, certifications, or other forms of guarantee.

In the case of Underwriters' Laboratories, each extinguisher of a type which has been approved is marked with a distinctive inspection label. This label is usually in the form of a small brass plate attached to the extinguisher near the name plate or forming a part of the name plate itself. This does not mean that all fire-fighting devices which do not bear the Underwriters' Laboratories label are improperly designed and constructed, but that the presence of this label does assure the purchaser that a given extinguisher has been built in accordance with recognized standards. Portable fire extinguishers are suitable for combating three classes of incipient fires in the home. According to the National Board of Fire Underwriters, those classes of fires are as follows.

1. Class A fires—in ordinary combustible materials (such as wood, paper, textiles, rubbish, and so forth), where the quenching and cooling effects of quantities of water or solutions containing large percentages of water are of first importance.

2. Class B fires—flammable liquids, greases, and so on, where a blanketing effect is essential.

3. Class C fires—in electrical equipment, where the use of a nonconducting extinguishing agent is of first importance. The following table gives various types of available fire extinguishers, the kinds of fires they can be used on, and how they are started and how far they will operate.

Table 15

FIRE EXTINGUISHER FACTS

Type	Kinds of Fires	How to Start	Discharge
Soda acid	Class A	Turn over	
Water pump	Class A	Pump by hand	30'–40' for 50–55 sec.
Gas cartridge	Class A and small Class B	Turn over and pump	(2½-gal. size)
Foam	Class A and Class B	Turn over	
Carbon dioxide	Class B, Class C and occasionally Class A	Pull the pin and open the valve	6'–8' for about 42 sec. (15-lb. size)
Vaporizing liquid	Class B, Class C and occasionally Class A	Turn the handle, pump by hand	20'–30' for 45 sec. (1-qt. size)
Dry chemical	Class B, Class C and occasionally Class A	Pull pin and open valve (or press the lever), then squeeze the nozzle valve	About 14' for 22–25 sec. (30-lb. size)

Note: Do not use water-base extinguishers on electrical fires.

Since no one type of extinguisher is equally effective against all types of fires, it is best to use one which is effective against oil, grease, and electrical fires and partially effective against rubbish, wood, and paper fires. These include carbon dioxide, vaporizing liquid, and dry chemical. However, in a large house, for specific locations, other types should be included. In the basement, for example, add a water pump tank, since this is the area where rubbish and paper are usually collected and become a fire hazard. Keep two buckets of clean sand, one near furnace and one near entrance to basement for use against small spit fires of flammable liquid.

A small home fire alarm can give the first warning of a fire. Since a large proportion of all fires start in the basement, this would be a good place to install one. Of course, other parts of the house can be similarly protected. There are three types of alarms: the manual windup, battery-operated, and electrically operated. The manual windup is least subject to failure. The electrically operated alarm will not work during power failure or electrical failures on the line it is wired on. For one model, its effective area can be extended by simply adding more wire with fire-sensitive elements.

What to Do in Case of Fire

Each member of a household should understand how to send in a fire alarm to the fire department. In many cities the fire alarm may be sent in by telephone or from a street fire-alarm box. Some cities require that the alarm be sent in by telephone, and others require that a fire-alarm box be used. Seconds count at the time of a fire, so the proper method should be definitely known and used.

If sending in a fire alarm by telephone is required or permitted, the telephone number of the fire department should occupy a conspicuous and permanent place at each telephone or telephone extension in the home. In giving information about a fire over the telephone, one should carefully consider what he is doing. What the fire department wants and should know is (*a*) the number of the house, (*b*) the name of the street or road, (*c*) the nearest street corner, and (*d*) the number of the telephone from which the call is made. A few seconds spent in giving this information are not wasted.

If sending a fire alarm from a fire-alarm box is required or permitted, the location and method of use of the nearest fire-alarm box should be definitely known. Also, if such a method is employed, someone should be stationed in the vicinity of the fire-alarm box or along the route of the responding fire department company to direct it to the fire.

Saving the lives of the occupants of a building on fire should receive first consideration. Many lives have been lost in attempts to put out fires or to save personal belongings.

In case of fire:

1. Collect your thoughts. Keep your mind on what you are doing. Act quickly.

2. Unless you are very sure that you can handle the fire without help, notify the fire department or have someone else do this. Many have been sure until too late.

3. Summon help if anyone is within calling distance.

4. If the blaze is small and you think you can put it out by devices which are available, either

    a. Use a suitable fire extinguisher, or

    b. Use a woolen blanket or rug to smother the fire. Keep the air from the fire, or

    c. Direct water from a garden hose on the fire if such a hose is available. If it's not, throw water from a pail, using a dipper or a broom. Do not use water on an oil or grease fire; use sand or earth from flowerpots. Water, especially in small amounts, will cause spattering of burning grease.

    d. Beat down any draperies, curtains, or light materials causing the blaze, using a wet broom or a long pole. Using the bare hands may result in serious burns.

5. Tie a wet towel or any other material (preferably of wool) over the mouth and nose if you are fighting the fire and are exposed to smoke or flames. More people lose their lives by suffocation than through burning.

6. Place yourself so that you can retreat in the direction of a safe exit without passing through the burning area. Unless you can do something worth while, get out of the building.

7. If necessary to go through a room full of smoke, keep close to the floor and crawl on the hands and knees, having covered the mouth and nose with a wet cloth. The drafts and currents cause the smoke to rise, and the air nearest the floor is usually the purest.

8. If you have to retreat and all occupants are out of the building or burning portion thereof, cut off the draft by closing doors and windows.

9. Do not jump from a high window unless into a life net. To use a rope or life line, twist the rope or life line around one leg and, holding the feet together, regulate the speed of descent. Otherwise the hands may be painfully injured by friction with the rope or life line, especially if the height is great. Sheets and other articles of bedding will often provide a life line if knots are carefully made so that they will not slip. An extra loop in the knot may avoid this danger. Tie the rope or life line to a bed or other article of furniture which will not pull through the window. The rope or life line should not be thrown out of the window until the instant it is needed. Getting out from an upper story onto a porch or veranda has saved many lives. Such action also affords temporary relief from smoke and heat and also attracts rescuers.

Persons with Clothing Afire

When a person's clothing catches fire, the first consideration is that the flame or hot gases should not be inhaled. If your clothing is on fire do not run, as running fans the flames and makes conditions worse. Smother the flames by wrapping yourself in a rug, blanket, portiere, or woolen coat and roll on the floor. While rolling on the floor scream for help. If the article of clothing which is on fire can be easily stripped off, this should, of course, be done. If a shower bath or pail of water is handy, use it and then roll in the spilled water.

If the clothing of another person takes fire, use the same measures. If the person is excited because of fear caused by the blazing clothing, it may be necessary to trip him to make him lie down. Then, if water or a fire extinguisher is handy, apply it at once, being careful not to direct the stream from the extinguisher on the face. After the flames of a person's burning clothing are extinguished and the clothing has been drenched with water, do not remove the clothing from burnt skin until an ointment is available to apply to the burn. Avoid tearing the skin.

BURGLARPROOF YOUR HOME

Burglaries are an emergency that little can be done about, once they occur. Prevention is about the *only* thing that can stop this emergency. Here are some useful precautions you can take that will protect your home and your valuables while you are away on vacation or a long week end. These are the principal errors people make which allow enterprising burglars to practice their criminal livelihood successfully.

1. Leaving a home with exterior doors or windows unlocked.

2. Failure to equip *both* front and back doors (in fact, all outside doors) with secure, high-quality locks.

3. Failure to notify the newsboy that the family is on vacation. Piled-up newspapers outside the door are an indication to the burglar that the "coast is clear."

4. Failure to notify the milk company by telephone or letter to stop milk deliveries during vacation periods. A note in an empty bottle saying that the family will be away for several days will stop delivery of milk, but it will also tell a snooper that he has a green light to burglarize the house.

5. Leaving a note for prospective guests in the mailbox saying, "Key is under doormat—make yourself at home."

6. Notifying the local newspaper that you plan to go on vacation. Thieves are quick to take advantage of such accommodating news items. It is better, after you return, to tell the newspaper that you have been on vacation and what you did.

Here are some things you can do to make things very difficult for house-breakers:

1. Keep at least two interior lights on when you leave the house for the evening or use an automatic lighting device. An unlit home is a signal to the nighttime burglar that he can move in more easily.

2. Leave the shades up when vacating the house, and notify neighbors and police that you are taking a trip. A light in the house during your absence will then warn those you have alerted that prowlers are in your

home. Ask neighbors to pick up all mail and circulars that may have been placed at your front door so that your house has a "lived-in" look.

3. Call police to check on all strange solicitors not carrying proper credentials. Many thieves pose as salesmen or repairmen while "casing" an area for future lucrative jobs. Never allow a salesman or repairman without good credentials to enter your home.

4. Make certain that basement and second-story windows are just as securely locked as those on the first floor. Keep ladders locked up in the garage, or if they must be kept outside, securely fasten them to the side of the house or garage with a length of chain and a pin-tumbler padlock of good quality.

5. While talking to a strange caller at your door, stand in front of the locking mechanism. A favorite trick of burglars is to engage a prospect in conversation while flicking the push buttons below the bolt of a mortise lock and thus unlocking the door. The burglar hopes that the householder will not notice that the door is unlocked, and he will return later. If the door is still unlatched, he finds a clear path to the interior of the house.

6. Most important of all, make certain that strong, reliable pin-tumbler cylinder locks are on all exterior doors. The pin-tumbler-type cylinder lock makes good lock security available to everyone at a reasonable price. Do not depend on cheaply made locks to protect your valuables.

7. A very economical method of protecting your exterior doors from intruders is to install auxiliary night latches with a deadlocking mechanism (bolt locks) on these doors. On glass doors, double cylinder locks should be installed.

8. With the possibility in mind that you may slip up on one or more of these rules, it is wise to keep a record of the serial numbers and descriptions of all your valuables. In many cases police can track down a burglar if this is done, as pawnshops and secondhand dealers are required by law to file sales reports with the police. Of course, the best way to prevent being robbed is *not* to keep valuables in your home, but instead store them in a safe deposit box in your bank. The burglars count on homeowners' ignoring this sound rule. Nevertheless, if you remember that most burglaries are made easy by the homeowner's own carelessness or failure to use his common sense, you can do a lot to improve the situation.

OUTDOOR PROBLEMS

There are several outdoor emergencies that you should be able to handle. Here are major ones.

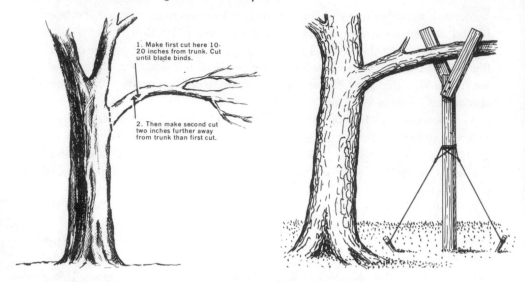

1. Make first cut here 10-20 inches from trunk. Cut until blade binds.

2. Then make second cut two inches further away from trunk than first cut.

A cracked tree limb is hazardous and should be removed as soon as weather permits. (Left) The safest way is to make two separate cuts, as shown by the arrows. This takes a little longer than a single cut, but you will not damage the tree, yourself, or anyone else. (Right) Sometimes a branch may be supported until the cut is made.

Removing a Broken Tree Limb or Tree

A badly cracked, heavy limb is dangerous and should be removed as soon as possible. If the limb is up high or very long, leave the job to a tree surgeon. And do not risk being a tree doctor if it's anywhere near power lines. That situation definitely requires professional skill.

When a tree's heavy branch sags dangerously toward the roof or any area, lash it in place. It is not too tough a job to toss some heavy lines over branches and secure the ends in two or more directions to stout trees nearby. Avoid using porch railings and lawn lampposts as anchors. In the absence of any substantial anchors, you can always drive car or truck to within safe range and secure the line to an axle. It's very unlikely you would be able to drive stakes into frozen ground.

Until the limb is removed, it's wise to rig up a barrier around the tree. Nothing fancy is required: a couple of boxes or sawhorses with a plank resting on top will do the job. If the tree is near a public street or sidewalk, the barrier should be illuminated by lanterns at night and your police or fire department contacted.

You will need a sharp crosscut saw to remove the limb. (Far better is one of the open-tooth saws specially made for cutting live wood.) Do not use an ax or hatchet. The risk of injury to yourself—or the tree—makes either tool a poor choice. Even if the limb is within reach, use a ladder for a more effective working position. Place it so you can make a cut on the underside of the limb, 10 to 20 inches from the trunk. If possible, enlist a neighbor's aid. Though it may seem obvious, do not lean the ladder against the part of the limb you are going to remove. And make certain the falling limb will not endanger you or anyone else.

Saw until the blade binds. This indicates the limb is starting to drop. Now make a second cut, on the top of the limb, about 2 inches farther away from the trunk than the first cut. Saw until the limb drops. This will leave a short stump which should be cut off as close as possible to the trunk. Cut carefully to avoid damaging the bark, and support the piece when it is about to fall so that wood will not be torn from the trunk. Treat the cut with a coat of the special wound paint sold by most nurseries. If sawing reveals rot, wait for nice weather, and remove it before painting.

A tree blown down, resting against the roof or outside wall, can cause additional damage, unless it is secured. Should the tree be propped against the house, use large pieces of timber to hold the tree up. Place one end of the timber against the foundation of the house and the other against the tree trunk to take the weight off the top of the tree resting against the house. Use guy wires and turnbuckles to brace the tree to prevent it from shifting in the fallen position.

Afterward, cut the tree for easy removal. First cut the tree between the timber support and house. Do not cut along the base of the tree; it will only increase the pressure against the house and cause more damage. Cut the top sections first; then cut the rest.

Strengthening Weakened Fences

Rotted posts make for wobbly fences, but the remedy does not necessarily mean a replacement job or a costly outlay. If the fence line is straight, without sags at the posts, any wobble can be overcome by driving wood stakes into the earth at each side, firming the foundation. Cut these stakes from 1-inch stock (cedar pickets could be used here), and chop a point at one end. Setting the stake close against the post, drive it into the ground, allowing 6 inches to remain exposed. Touch up with paint of the same color as the fence.

If a heavier 4 x 4 post has rotted and snapped at grade level (so that the top is just resting on its stump), you can replace the submerged section only with a sort of patching repair that makes it good as new. The first thing to do is saw off a few more inches of the remaining post, produc-

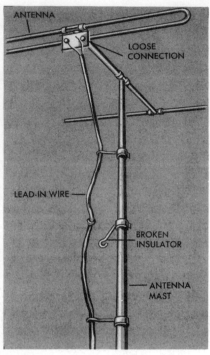

When your TV antenna suffers weather damage, it may interfere with reception. Here is what you must know to cure three of the most common storm-damaged TV aerial troubles: (Top left) To splice a broken antenna wire, cut the ends into matching L shapes. Strip each wire bare for a distance of ¾ inch. (Bottom left) Twist the ends together securely; then tape them. (Right) One antenna, two troubles: A loose connection where the wire meets the antenna causes a picture flicker. A broken insulator or standoff allows the wire to move about, making the picture bounce.

ing a squared end. Then move the post to one side, out of the way, and remove the rotted stump by digging with a shovel and prying with a pinch bar. When you have got it out, enlarge the cavity somewhat and place a flat rock at the bottom of the hole. Then cut a new piece of 4 x 4, equal in length to the distance from the rock base to the fresh cut of the old post (with the old post braced in a level position over the hole). Nail 4-inch-wide overlapping strips to two or more sides, at the end of the new section, and soak everything with a preservative compound.

Now, you can place the new section in the hole and pour a 1-foot base of concrete (1 part of cement, 3 parts of sand, and 3 parts of gravel), and after it sets, backfill the hole. Be sure to use flathead steel nails or copper nails on the overlapping strips that join the new and old post sections. Touch up the exposed, new section with paint to match.

As a rule, it is the end of a rail which rots first. Nails rust out, and rain is carried into the end grain through these openings. If no more than an inch or two of the rail ends are damaged, you may make an attempt at salvage and repair. Cut off the rotted end of the upper and lower rails equally and nail a length of 2 x 4 to them; then nail the 2 x 4 to the post. Broken or rotted pickets are best replaced individually, using a discarded one as a model for forming new ones. They can quickly be cut from standard stock obtainable in your lumberyard.

Mowers That Do Not Work

Garden tools are *not* emergency tools. But if the grass becomes long, there is one emergency that can cause trouble—and that is a mower that does not work.

If you own a power mower, you have undoubtedly had the experience of taking the mower out, yanking the starting rope, and having nothing happen. Then you yank again, and again nothing happens. After the third or fourth time, you are ready to pull the mower apart. Stop! Before you do that, use the following check list.

1. Open the cover on the gasoline tank. Is there enough gas? Even if the tank is filled part of the way, get that can of gasoline and fill the tank up.

2. How about the choke? Is it open or closed? Have you flooded the engine so it will have to stand awhile before it can be started? If you have not choked the engine, do so now and try again. If you have flooded the engine, let it stand awhile and then try again.

3. Maybe it's the spark plug; is it in working order? Of course, you cannot tell, if the engine is not running. But here is a test for you. Dis-

connect the wire to the top of the spark plug and sand it and the top of the plug clean. Now, holding the end of the wire about ¼ inch away from the top of the plug, turn the engine over. There should be a large spark! If there is not, the spark plug or the magneto (it's located under the blower housing) is at fault. You can check the spark plug easily by replacing it or taking it to your automobile service station, where it can be tested. If it's the spark plug, you can do the job yourself. But if it's the magneto that is at fault, better have a lawnmover serviceman take care of the mower unless you are very handy with tools and have the necessary equipment.

4. Try the fuel flow next. First, check the vent of the gasoline tank. There is a small hole in the top of the cover. It should be clean and open. Use a small pin to make certain. After that has been checked, take a screwdriver and turn the needle valve clockwise to increase the flow of gasoline to the mower. Open it all the way and then turn back one full turn counterclockwise. This will clear the gasoline line if it was clogged.

5. If, after you have tried all these steps, you still cannot start your power mower, it's time to call the repairman.

Other possible troubles are as follows.

Table 16

POWER MOWER EMERGENCIES

Engine will not run unless the choke is pulled all the way out.	Take a screwdriver and turn the needle valve counterclockwise one full turn. The fuel mixture was too lean, and you have to richen it.
Engine smokes excessively while running at any speed.	Take a screwdriver and turn the needle valve clockwise one-half turn. The fuel mixture was too rich. It may be necessary to make another half-turn if the smoking continues.
Engine misfires and sputters while operating.	First, check the spark plug. Make certain that the contacts on the top are clean; use sandpaper if necessary. If the engine still misses, remove the spark plug and have the gap checked. If the spark plug is working, the condenser is faulty and should be replaced by a repairman.
Engine misses—it does not run smoothly.	Here again, it may be spark plug trouble. Follow the same technique as if the engine misfired. Otherwise, the fault may be with the magneto; it should be replaced or repaired by a serviceman.
Runaway engine—it continues to drive the mower even in a stop position of the handle.	The idle-speed bar may be stuck or bent so that the engine is continually fed gasoline. If the bar is in working order, reset the idle-speed adjustment screw. Turn this screw clockwise one-half turn and try the engine again. If it is still running away, try another half turn and then another until the difficulty is corrected.

Small-Animal Control

Various small animals are undesirable near homes and in lawns or gardens either because of the damage they do or merely because of their presence. Some of these animals are, on the whole, beneficial, and it is only under special conditions that control measures are needed. In some cases, they may even cause an emergency situation.

Squirrels. Tree squirrels, both red and gray, as well as flying squirrels, sometimes become a nuisance by taking up quarters in attics, partitions, or spaces between floors, where they become noisy and, at times, destructive. Occasionally, these squirrels may nibble vegetables in the garden or feed on ripening fruit.

Squirrels in buildings may be trapped with ordinary snap-back rat traps baited with walnut meats or some similar food and set where the squirrels can easily reach them. They may be trapped unharmed for release elsewhere by the use of any live trap or box trap of suitable size. After the squirrels have been removed, the holes or crevices through which they gained entrance to the building should be closed tightly with wood, sheet metal, or heavy wire screening.

In attics and in summer homes unoccupied for the winter, a liberal sprinkling of naphthalene flakes may help to repel the squirrels. In some localities shooting is a simple way to control squirrel damage. But in some states the squirrel is protected by law and, before trapping or shooting, permission must be obtained from the local game protector.

Squirrels may sometimes be prevented from climbing fruit trees by the use of wide metal bands on the trunks. These should be about 2 feet wide, but are useless if the limbs can be reached from the ground or from nearby trees or other structures.

Chipmunks. Chipmunks are ordinarily harmless animals about the lawn or garden, feeding on nuts, seeds, and berries. Occasionally it may be necessary to reduce their numbers if they damage newly planted seedbeds or molest plants in garden areas. They are easily trapped in snap-back rat traps set near their burrows, which are holes in the ground, often at the base of a tree or stump or in a stone wall. Effective baits are rolled oats, corn, seeds, or peanut butter.

Woodchucks. Woodchucks feed on various grasses, clover, and succulent green plants. Occasionally they may live near gardens and extensively damage growing plants. Less frequently they may harm young fruit trees by eating or clawing the bark. Because the woodchuck relies for refuge on a burrow, it is relatively easy to control. The burrow may be identified by the mound of freshly dug soil at one of the entrances, as the woodchuck throws out soil frequently during the spring months. Often the animal may be seen entering its burrow.

In April or May, if care is taken in the identification of the burrow, woodchucks may be destroyed by fumigation with little danger to other valuable animals that sometimes occupy deserted "chuck" burrows. Since there are dangers connected with the use of chemicals and gas, this process is best left to trained individuals.

Additional ways to control woodchucks are shooting and trapping. If traps are used, two No. 1½ or No. 2 steel traps may be set at the burrow entrance. They should be concealed with a light covering of dry leaves or grass and firmly secured to prevent their being dragged into the burrow.

Rabbits. Occasionally cottontail rabbits eat the growing plants in home gardens. In winter they often destroy or injure ornamental shrubs, fruit trees, or berry bushes about the home. The best insurance against rabbits is a tight chicken-wire fence. Trapping may reduce rabbit numbers if several traps are used persistently. Any good box trap may be baited with apple or carrot and placed where the rabbits enter the garden. This may be near tall grass, weedy areas, or adjacent brush. Rabbits are most active from. twilight to early morning and usually hide during the day. Winter trapping is most effective.

A number of repellent formulas are recommended in *Conservation Bulletin* 11 of the United States Fish and Wildlife Service. Young fruit trees and shrubs may be successfully protected by individual wire guards.

Rabbits may be easily shot in country districts and in some suburban areas where a gun may be used with safety. This is one of the most effective ways to destroy them and is usually permitted by law when they are damaging crops. Your local game warden should be consulted.

Mice. The field mouse, one of the most prolific and widely distributed animals, is found wherever there is grass to feed on. It is active all year and constructs an intricate network of surface runways through the vegetation and surface litter. If numerous near gardens, these mice sometimes damage growing plants and ripening vegetables, eating into the exposed portion of beets, low-lying tomatoes, and the like.

Field mice are most easily controlled in small areas, such as gardens, by ordinary snap-back mousetraps; but, to be effective, a dozen or more traps should be used. The traps should be reset daily and freshly baited until no more mice are caught. A pinch of oatmeal sprinkled over the trigger of the trap is an effective bait.

The white-bellied, long-tailed deer mice live in wooded or shrubby areas and often inhabit hedgerows. They are active all year and lay up stores for the winter season, much as the squirrels do. They are easily controlled by the use of snap-back mousetraps. A dozen or more traps baited with oatmeal or peanut butter and placed in corners, along walls, and behind objects where the mice will find them will quickly destroy the resident mice.

The same measures that control deer mice will also control house mice.

Moles. Moles occasionally damage lawns, gardens, or golf greens through their tunneling activities. Moles are difficult to control because they live almost entirely in their networks of underground tunnels and will not accept baits readily. They can be controlled successfully only through the use of special mole traps which may be purchased from hardware dealers.

Bats. Our native bats are harmless and useful animals, feeding as they do on various types of flying insects. Occasionally, a colony of bats will take up residence in the attic or upper section of a building and become objectionable because of the odor they cause.

The surest method of control is to close all openings through which bats enter and leave the structure. All but one opening should be sealed with wood, screening, or sheet metal. This last opening should be sealed about $\frac{1}{2}$ hour after dark when most or all of the bats are out foraging for food. Sealing this last opening should effectively exclude the bats.

As an additional measure a generous quantity of naphthalene flakes spread over the roosting space helps to repel any bats that may gain entrance. Sometimes this measure alone will cause the bats to go elsewhere.

Rats. Laws have been passed against him, but the rat, being unable to read and so unaware that he is an outlaw, continues his destructive career unless cut down by poison, traps, or other agents. Periodic campaigns are conducted to arouse public sentiment against the pest, but too often the homeowner is convinced the rat is his neighbor's guest, never his own. However, you can make the news headlines in either of these ways at any time: your infant son or daughter may be bitten while asleep when a rat, drawn by even the faintest odor of milk, invades the nursery. Or you or your wife may by accident corner a rat on his travels and find yourself attacked and bitten severely before the frightened animal escapes. In either case—*call a doctor at once.* Rat bites are dangerous, for the rat sometimes carries rabies germs.

If you see one rat about your home, it's probable there are two and that the two will increase very shortly to ten. Thereafter the number will be limited only by the amount of food you make available and the shelters your home provides for nesting. Ratproofing embraces not only shutting rats out of the home but eliminating their hiding and nesting places and cutting off all food supply.

A home can be made ratproof by "building out" the rat. Every separate structure presents its individual problem, but there are two general principles that apply in all cases. First: the exterior of the house should be, ideally, of materials that rats cannot gnaw their way through. They can gnaw through wood, even stucco—but not through concrete, masonry, or metal. Since this is not always possible, those parts where rats can begin to make an entrance should be protected by metal gratings and screens. Second: structural interiors should contain no accessible dead spaces such as double walls, boxed-in plumbing, and boxed-in staircases. Unless these are guarded with metal, rats can readily gnaw their way in and will be difficult to get out.

All openings between floors and in partitions for the passage of pipes and wires should be closed with metal flashings. While it may seem that some openings are too small for a rat to get through, rats have been known to enter a 1-inch-square opening. And they are quick to enlarge any small hole if it promises a passage.

Though a newly completed home may be rat-free, they may come along later. Rats will be drawn by food first of all, and if enough is found, they will set about locating a nesting place. To eliminate the attraction of food, garbage must be kept in metal cans or destroyed at once. When feeding pets or poultry, be sure there are no "leftovers." True, they will vanish overnight, but that is very likely due to the effectiveness of rats in locating such food sources. Once fed, they will be back for more.

Inspection for signs of rats should be routine at the time of your regular spring and fall cleanup programs. If there are indications of rats, it's time to act to remove them. Trapping is one method. Cats and dogs help. However, in recent years greater reliance is being placed on red squill as a poison to eliminate rats. Red squill is harmless to pets and humans. If taken in error, it acts as its own emetic. To rats, however, it is fatal.

To prepare a bait of red squill, obtain some in powder form from a seed, drug, grocery, or hardware store. Make a thin paste by mixing it with water, mix the paste with ground fresh fish, canned meat, hamburger, or cereal. It can also be spread on slices of potatoes, bananas, or bread. Bait of this sort should be put out in an evening, as rats prefer feeding after sundown. Contrary to popular belief, rats do not like cheese. Rats poisoned by red squill will usually be found lying outdoors. Do not pick them up with bare hands, as fleas will live on dead or dying rats for several days and carry germs of disease with them. Incinerate or bury the victims. Red squill is available in various forms other than powder type. Its action is effective, however used.

Once you have eliminated the pests, repair to the damage they have done is in order. Then take the steps outlined to prevent their return.

Termites and Other Insects

The discovery that termites have invaded a house is often followed by blind panic, but rarely is there real cause for it. These pests usually give sufficient warning of their presence in time to let you take steps before damage is serious.

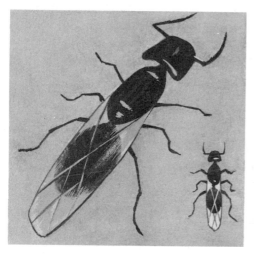

CARPENTER ANT
(inset, two-thirds adult life size)

WINGED TERMITE
(inset, two-thirds adult life size)

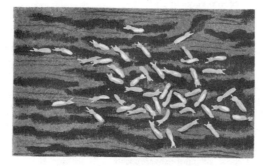

Termite workers and their effect on wood.

To spot termite invasion, look for the telltale tunnels that termites make to bridge masonry wherever it separates the wood framing members from the ground. If any wood framing members (particularly the sill plates) near the ground level show signs of deterioration, inspect them closely for termites or their tunnels. The secret of termite control lies in poisoning the soil, not the wood. Since termites cannot stand light or air and cannot bore through concrete, they must have a direct connection between soil and wood. They accomplish this connection through cracks in masonry foundations, through voids in block foundations, and through tunnels that they build themselves from mud and wood fiber. If these routes are sealed off, the termites inside the wood will die and others will not get in. Since many homes are constructed so that it's almost impossible to seal off these routes, the only other means of protection is chemicals. The chart below includes some of the most effective chemicals for combating termites. All chemicals mentioned are harmful in varying degrees to the skin, eyes, or lungs via the fumes, and some are flammable. Read the container labels carefully for directions on safe handling.

Table 17

CHEMICAL CONTROL OF INSECTS

Chemical	Formula	Dosage	Odor
Trichlorobenzene	Mix 1 gallon in 4 gallons of fuel oil, kerosene, or used crankcase oil.	1 gallon for each 2 cubic feet of soil to be treated.	Strong and long-lived.
Pentachlorophenol	Dissolve at rate of 2½ pounds of pentachlorophenol in either 1 gallon of pine oil or 2 gallons of an alkyl naphthalene. Dilute with fuel oil to make 7 gallons.	1 gallon for each 2 cubic feet of soil to be treated.	Slight.
Trichlorobenzene and Pentachlorophenol	Dissolve at rate of 1 pound of pentachlorophenol per 2½ gallons of trichlorobenzene. Dilute with fuel oil to make 30 gallons.	1 gallon for each 2 cubic feet to be treated.	Strong and persistent.
Sodium arsenite	Dissolve 10 pounds in 11 gallons of water.	1 gallon for each cubic foot of soil to be treated.	None.
Coal-tar creosote	1 part of coal-tar creosote to 2 parts of fuel oil.	2 gallons for each 5 cubic feet of soil.	Strong and long-lived.

In addition to the poisons listed in the chart, chlordane and dieldrin, which are sold as concentrates to be mixed with water, are also effective poisons. Although the oil-mixed treatments last longer, chlordane and dieldrin have the advantage of being odorless and nontoxic to plants. They should be mixed with water according to the directions on the container.

Pour the selected chemical into foundation block voids wherever they are accessible and where termites may have come up through them to reach the wood framing. The soil all around the house next to the foundation should also be treated with the chemical. Dig a trench 1 to 2 feet deep next to the foundation and pour the chemical in according to the dosage recommended in the chart. An alternative method is to make holes spaced 1 foot apart in the ground next to the foundation, using a crowbar or other long steel shaft. Then fill these holes with the chemical. For all interior applications in the basement, use a nonodorous chemical such as sodium arsenite, chlordane, or dieldrin, and spray it on instead of pouring it.

If you do not wish to attack the termite problem yourself, here are six facts to keep in mind when hiring a professional exterminator.

1. Investigate the organization thoroughly:

　　a. with the local Chamber of Commerce or Better Business Bureau;

　　b. with your local County Agricultural Agent;

　　c. with local, state, or national pest control organizations;

　　d. with the state license bureau if required in your state;

　　e. with actual references from persons for whom work was done in the past year or so.

2. Obtain, in writing, just what the exterminator plans to do and the materials he intends to use.

3. If a guarantee is offered, be sure of its terms, its length, and whether it is likely that the firm will be in existence as long as the guarantee.

4. Do not sign a statement that the work was properly done. You will not be able to tell whether it was or not. If, on loan applications, it is necessary to sign such a statement, it's doubly important that you know with whom you are dealing.

5. Make certain that the service is needed. Make your own inspection, and go along with the professional inspector and see what he discovers. Do not just take any statement that the service is necessary at face value.

6. Get bids from two or three services to make sure you are not being overcharged.

Ants. Despite their proverbial qualities of thrift and industry, ants are unwelcome trespassers both inside and outside the home. Just a few ant invaders found in the kitchen or dining room are enough to appall any tidy housewife. Outdoors, they are an unsightly menace, exposing grass roots and enlarging bare patches in your lawn by their labors. Fortunately, there are methods of controlling these pests.

Chlordane is the most generally effective insecticide to use against ants. It kills either on consumption or by contact and will prevent reinfestation for a long period. As previously stated, chlordane can be obtained as an oil- or water-base spray, a drench, a dust, or granules and is widely available under a variety of trade names; read the analysis statement on the label to see whether a product contains chlordane.

Preventing ants from entering the house is surely the most effective indoor control. Spray outside walls from the ground up to the windows with a 2 percent oil-base chlordane mixture; apply to the lower parts of window and door frames, underneath the porch, to the underside of the porch structure, and along all supports, posts, pillars, and pipes. Control of ants for a season should require no more than two applications of the spray. Care must be taken to keep the oil base from trees, shrubs, and lawn because it is injurious to plant life.

When ants are already inside the house, control can be accomplished by indirect application of the oil-base chlordane application. Place the mixture in front of their nests where the ants must crawl over it, and treat cracks and crevices in these areas. With a small paintbrush you can work effectively and avoid spray mist and drifting. When using an oil-base spray, observe these cautions; do not spray near an open flame because the oil is flammable, or near an asphalt tile because it will dissolve the asphalt.

To fight ants outside the house, drench an ant-infested soil area in the lawn or garden with a mixture of 1 tablespoonful of 50 percent chlordane wettable powder and 3 gallons of water. If nests are few and sparsely scattered, treat them individually by putting a mixture of 2 tablespoonfuls of 50 percent chlordane wettable powder and 1 gallon of water into each nest opening and drenching the environs of the nest for several feet back, soaking the chemical through the ground and into the nest with water. Chlordane is poisonous, so do *not* apply it to the foliage or fruit of plants.

Other Insects. Effective sprays are available for killing such insects as bedbugs, carpet beetles, centipedes, fleas, and spiders. A regular fly spray will kill houseflies, crickets, and spiders. Moths can be kept under control by employing moth crystals (paradichlorobenzene) and household sprays with a naphtha base.

For cockroaches, a stomach poison is the answer, as they are mostly immune to common household insecticides. Keep your pets and children out of the basement; put poison paste (several types are available at your supermarket) on slices of potato and place them around the basement perimeter walls, or sprinkle sodium fluoride along these edges.

The use of sprays to kill bees, hornets, and wasps may or may not be successful, depending on the species of the insect and how the chemical is employed. In most cases, it is desirable to remove the nest. If inside the house, strips of flypaper can be hung around the nest. This will trap many of the insects, and if the paper is replaced frequently, most if not all of them will be eliminated. The nest can then be pulled down, doused with kerosene, and burned. The vacuum cleaner, equipped with a long tube, can also be used. The tube should be held close to the nest opening so that the vacuum will suck in any insect entering or leaving. When the cleaner bag is filled, moth crystals can be sucked in to kill any insects still alive.

For an outside nest up under the eaves or in some similar place that is hard to get at you will require a ladder. Place it during the day and then, after dark (when the insects can't see and will still be in their nest), climb the ladder and with a long stick dislodge the nest free into a plastic or heavy paper bag. Immediately douse it with kerosene and set it on fire. For safety's sake, wear a hat and veil over your face, a long-sleeved woolen shirt, and heavy gloves.

Poisonous Plants

Poison ivy, poison sumac, and poison oak are three plants that can cause plenty of trouble. These plants may be eradicated by digging them out. Another method is spraying them with a solution composed of 3 pounds of salt dissolved in 1 gallon of slightly soapy water. The first spraying should take place as soon as the buds appear on the plant and should be followed by several later sprayings as the new leaves appear. Another spray may be made with crankcase oil diluted with kerosene or ordinary fuel oil. Oil sprays kill the leaves, but the roots must be dug out of the ground. Various chlorinated aliphatic acids are available commercially which kill these poisonous plants fairly rapidly.

Burn vines or bushes or roots which have been dug out only if *absolutely* essential, and then keep out of the smoke. The poison is vaporized by the heat of the fire and may produce symptoms over all parts of the body, and breathing the smoke may result in serious lung irritation.

Index

71 72 73 74 75   10 9 8 7 6 5 4 3 2 1